The First Step Act Of 2018 And Prison Reform: Recidivism Reduction Programs And Productive Activities Approved For Early Release Time Credit Incentive Programming

For Inmates Seeking To Maximize Early Release Time Credit Incentives

INTRODUCTION

January 29, 2020

This is the most current Federal Sentencing Alliance publication related to First Step Act Of 2018: Recidivism Reduction Programs And Productive Activities, as it incorporates recent releases by Attorney General Barr and the Bureau Of Prisons in January, 2020.

Federal Sentencing Alliance is pleased to provide you with a reformatted and easy to ready text of The First Step Act Of 2018, together with the released January 17, 2020 "List" of Evidence-based Recidivism Reduction Programs and Productive Activities, a reformatted version of the most recent Bureau Of Prisons Directory Of National Programs ("Programs Directory"), and a reformatted version of the most recent Bureau Of Prisons Inmate Occupational Training Directory ("Training Directory"). These reference guides are useful for researching BOP early release time credit incentive programming implementation.

This publication identifies *the* Evidence-based Recidivism Reduction Programs And Productive Activities that were *approved and vetted* for use by the Bureau Of Prisons implementation of early release time credit incentives, under the Attorney General Barr *System* referenced in the First Step Act. The List was released January 17, 2020.

To utilize these materials as reference guides, one would review the *List* to see which programs and activities are to be released nationally, or for a specific BOP facility. Next, one would go to the Bureau Of Prisons *Programs Directory* for a description of what those programs and activities entail, and the goals to be achieved upon successful completion. Lastly one would go to the last Bureau Of Prisons *Training Directory*, which describes which programs and activities were available at Bureau Of Prison facilities as of March 31, 2017.

In the event a new 2020 Program Directory or Training Directory is published by the Bureau Of Prisons, this publication will be amended to include those most recent directories, when they are available. For now, the 2017 Program and Training Directories are current.

Continuing Risk And Needs Assessment System Delays-

On July 20, 2019 United States Attorney General William Barr announced, via the publication of a document titled "The First Step Act Of 2018: Risk And Needs Assessment System" ("System"), that the final approved, catalogued, and vetted list of recidivism reduction programs and productive activities ("List") that could be used by inmates to earn time credits under the First Step Act Of 2018, would NOT be released until January, 2020. Many inmates were hopeful, as was the Author, that the Attorney General's List would have been released on or before July 20, 2019. Yet this List was not released until January 17, 2020.

The First Step Act Of 2018 mandated that new evidence-based recidivism reduction programs be substantively approved and vetted, prior to release of the "System". That did not occur in a timely manner. Although several legal scholars have complained about implementation delays in the past year, nobody has really quantified 'why' there was a 6 month delay right out of the starting gate, and what effect that had on both inmates and taxpayers in 2019, for failure of timely implementation. Congress realized that the System could not be released without programs and activities being first approved and vetted within 210 day of December 21, 2018, and made that specific function a prerequisite to release of the system. See 18 U.S.C. §§ 3633(a)(3)(5)(2019).

The reason Congress made that a *prerequisite* is because there can be no *Needs Assessment* component to a released *System* can occur by definition, without first having the approved and vetted programs and activities upon which that needs component can be based. That is common sense.

It should come as no surprise then that the Attorney General's July 20, 2019 press release titled: "First Step Act Of 2018: Risk And Needs Assessment System" was not really a System release whatsoever, because it contained absolutely no needs components. Somehow these deficiencies have not been complained about by the Congress and have not been reported upon by the Press. 2019 was a lost cause for First Step Act Of 2018 early release time credit incentives, which is a shame. The Bureau Of Prisons *could have*, but *did not* engage in First Step Act Of 2018 early release time credit incentives in 2019. Someone should be asking the proverbial question "why", as Congress intended that First Step Act benefits be realized immediately, on and after December 21, 2018. The 2019 delays are continuing into 2020 now.

On January 15, 2020, Attorney General Barr issued a Press Release titled *"Department of Justice Announces Enhancements to the Risk Assessment System and Updates on First Step Act Implementation"*, stating that the Bureau Of Prisons would be releasing a List of approved recidivism reduction programs and productive activities soon. Then on January 17, 2020, the Bureau Of Prisons Website released a List of Evidence-based Recidivism Reduction Programs And Productive Activities to be implemented pursuant to the First Step Act Of 2018. That List is republished below, as reformatted.

Programs List And Programs Directory-

The Program List uses broad terms like CBT (acronym for "Cognitive Behavioral Therapy"), which does not specify with detail, actual CBT programs being implemented, by actual name. The broad term "CBT" encompasses dozens of actual CBT named programs that exist. Most actual CBT programs are not listed with enough detail to identify any specific program within that broad spectrum by name. There are patents for many of these CBT Programs, so it would have been an easy matter to identify any particular program on the List with specificity. By definition, that means that CBT can mean any specific program that fits within a cognitive behavioral therapy treatment leading the participant to the individual goals to be achieved stated in the List. Unfortunately, that still does not identify the actual recidivism reduction program by name or with enough specificity to identify the actual CBT Program being implemented. This serves to keep the actual CBT Programs being implemented a nebulous concept for the time being; very *fluid*. The vague nature of the programs listed, again, suggests that they may be subject to change during the implementation processes.

Additionally, the Bureau Of Prisons will be completing a test project for some of the listed CBT Programs at a few of the Bureau Of Prison facilities nationally, before those are released to the remainder of BOPs facilities in 2021. That was Attorney General Barr's concept and was very briefly mentioned in the July 20, 2019 Press Release. One can ascertain which programs are being released nationally, and which ones are test facility programs for the next year, by looking at the four corners of the List.

Educational Programs Within Recidivism Reduction Programming Category-

The Author is pleased to see several Literacy Programs and Educational Programs listed as recidivism reduction programs, as opposed to productive activities. Educational programs have historically been categorized as productive activities. That particular designation will certainly broaden accessability to inmates trying to achieve early release time credit incentives once implemented for those who have been scored Medium recidivism risk or higher, pursuant to their first PATTERN risk assessment. The change also means that 100% of qualifying inmates (e.g. not disqualified due to the nature of the offense) can avail themselves of educational programs, including possibly correspondence courses through the mail-with prior BOP approval, for early release time credit incentives. These are an important source of early release time credit incentives, maybe the most important, as educational programming may be more accessible to eager inmates, as least in the short term. Definitely something to consider, with prior approval at your facility.

It remains to be seen *when* the Bureau Of Prisons will *actually and meaningfully* implement the List of Recidivism Reduction Programs and Productive Activities that appear on the January 17, 2020 BOP List for national implementation now, and if implemented soon, to what extent.

Many Missed Due Dates For Utilization And Implementation-

From a studied in depth review of the First Step Act Of 2018, and all of the related United States Code provisions amended in 2019, it appears that both the Attorney General and the Bureau Of Prisons *missed mandatory due dates* for recidivism reduction programs and productive activity utilization and implementation. Again, neither the Congress or the Press have complained about missed due dates causing delays in early release time credit incentives for 2019, which is remarkable.

In that regard, the Bureau Of Prisons *could have* utilized previously existing programs and activities at individual facilities nationwide for early release time credit incentives, as of December 21, 2018, but did not. Indeed the national programs and activities included in the new List reference a Programs Directory and Training Directory in existence since prior to 2017. Why were they not utilized in 2019 for early release earned time credit incentives under the First Step Act Of 2018? That factor alone caused 2019 to be a lost cause for application of early release time credit incentives, pursuant to the mandates of the First Step Act.

Next, the Attorney General's Office has still not released a *First Step Act Of 2018: Risk And Needs Assessment System* to the general public, notwithstanding that it was due to be released by Website publication on or before July 19, 2020. Yet, a document bearing that title was released on July 20, 2019 by the Attorney General's Office. The Bureau Of Prisons has very subtly stated in a December 31, 2019 public notice that no System has been released, because it's own due dates are *hinged* to Attorney General Barr's System release. *see "Good Conduct Time Credit Under The First Step Act"*, 82 FR 72274 (December 31, 2019)(Summary). It is difficult to see these missed deadline dates in a positive light, because they resemble buck passing and stalling for time. There is no viable reason why inmates could not have earned credits in 2019, as the Bureau Of Prisons *could have* permitted just that and did not.

These anomalies have created a variety of circular unanswered questions: 1.) How is it that the Attorney General's First Step Act Of 2018: Risk And Needs Assessment System, was released without a vetted and approved List of evidence-based recidivism reduction programs and productive activities on July 20, 2019, and why didn't anyone critically read the document to report that it contained no Needs Assessment System components; and 2.) Why did the Bureau Of Prisons ignore utilization of previously existing programs and activities during the preliminary phase in period of calendar year 2019, to permit eager inmates to benefit from their rights to earn early release time credit incentives, mandated by the First Step Act Of 2018.

For now *the List* has been released. When the programs and activities enumerated in *the List* will be *meaningfully implemented* remains to be seen. In the meantime, substantial inmate rights hang in the balance. The Courts have not yet weighed in on these issues. To further confuse the implementation issue, the Bureau Of Prisons has been given until January 15, 2022 for *maximum implementation* of recidivism reduction programs and productive activities (for all programs and activities and for all qualified inmates for maximum benefits), pursuant to the First Step Act, however, as previously stated, the Author believes that actual Bureau Of Prisons *utilization of early release time credit incentives* should have commenced on December 21, 2018.

A word about PATTERN Risk Assessment and Program and Activity Qualification-

Offenses ineligible for early release time credit incentive participation is found at 18 U. S. Code § 3632 (d)(D)(2019). Inmates convicted of those enumerated offenses, and there are many, do not qualify for participation in early release time credit incentive programming. Inmates are encouraged to look at the disqualification list to ensure their own qualification for early release time credit incentive programs, and to be prepared to argue, if possible, why they are qualified to participate, by filing internal Requests at their individual facilities for consideration.

PATTERN Tool Prototype and PATTERN Tool Amendments January 15, 2020-

The types of programs and/or activities that an inmate can participate in for earned time credits is dependent upon the results of their initial recidivism risk and needs assessment, that was completed prior to January 15, 2020 for all inmates in all BOP facilities.

Pursuant to the results from an assessment tool released on July 20, 2020 called the "Prisoner Assessment Tool Targeting Estimated Risk and Needs" or simply "PATTERN", all inmates were scored at these recidivism risk levels: minimal, low, medium, or high. Although, scoring PATTERN is not the focus of this publication, Federal Sentencing Alliance has published a related book titled: "Deconstructing The First Step Act of 2018 Risk and Needs Assessment System: For Inmates Seeking To Maximize Prison Time Credits" also available on Amazon.

The PATTERN tool appears easy to score once one has the relevant information to input to score, mostly available from one's Presentence Investigation Report ("PSR"). PATTERN is merely a series of questions that are factually answered and then scored. It resembles a questionnaire. The score determines whether one is deemed a minimal, low, medium, or high risk of recidivism by the Bureau Of Prisons. The scored risk level in turn determines which programs and activities, one otherwise qualified for, can participate in, provided those programs and activities are available at the facility where the inmate is housed. The PATTERN tool seems to be extremely liberal for most otherwise qualified federal inmates. Interestingly, the mathematical calculations explaining exactly how the PATTERN tool was derived scientifically was never released to the public. Moreover, the hypothetical calculation that was released to the public does not mathematically result in the risk category point levels enumerated in the PATTERN tool. This is why the Author considers the PATTERN tool in use to be very liberal. How the cut point levels were derived for the PATTERN tool remains a mystery.

On January 15, 2020 Attorney General Barr announced some tweaks made to the PATTERN tool prototype released on July 20, 2019. Although the amendments to the tool were announced, the actual amended PATTERN tool was not released to the public.

This is what AG Barr's July 15, 2020 Press Release says regarding amendments to the initial PATTERN Tool prototype, with the amended Pattern tool not yet released to the public:

> "In response to the public comments received and in coordination with the Independent Review Committee (IRC), the Justice Department has made

changes to PATTERN that enhance its effectiveness, fairness and transparency. These changes had only a slight effect on PATTERN's high-level of predictability and include:

Adding a dynamic measure of offender's "infraction free" period during his or her current term of incarceration;

Modifying programming measures by adding psychology treatment programs (Bureau Rehabilitation and Values Enhancement Program (BRAVE), Challenge, Skills Program, Sex Offender Treatment (both residential and non-residential), Steps Toward Awareness, Growth, and Emotional Strength Program (STAGES), and Step Down programs), the faith-based Life Connections Program (LCP), and the BOP's Drug Education program, to the "Number of programs completed (any)" measure and combine technical/vocational and Federal Prison Industries (UNICOR) into a new work programming measure; and

Removing Age of first arrest/conviction and voluntary surrender." *Id.*

All of those enumerated PATTERN tool modifications appear to mitigate points scored as opposed to aggravating points scored from the original prototype PATTERN. In other words, those modifications appear to further reduce a PATTERN score, but not increase it, which is a great thing.

For those inmates that achieve a PATTERN low or minimal recidivism risk assessment, engaging in *productive activities* will result in earned time credits. The First Step Act even provides for certain inmates to be considered to "deliver" productive activity programs to other inmates. What better way to engage early release time credit incentives than to actually be the one delivering those activities to others? Although that would require approval from the Warden, it is worth exploring for those inmates who believe they can teach others, while fitting within the parameters of productive activities otherwise authorized at an individual facility already. For those inmates that receive a medium or high recidivism risk assessment, engaging in recidivism reduction programming will result in earned time credits.

Circular Responsibilities-

Interestingly, Attorney General Barr made the January 15, 2020 Press Release on the same day that BOPs mandatory program implementation of the *new System* was to commence, pursuant to the tenets of the First Step Act; while BOP remained *mute*. One would have expected for the Bureau Of Prisons to state publicly *actual implementation* of the new Risk And Needs Assessment System on January 15, 2020 had begun nationally, but that did not occur. Again *see "Good Conduct Time Credit Under The First Step Act"*, 82 FR 72274 (December 31, 2019)(Summary), which could logically explain some of this anomaly. This notice suggests that the BOP does not consider the *System* released yet; so its own time clock has not yet started to run yet, being hinged upon a release of a *System.*

Federal Sentencing Alliance-

Federal Sentencing Alliance is not associated with the United States Congress, the Bureau Of Prisons, or any agency or department of the United States. The First Step Act Of 2018, it's implementation, and final parameters, is within the sound province of the Attorney General Of The United States, the Bureau Of Prisons, and other federal departments and agencies.

Any opinions expressed by Federal Sentencing Alliance should not be construed as legal advice. The analysis and opinions expressed by Federal Sentencing Alliance in this book regarding earned time credits for early release, based upon successful participation and completion of recidivism reduction programs and/or productive activities, represent the opinions of Federal Sentencing Alliance alone, intended to foster critical thinking regarding these topics. Because program implementation will be ongoing until 2022 there will be plenty of critical thinking in the process at various stages of implementation to finality.

Please see other Federal Sentencing Alliance publications available on Amazon by clicking on the blue Author link on any book screen.

TABLE OF CONTENTS

S. 756 - First Step Act of 2018
115th Congress (2017-2018)
Second Session

Begun and held at the City of Washington on Wednesday, the third day of January, two thousand and eighteen-

To reauthorize and amend the Marine Debris Act to promote international action to reduce marine debris, and for other purposes.

Be it enacted by the Senate and House of Representatives of the United States of America in Congress assembled,

SECTION 1. Short title; table of contents.

(a)   Short title.-This Act may be cited as the **First Step Act of 2018**.

(b)   Table of contents.-The table of contents for this Act is as follows:

TITLE III RESTRAINTS ON PREGNANT PRISONERS PROHIBITED

TITLE IV SENTENCING REFORM

TITLE V SECOND CHANCE ACT OF 2007 REAUTHORIZATION

TITLE VI MISCELLANEOUS CRIMINAL JUSTICE

TITLE I Recidivism reduction

SEC. 101. Risk and needs assessment system.

(a)   In general.-Chapter 229 of title 18, United States Code, is amended by inserting after subchapter C the following:

SUBCHAPTER D-RISK AND NEEDS ASSESSMENT SYSTEM

Sec.
3631. Duties of the Attorney General.
3632. Development of risk and needs assessment system.
3633. Evidence-based recidivism reduction program and recommendations.
3634. Report.
3635. Definitions.

§ 3631. Duties of the Attorney General

(a) In general.-The Attorney General shall carry out this subchapter in consultation with-

(1) the Director of the Bureau of Prisons;

(2) the Director of the Administrative Office of the United States Courts;

(3) the Director of the Office of Probation and Pretrial Services;

(4) the Director of the National Institute of Justice;

(5) the Director of the National Institute of Corrections; and

(6) the Independent Review Committee authorized by the First Step Act of 2018.

(b) Duties.-The Attorney General shall-

(1) conduct a review of the existing prisoner risk and needs assessment systems in operation on the date of enactment of this subchapter;

(2) develop recommendations regarding evidence-based recidivism reduction programs and productive activities in accordance with section 3633;

(3) conduct ongoing research and data analysis on-

(A) evidence-based recidivism reduction programs relating to the use of prisoner risk and needs assessment tools;

(B) the most effective and efficient uses of such programs;

(C) which evidence-based recidivism reduction programs are the most effective at reducing recidivism, and the type, amount, and intensity of programming that most effectively reduces the risk of recidivism; and

(D) products purchased by Federal agencies that are manufactured overseas and could be manufactured by prisoners participating in a prison work program without reducing job opportunities for other workers in the United States;

(4) on an annual basis, review, validate, and release publicly on the Department of Justice website the risk and needs assessment system, which review shall include-

(A) any subsequent changes to the risk and needs assessment system made after the date of enactment of this subchapter;

(B) the recommendations developed under paragraph (2), using the research conducted under paragraph (3);

(C) an evaluation to ensure that the risk and needs assessment system bases the assessment of each prisoner's risk of recidivism on indicators of progress and of regression that are dynamic and that can reasonably be expected to change while in prison;

(D) statistical validation of any tools that the risk and needs assessment system uses; and

(E) an evaluation of the rates of recidivism among similarly classified prisoners to identify any unwarranted disparities, including disparities among similarly classified prisoners of different demographic groups, in such rates;

(5) make any revisions or updates to the risk and needs assessment system that the Attorney General determines appropriate pursuant to the review under paragraph (4), including updates to ensure that any disparities identified in paragraph (4)(E) are reduced to the greatest extent possible; and

(6) report to Congress in accordance with section 3634.

§ 3632. Development of risk and needs assessment system

(a) In general.-Not later than 210 days after the date of enactment of this subchapter, the Attorney General, in consultation with the Independent Review Committee authorized by the First Step Act of 2018, shall develop and release publicly on the Department of Justice website a risk and needs assessment system (referred to in this subchapter as the 'System'), which shall be used to-

(1) determine the recidivism risk of each prisoner as part of the intake process, and classify each prisoner as having minimum, low, medium, or high risk for recidivism;

(2) assess and determine, to the extent practicable, the risk of violent or serious misconduct of each prisoner;

(3) determine the type and amount of evidence-based recidivism reduction programming that is appropriate for each prisoner and assign each prisoner to such programming accordingly, and based on the prisoner's specific criminogenic needs, and in accordance with subsection (b);

(4) reassess the recidivism risk of each prisoner periodically, based on factors including indicators of progress, and of regression, that are dynamic and that can reasonably be expected to change while in prison;

(5) reassign the prisoner to appropriate evidence-based recidivism reduction programs or productive activities based on the revised determination to ensure that-

(A) all prisoners at each risk level have a meaningful

opportunity to reduce their classification during the period of incarceration;

(B) to address the specific criminogenic needs of the prisoner; and

(C) all prisoners are able to successfully participate in such programs;

(6) determine when to provide incentives and rewards for successful participation in evidence-based recidivism reduction programs or productive activities in accordance with subsection (e);

(7) determine when a prisoner is ready to transfer into prerelease custody or super- vised release in accordance with section 3624; and

(8) determine the appropriate use of audio technology for program course materials with an understanding of dyslexia.

In carrying out this subsection, the Attorney General may use existing risk and needs assessment tools, as appropriate.

(b) Assignment of evidence-based recidivism reduction programs.-The System shall provide guidance on the type, amount, and intensity of evidence-based recidivism reduction programming and productive activities that shall be assigned for each prisoner, including-

(1) programs in which the Bureau of Prisons shall assign the prisoner to participate, according to the prisoner's specific criminogenic needs; and

(2) information on the best ways that the Bureau of Prisons can tailor the programs to the specific criminogenic needs of each prisoner so as to most effectively lower each prisoner's risk of recidivism.

(c) Housing and assignment decisions.-The System shall provide guidance on program grouping and housing assignment determinations and, after accounting for the safety of each prisoner and other individuals at the prison, provide that prisoners with a similar risk level be grouped together in housing and assignment decisions to the extent practicable.

(d) Evidence-Based recidivism reduction program incentives and productive activities rewards.-The System shall provide incentives and rewards for prisoners to participate in and complete evidence-based recidivism reduction programs as follows:

(1) PHONE AND VISITATION PRIVILEGES.-A prisoner who is successfully participating in an evidence-based recidivism reduction program shall receive-

(A) phone privileges, or, if available, video conferencing privileges, for up to 30 minutes per day, and up to 510 minutes per month; and

(B) additional time for visitation at the prison, as determined by the warden of the prison.

(2) TRANSFER TO INSTITUTION CLOSER TO RELEASE RESIDENCE.-A prisoner who is successfully participating in an evidence-based recidivism reduction program shall be considered by the Bureau of Prisons for placement in a facility closer to the prisoner's release residence upon request from the prisoner and subject to-

(A) bed availability at the transfer facility;

(B) the prisoner's security designation; and

(C) the recommendation from the warden of the prison at which the prisoner is incarcerated at the time of making the request.

(3) ADDITIONAL POLICIES.-The Director of the Bureau of Prisons shall develop additional policies to provide appropriate incentives for successful participation and completion of evidence-based recidivism reduction programming. The incentives shall include not less than 2 of the following:

(A) Increased commissary spending limits and product offerings.

(B) Extended opportunities to access the email system.

(C) Consideration of transfer to preferred housing units (including transfer to different prison facilities).

(D) Other incentives solicited from prisoners and determined appropriate by the Director.

(4) TIME CREDITS.-

(A) IN GENERAL.-A prisoner, except for an ineligible prisoner under subparagraph (D), who successfully completes evidence-based recidivism reduction programming or productive activities, shall earn time credits as follows:

(i) A prisoner shall earn 10 days of time credits for every 30 days of successful participation in evidence-based recidivism reduction programming or productive activities.

(ii) A prisoner determined by the Bureau of Prisons to be at a minimum or low risk for recidivating, who, over 2 consecutive assessments, has not increased their risk of recidivism, shall earn an additional 5 days of time credits for every 30 days of successful participation in evidence-based recidivism reduction programming or productive activities.

(B) AVAILABILITY.-A prisoner may not earn time credits under this paragraph for an evidence-based recidivism reduction program that the prisoner successfully completed-

(i) prior to the date of enactment of this subchapter; or

(ii) during official detention prior to the date that the prisoner's sentence commences under section 3585(a).

(C) APPLICATION OF TIME CREDITS TOWARD PRERELEASE CUSTODY OR SUPERVISED RELEASE.-Time credits earned under this paragraph by prisoners who success- fully participate in recidivism reduction programs or productive activities shall be applied toward time in prerelease custody or supervised release. The Director of the Bureau of Prisons shall transfer eligible prisoners, as determined under section 3624(g), into prerelease custody or supervised release.

(D) INELIGIBLE PRISONERS.-A prisoner is ineligible to receive time credits under this paragraph if the prisoner is serving a sentence for a conviction under any of the following provisions of law:

(i) Section 32, relating to destruction of aircraft or aircraft facilities.

(ii) Section 33, relating to destruction of motor vehicles or motor vehicle facilities.

(iii) Section 36, relating to drive-by shootings.

(iv) Section 81, relating to arson within special maritime and territorial jurisdiction.

(v) Section 111(b), relating to assaulting, resisting, or impeding certain officers or employees using a deadly or dangerous weapon or inflicting bodily injury.

(vi) Paragraph (1), (7), or (8) of section 113(a), relating to assault with intent to commit murder, assault resulting in substantial bodily injury to a spouse or intimate partner, a dating partner, or an individual who has not attained the age of 16 years, or assault of a spouse, intimate partner, or dating partner by strangling, suffocating, or attempting to strangle or suffocate.

(vii) Section 115, relating to influencing, impeding, or retaliating against a Federal official by injuring a family member, except for a threat made in violation of that section.

(viii) Section 116, relating to female genital mutilation.

(ix) Section 117, relating to domestic assault by a habitual offender.

(x) Any section of chapter 10, relating to biological weapons.

(xi) Any section of chapter 11B, relating to chemical weapons.

(xii) Section 351, relating to Congressional, Cabinet, and Supreme Court assassination, kidnapping, and assault.

(xiii) Section 521, relating to criminal street gangs.

(xiv) Section 751, relating to prisoners in custody of an institution or officer.

(xv) Section 793, relating to gathering, transmitting, or losing defense information.

(xvi) Section 794, relating to gathering or delivering defense information to aid a foreign government.

(xvii) Any section of chapter 39, relating to explosives and other dangerous articles, except for section 836 (relating to the transportation of fireworks into a State prohibiting sale or use).

(xviii) Section 842(p), relating to distribution of information relating to explosives, destructive devices, and weapons of mass destruction, but only if the conviction involved a weapon of mass destruction (as defined in section 2332a(c)).

(xix) Subsection (f)(3), (h), or (i) of section 844, relating to the use of fire or an explosive.

(xx) Section 871, relating to threats against the President and successors to the Presidency.

(xxi) Section 879, relating to threats against former Presidents and certain other per- sons.

(xxii) Section 924(c), relating to unlawful possession or

use of a firearm during and in relation to any crime of violence or drug trafficking crime.

(xxiii) Section 1030(a)(1), relating to fraud and related activity in connection with computers.

(xxiv) Section 1091, relating to genocide.

(xxv) Any section of chapter 51, relating to homicide, except for section 1112 (relating to manslaughter), 1113 (relating to attempt to commit murder or manslaughter, but only if the conviction was for an attempt to commit manslaughter), 1115 (relating to misconduct or neglect of ship officers), or 1122 (relating to protection against the human immunodeficiency virus).

(xxvi) Any section of chapter 55, relating to kidnapping.

(xxvii) Any offense under chapter 77, relating to peonage, slavery, and trafficking in persons, except for sections 1593 through 1596.

(xxviii) Section 1751, relating to Presidential and Presidential staff assassination, kid- napping, and assault.

(xxix) Section 1791, relating to providing or possessing contraband in prison.

(xxx) Section 1792, relating to mutiny and riots.

(xxxi) Section 1841(a)(2)(C), relating to intentionally killing or attempting to kill an unborn child.

(xxxii) Section 1992, relating to terrorist attacks and other violence against railroad carriers and against mass transportation systems on land, on water, or through the air.

(xxxiii) Section 2113(e), relating to bank robbery

resulting in death.

(xxxiv) Section 2118(c), relating to robberies and burglaries involving controlled sub- stances resulting in assault, putting in jeopardy the life of any person by the use of a dangerous weapon or device, or death.

(xxxv) Section 2119, relating to taking a motor vehicle (commonly referred to as 'car jacking').

(xxxvi) Any section of chapter 105, relating to sabotage, except for section 2152.

(xxxvii) Any section of chapter 109A, relating to sexual abuse.

(xxxviii) Section 2250, relating to failure to register as a sex offender.

(xxxix) Section 2251, relating to the sexual exploitation of children.

(xl) Section 2251A, relating to the selling or buying of children.

(xli) Section 2252, relating to certain activities relating to material involving the sexual exploitation of minors.

(lii) Section 57(b) of the Atomic Energy Act of 1954 **(42 U.S.C. 2077(b))**, relating to the engagement or participation in the development or production of special nuclear material.

(liii) Section 92 of the Atomic Energy Act of 1954 **(42 U.S.C. 2122)**, relating to prohibitions governing atomic weapons.

(liv) Section 101 of the Atomic Energy Act of 1954 **(42 U.S.C. 2131)**, relating to the atomic energy license requirement.

(lv) Section 224 or 225 of the Atomic Energy Act of 1954 **(42 U.S.C. 2274, 2275)**, relating to the communication or receipt of restricted data.

(lvi) Section 236 of the Atomic Energy Act of 1954 **(42 U.S.C. 2284)**, relating to the sabotage of nuclear facilities or fuel.

(lvii) Section 60123(b) of title 49, relating to damaging or destroying a pipeline facility, but only if the conduct which led to the conviction involved a substantial risk of death or serious bodily injury.

(lviii) Section 401(a) of the Controlled Substances Act **(21 U.S.C. 841)**, relating to manufacturing or distributing a controlled substance in the case of a conviction for an offense described in subparagraph (A), (B), or (C) of subsection (b)(1) of that section for which death or serious bodily injury resulted from the use of such substance.

(lix) Section 276(a) of the Immigration and Nationality Act **(8 U.S.C. 1326)**, relating to the reentry of a removed alien, but only if the alien is described in paragraph (1) or (2) of subsection (b) of that section.

(lx) Section 277 of the Immigration and Nationality Act **(8 U.S.C. 1327)**, relating to aiding or assisting certain aliens to enter the United States.

(lxi) Section 278 of the Immigration and Nationality Act **(8 U.S.C. 1328)**, relating to the importation of an alien into the United States for an immoral purpose.

(lxii) Any section of the Export Administration Act of 1979 **(50 U.S.C. 4611 et seq.)**

(lxiii) Section 206 of the International Emergency Economic Powers Act **(50 U.S.C. 1705)**.

(lxiv) Section 601 of the National Security Act of 1947 **(50 U.S.C. 3121)**, relating to the protection of identities of certain United States undercover intelligence officers, agents, informants, and sources.

(lxv) Subparagraph (A)(i) or (B)(i) of section 401(b)(1) of the Controlled Substances Act **(21 U.S.C. 841(b)(1))** or paragraph (1)(A) or (2)(A) of section 1010(b) of the Controlled Substances Import and Export Act **(21 U.S.C. 960(b))**, relating to manufacturing, distributing, dispensing, or possessing with intent to manufacture, distribute, dispense, or knowingly importing or exporting, a mixture or substance containing a detectable amount of heroin if the sentencing court finds that the offender was an organizer, leader, manager, or supervisor of others in the offense, as determined under the guidelines promulgated by the United States Sentencing Commission.

(lxvi) Subparagraph (A)(vi) or (B)(vi) of section 401(b)(1) of the Controlled Substances Act **(21 U.S.C. 841(b)(1))** or paragraph (1)(F) or (2)(F) of section 1010(b) of the Con- trolled Substances Import and Export Act **(21 U.S.C. 960(b))**, relating to manufacturing, distributing, dispensing, or possessing with intent to manufacture, distribute, or dispense, a mixture or substance containing a detectable amount of N-phenyl- N-[1-(2-phenylethyl)-4-piperidinyl] propanamide, or any analogue thereof.

(lxvii) Subparagraph (A)(viii) or (B)(viii) of section 401(b)(1) of the Controlled Sub- stances Act **(21 U.S.C. 841(b)(1))** or paragraph (1)(H) or (2)(H) of section 1010(b) the Controlled Substances Import and Export Act **(21 U.S.C. 960(b))**, relating to manufacturing, distributing, dispensing, or possessing with intent to manufacture, distribute, or dispense, or knowingly importing or exporting, a mixture of substance containing a detectable amount of methamphetamine, its salts, isomers, or salts of its isomers, if the sentencing court finds that the offender was an organizer, leader, manager, or supervisor of others in the offense, as determined under the guidelines promulgated by the United States Sentencing Commission.

(lxviii) Subparagraph (A) or (B) of section 401(b)(1) of the Controlled Substances Act **(21 U.S.C. 841(b)(1))** or paragraph (1) or (2) of section 1010(b) of the Controlled Substances Import and Export Act **(21 U.S.C. 960(b))**, relating to manufacturing, distributing, dispensing, or possessing with intent to manufacture, distribute, or dispense, a controlled substance, or knowingly importing or exporting a controlled substance, if the sentencing court finds that-

(I) the offense involved a mixture or substance containing a detectable amount of N-phenyl-N-[1-(2-phenylethyl)-4-piperidinyl] propanamide, or any analogue thereof; and

(II) the offender was an organizer, leader, manager, or supervisor of others in the offense, as determined under the guidelines promulgated by the United States Sentencing Commission.

(E) DEPORTABLE PRISONERS INELIGIBLE TO APPLY TIME CREDITS.-

(i) IN GENERAL.-A prisoner is ineligible to apply time credits under subparagraph (C) if the prisoner is the subject of a final order of removal under any provision of the immigration laws (as such term is defined in section 101(a)(17) of the Immigration and Nationality Act **(8 U.S.C. 1101(a)(17)))**.

(ii) PROCEEDINGS.-The Attorney General, in consultation with the Secretary of Home- land Security, shall ensure that any alien described in section 212 or 237 of the Immigration and Nationality Act **(8 U.S.C. 1182, 1227)** who seeks to earn time credits are subject to proceedings described in section 238(a) of that Act **(8 U.S.C. 1228(a))** at a date as early as practicable during the prisoner's incarceration.

(5) RISK REASSESSMENTS AND LEVEL ADJUSTMENT.-A prisoner who successfully participates in evidence-based recidivism reduction programming or productive activities shall receive periodic risk reassessments not less often than annually, and a prisoner determined to be at a medium or high risk of recidivating and who has less than 5 years until his or her projected release date shall receive more frequent risk reassessments. If the reassessment shows that the prisoner's risk of recidivating or specific needs have changed, the Bureau of Prisons shall update the determination of the prison- er's risk of recidivating or information regarding the prisoner's specific needs and reassign the prisoner to appropriate evidence-based recidivism reduction programming or productive activities based on such changes.

(6) RELATION TO OTHER INCENTIVE PROGRAMS.-The incentives described in this subsection shall be in addition to any other rewards or incentives for which a prisoner may be eligible.

(e) Penalties.-The Director of the Bureau of Prisons shall develop guidelines for the reduction of rewards and incentives earned under subsection (d) for prisoners who violate prison rules or evidence-based recidivism reduction program or productive activity rules, which shall provide-

(1) general levels of violations and resulting reductions;

(2) that any reduction that includes the loss of time credits shall require written notice to the prisoner, shall be limited to time credits that a prisoner earned as of the date of the prisoner's rule violation, and shall not include any future time credits that the prisoner may earn; and

(3) for a procedure to restore time credits that a prisoner lost as a result of a rule violation, based on the prisoner's individual progress after the date

of the rule violation.

(f) Bureau of Prisons training.-The Attorney General shall develop and implement training programs for Bureau of Prisons officers and employees responsible for administering the System, which shall include-

(1) initial training to educate officers and employees on how to use the System in an appropriate and consistent manner, as well as the reasons for using the System;

(2) continuing education;

(3) periodic training updates; and

(4) a requirement that such officers and employees demonstrate competence in administering the System, including interrater reliability, on a biannual basis.

(g) Quality assurance.-In order to ensure that the Bureau of Prisons is using the System in an appropriate and consistent manner, the Attorney General shall monitor and assess the use of the System, which shall include conducting annual audits of the Bureau of Prisons regarding the use of the System.

(h) Dyslexia screening.-

(1) SCREENING.-The Attorney General shall incorporate a dyslexia screening program into the System, including by screening for dyslexia during-

(A) the intake process; and

(B) each periodic risk reassessment of a prisoner.

(2) TREATMENT.-The Attorney General shall incorporate programs designed to treat dyslexia into the evidence-based recidivism reduction programs or productive activities required to be implemented under this section. The Attorney General may also incorporate programs designed to treat other learning disabilities.

§ 3633. Evidence-based recidivism reduction program and recommendations

(a) In general.-Prior to releasing the System, in consultation with the Independent Review Committee authorized by the First Step Act of 2018, the Attorney General shall-

(1) review the effectiveness of evidence-based recidivism reduction programs that exist as of the date of enactment of this subchapter in prisons operated by the Bureau of Pris- ons;

(2) review available information regarding the effectiveness of evidence-based recidivism reduction programs and productive activities that exist in State-operated prisons throughout the United States;

(3) identify the most effective evidence-based recidivism reduction programs;

(4) review the policies for entering into evidence-based recidivism reduction partner- ships described in section 3621(h)(5); and

(5) direct the Bureau of Prisons regarding-

(A) evidence-based recidivism reduction programs;

(B) the ability for faith-based organizations to function as a provider of educational evidence-based programs outside of the religious classes and services provided through the Chaplaincy; and

(C) the addition of any new effective evidence-based recidivism reduction programs that the Attorney General finds.

(b) Review and recommendations regarding dyslexia mitigation.-In carrying out sub- section (a), the Attorney General shall consider the prevalence and mitigation of dyslexia in prisons, including by-

(1) reviewing statistics on the prevalence of dyslexia, and the effectiveness of any pro- grams implemented to mitigate the effects of dyslexia, in prisons operated by the Bureau of Prisons and State-operated prisons throughout the United States; and

(2) incorporating the findings of the Attorney General under paragraph (1) of this sub- section into any directives given to the Bureau of Prisons under paragraph (5) of subsection (a).

§ 3634. Report

Beginning on the date that is 2 years after the date of enactment of this subchapter, and annually thereafter for a period of 5 years, the Attorney General shall submit a report to the Committees on the Judiciary of the Senate and the House of Representatives and the Subcommittees on Commerce, Justice, Science, and Related Agencies of the Committees on Appropriations of the Senate and the House of Representatives that contains the following:

(1) A summary of the activities and accomplishments of the Attorney General in carrying out this Act.

(2) A summary and assessment of the types and effectiveness of the evidence-based recidivism reduction programs and productive activities in prisons operated by the Bureau of Prisons, including-

(A) evidence about which programs have been shown to reduce recidivism;

(B) the capacity of each program and activity at each prison, including the number of prisoners along with the recidivism risk of each prisoner enrolled in each program; and

(C) identification of any gaps or shortages in capacity of such programs and activities.

(3) Rates of recidivism among individuals who have been released from Federal prison, based on the following criteria:

(A) The primary offense of conviction.

(B) The length of the sentence imposed and served.

(C) The Bureau of Prisons facility or facilities in which the prisoner's sentence was served.

(D) The evidence-based recidivism reduction programming that the prisoner success- fully completed, if any.

(E) The prisoner's assessed and reassessed risk of recidivism.

(F) The productive activities that the prisoner successfully completed, if any.

(4) The status of prison work programs at facilities operated by the Bureau of Prisons, including-

(A) a strategy to expand the availability of such programs without reducing job opportunities for workers in the United States who are not in the custody of the Bureau of Prisons, including the feasibility of prisoners manufacturing products purchased by Federal agencies that are manufactured overseas;

(B) an assessment of the feasibility of expanding such programs, consistent with the strategy required under subparagraph (A), with the goal that 5 years after the date of enactment of this subchapter, not less than 75 percent of eligible minimum- and low- risk offenders have the opportunity to participate in a prison work program for not less than 20 hours per week; and

(C) a detailed discussion of legal authorities that would be useful or necessary to achieve the goals described in subparagraphs (A) and (B).

(5) An assessment of the Bureau of Prisons' compliance with section 3621(h).

(6) An assessment of progress made toward carrying out the purposes of this subchapter, including any savings associated with-

(A) the transfer of prisoners into prerelease custody or supervised release under section 3624(g), including savings resulting from the avoidance or deferral of future construction, acquisition, and operations costs; and

(B) any decrease in recidivism that may be attributed to the System or the increase in evidence-based recidivism reduction programs required under this subchapter.

(7) An assessment of budgetary savings resulting from this subchapter, including-

(A) a summary of the amount of savings resulting from the transfer of prisoners into prerelease custody under this chapter, including savings resulting from the avoidance or deferral of future construction, acquisition, or operations costs;

(B) a summary of the amount of savings resulting from any decrease in recidivism that may be attributed to the implementation of the risk and needs assessment system or the increase in recidivism reduction programs and productive activities required by this subchapter;

(C) a strategy to reinvest the savings described in subparagraphs (A) and (B) in other-

(i) Federal, State, and local law enforcement activities; and

(ii) expansions of recidivism reduction programs and productive activities in the Bureau of Prisons; and

(D) a description of how the reduced expenditures on Federal corrections and the budgetary savings resulting from this subchapter are currently being used and will be used to-

(i) increase investment in law enforcement and crime prevention to combat gangs of national significance and high-level drug traffickers through the High Intensity Drug Trafficking Areas Program and other task forces;

(ii) hire, train, and equip law enforcement officers and prosecutors; and

(iii) promote crime reduction programs using evidence-based practices and strategic planning to help reduce crime and criminal recidivism.

(8) Statistics on-

(A) the prevalence of dyslexia among prisoners in prisons operated by the Bureau of Prisons; and

(B) any change in the effectiveness of dyslexia mitigation programs among such prisoners that may be attributed to the incorporation of dyslexia screening into the System and of dyslexia treatment into the evidence-based recidivism reduction programs, as required under this chapter.

§ 3635. Definitions

In this subchapter the following definitions apply:

(1) DYSLEXIA.-The term 'dyslexia' means an unexpected difficulty in reading for an individual who has the intelligence to be a much better reader, most commonly caused by a difficulty in the phonological processing (the appreciation of the individual sounds of spoken language), which affects the ability of an individual to speak, read, and spell.

(2) DYSLEXIA SCREENING PROGRAM.-The term 'dyslexia screening program' means a screening program for dyslexia that is-

(A) evidence based (as defined in section 8101(21) of the Elementary and Secondary Education Act of 1965 (20 U.S.C. 7801(21))) with proven psychometrics for validity;

(B) efficient and low-cost; and

(C) readily available.

(3) EVIDENCE-BASED RECIDIVISM REDUCTION PROGRAM.-The term 'evidence-based recidivism reduction program' means either a group or individual activity that-

(A) has been shown by empirical evidence to reduce recidivism or is based on research indicating that it is likely to be effective in reducing recidivism;

(B) is designed to help prisoners succeed in their communities upon release from prison; and

(C) may include-

(i) social learning and communication, interpersonal, anti bullying, rejection response, and other life skills;

(ii) family relationship building, structured parent-child interaction, and parenting skills;

(iii) classes on morals or ethics;

(iv) academic classes;

(v) cognitive behavioral treatment;

(vi) mentoring;

(vii) substance abuse treatment;

(viii) vocational training;

(ix) faith-based classes or services;

(x) civic engagement and reintegrative community services;

(xi) a prison job, including through a prison work program;

(xii) victim impact classes or other restorative justice programs; and

(xiii) trauma counseling and trauma-informed support programs.

(4) PRISONER.-The term 'prisoner' means a person who has been sentenced to a term of imprisonment pursuant to a conviction for a Federal

criminal offense, or a person in the custody of the Bureau of Prisons.

(5) PRODUCTIVE ACTIVITY.-The term 'productive activity' means either a group or individual activity that is designed to allow prisoners determined as having a minimum or low risk of recidivating to remain productive and thereby maintain a minimum or low risk of recidivating, and may include the delivery of the programs described in paragraph (1)[1] to other prisoners.

(6) RISK AND NEEDS ASSESSMENT TOOL.- The term 'risk and needs assessment tool' means an objective and statistically validated method through which information is collected and evaluated to determine-

(A) as part of the intake process, the risk that a prisoner will recidivate upon release from prison;

(B) the recidivism reduction programs that will best minimize the risk that the prisoner will recidivate upon release from prison; and

(C) the periodic reassessment of risk that a prisoner will recidivate upon release from prison, based on factors including indicators of progress and of regression, that are dynamic and that can reasonably be expected to change while in prison..

(b)   Clerical amendment.-The table of subchapters for chapter 229 of title 18, United States Code, is amended by adding at the end the following:

"D. Risk and Needs Assessment 3631."

SEC. 102. Implementation of system and recommendations by Bureau of Prisons.

(a)   Implementation of system generally.- **Section 3621 of title 18**, United States Code, is amended by adding at the end the following:

"(h) Implementation of risk and needs assessment system.-

---

[1] But See 18 U.S.Code 3635 (2019), n. 1., Probably should be paragraph (3). *Id.*

(1) IN GENERAL.-Not later than 180 days after the Attorney General completes and releases the risk and needs assessment system (referred to in this subsection as the 'System') developed under subchapter D, the Director of the Bureau of Prisons shall, in accordance with that subchapter-

(A) implement and complete the initial intake risk and needs assessment for each prisoner (including for each prisoner who was a prisoner prior to the effective date of this subsection), regardless of the prisoner's length of imposed term of imprisonment, and begin to assign prisoners to appropriate evidence-based recidivism reduction programs based on that determination;

(B) begin to expand the effective evidence-based recidivism reduction programs and productive activities it offers and add any new evidence based recidivism reduction programs and productive activities necessary to effectively implement the System; and

(C) begin to implement the other risk and needs assessment tools necessary to effectively implement the System over time, while prisoners are participating in and completing the effective evidence-based recidivism reduction programs and productive activities.

(2) PHASE-IN.-In order to carry out paragraph (1), so that every prisoner has the opportunity to participate in and complete the type and amount of evidence-based recidivism reduction programs or productive activities they need, and be reassessed for recidivism risk as necessary to effectively implement the System, the Bureau of Prisons shall-

(A) provide such evidence-based recidivism reduction programs and productive activities for all prisoners before the date that is 2 years after the date on which the Bureau of Prisons completes a risk and needs assessment for each prisoner under paragraph (1) (A); and

(B) develop and validate the risk and needs assessment tool to be used in the reassessments of risk of recidivism, while prisoners are participating in and completing evidence-based recidivism reduction programs and productive activities.

(3) PRIORITY DURING PHASE-IN.-During the 2-year period described in paragraph (2) (A), the priority for such programs and activities shall be accorded based on a prisoner's proximity to release date.

(4) PRELIMINARY EXPANSION OF EVIDENCE-BASED RECIDIVISM REDUCTION PROGRAMS AND AUTHORITY TO USE INCENTIVES.-Beginning on the date of enactment of this subsection, the Bureau of Prisons may begin to expand any evidence-based recidivism reduction programs and productive activities that exist at a prison as of such date, and may offer to prisoners who successfully participate in such programs and activities the incentives and rewards described in subchapter D.

(5) RECIDIVISM REDUCTION PARTNERSHIPS.- In order to expand evidence-based recidivism reduction programs and productive activities, the Attorney General shall develop policies for the warden of each prison of the Bureau of Prisons to enter into partnerships, subject to the availability of appropriations, with any of the following:

(A) Nonprofit and other private organizations, including faith-based, art, and community-based organizations that will deliver recidivism reduction programming on a paid or volunteer basis.

(B) Institutions of higher education (as defined in section 101 of the Higher Education Act of 1965 **(20 U.S.C. 1001))** that will deliver instruction on a paid or volunteer basis.

(C) Private entities that will-

(i) deliver vocational training and certifications;

(ii) provide equipment to facilitate vocational training or employment opportunities for prisoners;

(iii) employ prisoners; or

(iv) assist prisoners in prerelease custody or supervised release in finding employment.

(D) Industry-sponsored organizations that will deliver

workforce development and training, on a paid or volunteer basis.

(6) REQUIREMENT TO PROVIDE PROGRAMS TO ALL PRISONERS; PRIORITY.-The Director of the Bureau of Prisons shall provide all prisoners with the opportunity to actively participate in evidence-based recidivism reduction programs or productive activities, according to their specific criminogenic needs, throughout their entire term of incarceration. Priority for participation in recidivism reduction programs shall be given to medium-risk and high-risk prisoners, with access to productive activities given to minimum-risk and low-risk prisoners.

(7) DEFINITIONS.-The terms in this subsection have the meaning given those terms in section 3635."

(b) Prerelease custody.-

(1) IN GENERAL.-**Section 3624 of title 18**, United States Code, is amended-

(A) in subsection (b)(1)-

(i) by striking , beyond the time served, of up to 54 days at the end of each year of the prisoner's term of imprisonment, beginning at the end of the first year of the term, and inserting of up to 54 days for each year of the prisoner's sentence imposed by the court,; and

(ii) by striking credit for the last year or portion of a year of the term of imprisonment shall be prorated and credited within the last six weeks of the sentence and inserting credit for the last year of a term of imprisonment shall be credited on the first day of the last year of the term of imprisonment; and

(B) by adding at the end the following:

"(g) Prerelease custody or supervised release for risk and needs assessment system participants.-

(1) ELIGIBLE PRISONERS.-This subsection applies in the case of a prisoner (as such term is defined in section 3635) who-

     (A) has earned time credits under the risk and needs assessment system developed under subchapter D (referred to in this subsection as the 'System') in an amount that is equal to the remainder of the prisoner's imposed term of imprisonment;

     (B) has shown through the periodic risk reassessments a demonstrated recidivism risk reduction or has maintained a minimum or low recidivism risk, during the prisoner's term of imprisonment;

     (C) has had the remainder of the prisoner's imposed term of imprisonment computed under applicable law; and

     (D)

          (i) in the case of a prisoner being placed in prerelease custody, the prisoner-

               (I) has been determined under the System to be a minimum or low risk to recidivate pursuant to the last 2 reassessments of the prisoner; or

               (II) has had a petition to be transferred to prerelease custody or supervised release approved by the warden of the prison, after the warden's determination that-

                    (aa) the prisoner would not be a danger to society if transferred to prerelease custody or supervised release;

                    (bb) the prisoner has made a good faith effort to lower their recidivism risk through participation in recidivism reduction programs or productive activities; and

                    (cc) the prisoner is unlikely to recidivate; or

(ii) in the case of a prisoner being placed in supervised release, the prisoner has been determined under the System to be a minimum or low risk to recidivate pursuant to the last reassessment of the prisoner.

(2) TYPES OF PRERELEASE CUSTODY.-A prisoner shall be placed in prerelease custody as follows:

(A) HOME CONFINEMENT.-

(i) IN GENERAL.-A prisoner placed in prerelease custody pursuant to this subsection who is placed in home confinement shall-

(I) be subject to 24-hour electronic monitoring that enables the prompt identification of the prisoner, location, and time, in the case of any violation of subclause (II);

(II) remain in the prisoner's residence, except that the prisoner may leave the prisoner's home in order to, subject to the approval of the Director of the Bureau of Prisons-

(aa) perform a job or job-related activities, including an apprenticeship, or participate in job-seeking activities;

(bb) participate in evidence-based recidivism reduction programming or productive activities assigned by the System, or similar activities;

(cc) perform community service;

(dd) participate in crime victim restoration activities;

(ee) receive medical treatment;

(ff) attend religious activities; or

(gg) participate in other family related activities that facilitate the prisoner's successful reentry such as a family funeral, a family wedding, or to visit a family member who is seriously ill; and

(III) comply with such other conditions as the Director determines appropriate.

(ii) ALTERNATE MEANS OF MONITORING.-If the electronic monitoring of a prisoner described in clause (i)(I) is infeasible for technical or religious reasons, the Director of the Bureau of Prisons may use alternative means of monitoring a prisoner placed in home confinement that the Director determines are as effective or more effective than the electronic monitoring described in clause (i)(I).

(iii) MODIFICATIONS.-The Director of the Bureau of Prisons may modify the conditions described in clause (i) if the Director determines that a compelling reason exists to do so, and that the prisoner has demonstrated exemplary compliance with such conditions.

(iv) DURATION.-Except as provided in paragraph (4), a prisoner who is placed in home confinement shall remain in home confinement until the prisoner has served not less than 85 percent of the prisoner's imposed term of imprisonment.

(B) RESIDENTIAL REENTRY CENTER.-A prisoner placed in prerelease custody pursuant to this subsection who is placed at a residential reentry center shall be subject to such conditions as the Director of the Bureau of Prisons determines appropriate.

(3) SUPERVISED RELEASE.-If the sentencing court included as a part of the prisoner's sentence a requirement that the prisoner be placed on a term

of supervised release after imprisonment pursuant to section 3583, the Director of the Bureau of Prisons may transfer the prisoner to begin any such term of supervised release at an earlier date, not to exceed 12 months, based on the application of time credits under section 3632.

(4) DETERMINATION OF CONDITIONS.-In determining appropriate conditions for prisoners placed in prerelease custody pursuant to this subsection, the Director of the Bureau of Prisons shall, to the extent practicable, provide that increasingly less restrictive conditions shall be imposed on prisoners who demonstrate continued compliance with the conditions of such prerelease custody, so as to most effectively prepare such prisoners for reentry.

(5) VIOLATIONS OF CONDITIONS.-If a prisoner violates a condition of the prisoner's prerelease custody, the Director of the Bureau of Prisons may impose such additional conditions on the prisoner's prerelease custody as the Director of the Bureau of Prisons determines appropriate, or revoke the prisoner's prerelease custody and require the prisoner to serve the remainder of the term of imprisonment to which the prisoner was sentenced, or any portion thereof, in prison. If the violation is nontechnical in nature, the Director of the Bureau of Prisons shall revoke the prisoner's prerelease custody.

(6) ISSUANCE OF GUIDELINES.-The Attorney General, in consultation with the Assistant Director for the Office of Probation and Pretrial Services, shall issue guidelines for use by the Bureau of Prisons in determining-

(A) the appropriate type of prerelease custody or supervised release and level of supervision for a prisoner placed on prerelease custody pursuant to this subsection; and

(B) consequences for a violation of a condition of such prerelease custody by such a prisoner, including a return to prison and a reassessment of evidence-based recidivism risk level under the System.

(7) AGREEMENTS WITH UNITED STATES PROBATION AND PRETRIAL SERVICES.- The Director of the Bureau of Prisons shall, to the greatest extent practicable, enter into agreements with United States Probation and Pretrial Services to supervise prisoners placed in home confinement under this subsection. Such agreements shall-

(A) authorize United States Probation and Pretrial Services to exercise the authority granted to the Director pursuant to paragraphs (3) and (4); and

(B) take into account the resource requirements of United States Probation and Pretrial Services as a result of the transfer of Bureau of Prisons prisoners to prerelease custody or supervised release.

(8) ASSISTANCE.-United States Probation and Pretrial Services shall, to the greatest extent practicable, offer assistance to any prisoner not under its supervision during pre release custody under this subsection.

(9) MENTORING, REENTRY, AND SPIRITUAL SERVICES.-Any prerelease custody into which a prisoner is placed under this subsection may not include a condition prohibiting the prisoner from receiving mentoring, reentry, or spiritual services from a person who provided such services to the prisoner while the prisoner was incarcerated, except that the warden of the facility at which the prisoner was incarcerated may waive the requirement under this paragraph if the warden finds that the provision of such ser- vices would pose a significant security risk to the prisoner, persons who provide such services, or any other person. The warden shall provide written notice of any such waiver to the person providing such services and to the prisoner.

(10) TIME LIMITS INAPPLICABLE.- The time limits under subsections (b) and (c) shall not apply to prerelease custody under this subsection.

(11) PRERELEASE CUSTODY CAPACITY.-The Director of the Bureau of Prisons shall ensure there is sufficient prerelease custody capacity to accommodate all eligible prisoners..

(2) EFFECTIVE DATE.-The amendments made by this subsection shall take effect beginning on the date that the Attorney General completes and releases the risk and needs assessment system under subchapter D of chapter 229 of title 18, United States Code, as added by section 101(a) of this Act.

(3) APPLICABILITY.- The amendments made by this subsection shall apply with respect to offenses committed before, on, or after the date of enactment of this Act, except that such amendments shall not apply with respect to

offenses committed before November 1, 1987.

SEC. 103. GAO Report

Not later than 2 years after the Director of the Bureau of Prisons implements the risk and needs assessment system under section 3621 of title 18, United States Code, and every 2 years thereafter, the Comptroller General of the United States shall conduct an audit of the use of the risk and needs assessment system at Bureau of Prisons facilities. The audit shall include analysis of the following:

(1) Whether inmates are being assessed under the risk and needs assessment system with the frequency required under such section 3621 of title 18, United States Code.

(2) Whether the Bureau of Prisons is able to offer recidivism reduction programs and productive activities (as such terms are defined in section 3635 of title 18, United States Code, as added by section 101(a) of this Act).

(3) Whether the Bureau of Prisons is offering the type, amount, and intensity of recidivism reduction programs and productive activities for prisoners to earn the maximum amount of time credits for which they are eligible.

(4) Whether the Attorney General is carrying out the duties under section 3631(b) of title 18, United States Code, as added by section 101(a) of this Act.

(5) Whether officers and employees of the Bureau of Prisons are receiving the training described in section 3632(f) of title 18, United States Code, as added by section 101(a) of this Act.

(6) Whether the Bureau of Prisons offers work assignments to all prisoners who might benefit from such an assignment.

(7) Whether the Bureau of Prisons transfers prisoners to prerelease custody or super- vised release as soon as they are eligible for such a transfer under section 3624(g) of title 18, United States Code, as added by section 102(b) of this Act.

(8) The rates of recidivism among similarly classified prisoners to identify any unwarranted disparities, including disparities among similarly classified prisoners of different demographic groups, in such rates.

SEC. 104. Authorization of appropriations.

(a) In general.-There is authorized to be appropriated to carry out this title $75,000,000 for each of fiscal years 2019 through 2023. Of the amount appropriated under this subsection, 80 percent shall be reserved for use by the Director of the Bureau of Prisons to implement the system under section 3621(h) of title 18, United States Code, as added by section 102(a) of this Act.

(b) Savings.-It is the sense of Congress that any savings associated with reductions in recidivism that result from this title should be reinvested-

(1) to supplement funding for programs that increase public safety by providing resources to State and local law enforcement officials, including for the adoption of innovative technologies and information sharing capabilities;

(2) into evidence-based recidivism reduction programs offered by the Bureau of Prisons; and

(3) into ensuring eligible prisoners have access to such programs and productive activities offered by the Bureau of Prisons.

SEC. 105. Rules Of Construction.

Nothing in this Act, or the amendments made by this Act, may be construed to provide authority to place a prisoner in prerelease custody or supervised release who is serving a term of imprisonment pursuant to a conviction for an offense under the laws of one of the 50 States, or of a territory or possession of the United States or to amend or affect the enforcement of the immigration laws, as defined in section 101 of the Immigration and Nationality Act **(8 U.S.C. 1101).**

SEC. 106. Faith Based Considerations

(a) In general.- In considering any program, treatment, regimen, group, company, charity, person, or entity of any kind under any provision of this Act, or the amendments made by this Act, the fact that it may be or is faith-based may not be a basis for any discrimination against it in any manner or for any purpose.

(b) Eligibility for earned time credit.-Participation in a faith-based program, treatment, or regimen may qualify a prisoner for earned time credit under subchapter D of chapter 229 of title 18, United States Code, as added by section 101(a) of this Act, however, the Director of the Bureau of Prisons shall ensure that non-faith-based programs that qualify for earned time credit are offered at each Bureau of Prisons facility in addition to any such faith-based programs.

(c) Limitation on activities.-A group, company, charity, person, or entity may not engage in explicitly religious activities using direct financial assistance made available under this title or the amendments made by this title.

(d) Rule of construction.-Nothing in this Act, or the amendments made by this Act, may be construed to amend any requirement under Federal law or the Constitution of the United States regarding funding for faith-based programs or activities.

SEC. 107. Independent Review Committee.

(a) In general.-The Attorney General shall consult with an Independent Review Committee in carrying out the Attorney General's duties under sections 3631(b), 3632 and 3633 of title 18, United States Code, as added by section 101(a) of this Act.

(b) Formation of Independent Review Committee.-The National Institute of Justice shall select a nonpartisan and nonprofit organization with expertise in the study and development of risk and needs assessment tools to host the Independent Review Committee. The Independent Review Committee shall be established not later than 30 days after the date of enactment of this Act.

(c) Appointment of Independent Review Committee.-The organization selected by the National Institute of Justice shall appoint not fewer than 6 members to the Independent Review Committee.

(d) Composition of the Independent Review Committee.-The members of the Independent Review Committee shall all have expertise in risk and needs assessment systems and shall include-

(1) 2 individuals who have published peer-reviewed scholarship about risk and needs assessments in both corrections and community settings;

(2) 2 corrections practitioners who have developed and implemented a risk assessment tool in a corrections system or in a community supervision setting, including 1 with prior experience working within the Bureau of Prisons; and

(3) 1 individual with expertise in assessing risk assessment implementation.

(e) Duties of the Independent Review Committee.-The Independent Review Committee shall assist the Attorney General in carrying out the Attorney General's duties under sections 3631(b), 3632 and 3633 of title 18, United States Code, as added by section 101 (a) of this Act, including by assisting in-

(1) conducting a review of the existing prisoner risk and needs assessment systems in operation on the date of enactment of this Act;

(2) developing recommendations regarding evidence-based recidivism reduction programs and productive activities;

(3) conducting research and data analysis on-

(A) evidence-based recidivism reduction programs relating to the use of prisoner risk and needs assessment tools;

(B) the most effective and efficient uses of such programs; and

(C) which evidence-based recidivism reduction programs are the most effective at reducing recidivism, and the type, amount, and intensity of programming that most effectively reduces the risk of recidivism; and

(4) reviewing and validating the risk and needs assessment system.

(f) Bureau of Prisons cooperation.-The Director of the Bureau of Prisons shall assist the Independent Review Committee in performing the Committee's duties and promptly respond to requests from the Committee for access to Bureau of Prisons facilities, personnel, and information.

(g) **Report.-Not later than 2 years after the date of enactment of this Act, the Independent Review Committee shall submit to the Committee on the Judiciary and the Subcommittee on Commerce, Justice, Science, and Related Agencies of the Committee on Appropriations of the Senate and the Committee on the Judiciary and the Subcommittee on Commerce, Justice, Science, and Related Agencies of the Committee on Appropriations of the House of Representatives a report that includes-**

(1) a list of all offenses of conviction for which prisoners were ineligible to receive time credits under section 3632(d)(4)(D) of title 18, United States Code, as added by section 101(a) of this Act, and for each offense the number of prisoners excluded, including demographic percentages by age, race, and sex;

(2) the criminal history categories of prisoners ineligible to receive time credits under section 3632(d)(4)(D) of title 18, United States Code, as added by section 101(a) of this Act, and for each category the number of prisoners excluded, including demographic percentages by age, race, and sex;

(3) the number of prisoners ineligible to apply time credits under section 3632(d)(4)(D) of title 18, United States Code, as added by section 101(a) of this Act, who do not participate in recidivism reduction programming or productive activities, including the demo- graphic percentages by age, race, and sex;

(4) any recommendations for modifications to section 3632(d)(4)(D) of title 18, United States Code, as added by section 101(a) of this Act, and any other recommendations regarding recidivism reduction.

(h) Termination.-The Independent Review Committee shall terminate on the date that is 2 years after the date on which the risk and needs assessment system authorized by sections 3632 and 3633 of title 18, United States Code, as added by section 101(a) of this Act, is released.

TITLE II Bureau of Prisons secure firearms storage

SEC. 201. Short Title.

This title may be cited as the Lieutenant Osvaldo Albarati Correctional Officer Self-Protection Act of 2018.

SEC. 202. Secure Firearms Storage.

(a) In general.-Chapter 303 of title 18, United States Code, is amended by adding at the end the following:

§ 4050. Secure firearms storage

(a) Definitions.-In this section-

(1) the term 'employee' means a qualified law enforcement officer employed by the Bureau of Prisons; and

(2) the terms 'firearm' and 'qualified law enforcement officer' have the meanings given those terms under section 926B.

(b) Secure firearms storage.-The Director of the Bureau of Prisons shall ensure that each chief executive officer of a Federal penal or correctional institution-

(1)
(A) provides a secure storage area located outside of the secure perimeter of the institution for employees to store firearms; or

(B) allows employees to store firearms in a vehicle lockbox approved by the Director of the Bureau of Prisons; and

(2) notwithstanding any other provision of law, allows employees to carry concealed firearms on the premises outside of the secure perimeter of the institution..

(b) Technical and conforming amendment.-The table of sections for chapter 303 of title 18, United States Code, is amended by adding at the end the following:

"4050. Secure firearms storage."

TITLE III Restraints on pregnant prisoners prohibited

SEC. 301. Use of restraints on prisoners during the period of pregnancy and postpartum recovery prohibited.

(a) In general.-Chapter 317 of title 18, United States Code, is amended by inserting after section 4321 the following:

§ 4322. Use of restraints on prisoners during the period of pregnancy, labor, and postpartum recovery prohibited

(a) Prohibition.-Except as provided in subsection (b), beginning on the date on which pregnancy is confirmed by a healthcare professional, and ending at the conclusion of postpartum recovery, a prisoner in the custody of the Bureau of Prisons, or in the custody of the United States Marshals Service pursuant to section 4086, shall not be placed in restraints.

(b) Exceptions.-

(1) IN GENERAL.-The prohibition under subsection (a) shall not apply if-

(A) an appropriate corrections official, or a United States marshal, as applicable, makes a determination that the prisoner-

(i) is an immediate and credible flight risk that cannot reasonably be prevented by other means; or

(ii) poses an immediate and serious threat of harm to herself or others that cannot reasonably be prevented by other means; or

(B) a healthcare professional responsible for the health and safety of the prisoner determines that the use of restraints is appropriate for the medical safety of the prisoner.

(2) LEAST RESTRICTIVE RESTRAINTS.-In the case that restraints are used pursuant to an exception under paragraph (1), only the least restrictive restraints necessary to pre- vent the harm or risk of escape described in paragraph

(1) may be used.

(3) APPLICATION.-

(A) IN GENERAL.-The exceptions under paragraph (1) may not be applied-

(i) to place restraints around the ankles, legs, or waist of a prisoner;

(ii) to restrain a prisoner's hands behind her back;

(iii) to restrain a prisoner using 4-point restraints; or

(iv) to attach a prisoner to another prisoner.

(B) MEDICAL REQUEST.-Notwithstanding paragraph (1), upon the request of a healthcare professional who is responsible for the health and safety of a prisoner, a corrections official or United States marshal, as applicable, shall refrain from using restraints on the prisoner or shall remove restraints used on the prisoner.

(c) Reports.-

(1) REPORT TO THE DIRECTOR AND HEALTHCARE PROFESSIONAL.-If a corrections official or United States marshal uses restraints on a prisoner under subsection (b)(1), that official or marshal shall submit, not later than 30 days after placing the prisoner in restraints, to the Director of the Bureau of Prisons or the Director of the United States Marshals Service, as applicable, and to the healthcare professional responsible for the health and safety of the prisoner, a written report that describes the facts and circum- stances surrounding the use of restraints, and includes-

(A) the reasoning upon which the determination to use restraints was made;

(B) the details of the use of restraints, including the type of restraints used and length of time during which restraints were used; and

(C) any resulting physical effects on the prisoner observed by or known to the corrections official or United States marshal, as applicable.

(2) SUPPLEMENTAL REPORT TO THE DIRECTOR.-Upon receipt of a report under para- graph (1), the healthcare professional responsible for the health and safety of the prisoner may submit to the Director such information as the healthcare professional determines is relevant to the use of restraints on the prisoner.

(3) REPORT TO JUDICIARY COMMITTEES.-

(A) IN GENERAL.-Not later than 1 year after the date of enactment of this section, and annually thereafter, the Director of the Bureau of Prisons and the Director of the United States Marshals Service shall each submit to the Judiciary Committee of the Senate and of the House of Representatives a report that certifies compliance with this section and includes the information required to be reported under paragraph (1).

(B) PERSONALLY IDENTIFIABLE INFORMATION.-The report under this paragraph shall not contain any personally identifiable information of any prisoner.

(d) Notice.-Not later than 48 hours after the confirmation of a prisoner's pregnancy by a healthcare professional, that prisoner shall be notified by an appropriate healthcare professional, corrections official, or United States marshal, as applicable, of the restrictions on the use of restraints under this section.

(e) Violation reporting process.-The Director of the Bureau of Prisons, in consultation with the Director of the United States Marshals Service, shall establish a process through which a prisoner may report a violation of this section.

(f) Training.-

(1) IN GENERAL.-The Director of the Bureau of Prisons and the Director of the United States Marshals Service shall each develop training guidelines regarding the use of restraints on female prisoners during the period of pregnancy, labor, and postpartum recovery, and shall incorporate such guidelines into appropriate training programs. Such training guidelines shall include-

(A) how to identify certain symptoms of pregnancy that require immediate referral to a healthcare professional;

(B) circumstances under which the exceptions under subsection (b) would apply;

(C) in the case that an exception under subsection (b) applies, how to apply restraints in a way that does not harm the prisoner, the fetus, or the neonate;

(D) the information required to be reported under subsection (c); and

(E) the right of a healthcare professional to request that restraints not be used, and the requirement under subsection (b)(3)(B) to comply with such a request.

(2) DEVELOPMENT OF GUIDELINES.-In developing the guidelines required by para- graph (1), the Directors shall each consult with healthcare professionals with expertise in caring for women during the period of pregnancy and postpartum recovery.

(g) Definitions.-For purposes of this section:

(1) POSTPARTUM RECOVERY.-The term 'postpartum recovery' means the 12-week period, or longer as determined by the healthcare professional responsible for the health and safety of the prisoner, following delivery, and shall include the entire period that the prisoner is in the hospital or infirmary.

(2) PRISONER.-The term 'prisoner' means a person who has been sentenced to a term of imprisonment pursuant to a conviction for a Federal criminal offense, or a person in the custody of the Bureau of Prisons, including a person in a Bureau of Prisons contracted facility.

(3) RESTRAINTS.-The term 'restraints' means any physical or mechanical device used to control the movement of a prisoner's body, limbs, or both.

(b) Clerical amendment.-The table of sections for chapter 317 of title 18,

United States Code, is amended by adding after the item relating to section 4321 the following:

"**4322.** Use of restraints on prisoners during the period of pregnancy, labor, and postpartum recovery prohibited."

TITLE IV Sentencing Reform

SEC. 401. Reduce and restrict enhanced sentencing for prior drug felonies.

(a) Controlled Substances Act amendments.-The Controlled Substances Act (21 U.S.C. 801 et seq.) is amended-

(1) in section 102 **(21 U.S.C. 802)**, by adding at the end the following:

"**(57) The term 'serious drug felony' means** an offense described in section 924(e)(2) of title 18, United States Code, for which-

(A) the offender served a term of imprisonment of more than 12 months; and

(B) the offender's release from any term of imprisonment was within 15 years of the commencement of the instant offense.

(58) The term 'serious violent felony' means-

(A) an offense described in section 3559(c)(2) of title 18, United States Code, for which the offender served a term of imprisonment of more than 12 months; and

(B) any offense that would be a felony violation of section 113 of title 18, United States Code, if the offense were committed in the special maritime and territorial jurisdiction of the United States, for which the offender served a term of imprisonment of more than 12 months."; and

(2) in section 401(b)(1) **(21 U.S.C. 841(b)(1))**-

(A) in subparagraph (A), in the matter following clause (viii)-

(i) by striking "If any person commits such a violation after a prior conviction for a felony drug offense has become final, such person shall be sentenced to a term of imprisonment which may not be less than 20 years" and inserting the following: "If any person commits such a violation after a prior conviction for a serious drug felony or serious violent felony has become final, such person shall be sentenced to a term of imprisonment of not less than 15 years"; and

(ii) by striking after two or more prior convictions for a felony drug offense have become final, such person shall be sentenced to a mandatory term of life imprisonment without release and inserting the following: after 2 or more prior convictions for a serious drug felony or serious violent felony have become final, such person shall be sentenced to a term of imprisonment of not less than 25 years; and

(B) in subparagraph (B), in the matter following clause (viii), by striking If any person commits such a violation after a prior conviction for a felony drug offense has become final and inserting the following: If any person commits such a violation after a prior conviction for a serious drug felony or serious violent felony has become final."

(b) Controlled Substances Import and Export Act amendments.-Section 1010(b) of the Controlled Substances Import and Export Act **(21 U.S.C. 960(b))** is amended-

(1) in paragraph (1), in the matter following subparagraph (H), by striking If any per- son commits such a violation after a prior conviction for a felony drug offense has become final, such person shall be sentenced to a term of imprisonment of not less than 20 years and inserting If any person commits such a violation after a prior conviction for a serious drug felony or serious violent felony has become final, such person shall be sentenced to a term of imprisonment of not less than 15 years; and

(2) in paragraph (2), in the matter following subparagraph (H), by striking felony drug offense and inserting serious drug felony or serious violent

felony.

(c) Applicability to pending cases.-This section, and the amendments made by this section, shall apply to any offense that was committed before the date of enactment of this Act, if a sentence for the offense has not been imposed as of such date of enactment.

SEC. 402. Broadening of existing safety valve.

(a) Amendments.-Section 3553 of title 18, United States Code, is amended-

(1) in subsection (f)-

(A) in the matter preceding paragraph (1)-

(i) by striking or section 1010 and inserting , section 1010; and

(ii) by inserting , or section 70503 or 70506 of title 46 after 963);

(B) by striking paragraph (1) and inserting the following:

(1) the defendant does not have-

(A) more than 4 criminal history points, excluding any criminal history points resulting from a 1-point offense, as determined under the sentencing guidelines;

(B) a prior 3-point offense, as determined under the sentencing guidelines; and

(C) a prior 2-point violent offense, as determined under the sentencing guidelines; and

(1) by adding at the end the following:

"Information disclosed by a defendant under this subsection may not be used to enhance the sentence of the defendant unless the information relates to a violent offense."; and

(2) by adding at the end the following:

"(g) Definition of violent offense.-As used in this section, the term 'violent offense' means a crime of violence, as defined in section 16, that is punishable by imprisonment."

(b) Applicability.- The amendments made by this section shall apply only to a conviction entered on or after the date of enactment of this Act.

SEC. 403. CLARIFICATION OF SECTION 924(c) OF TITLE 18, UNITED STATES CODE.

(a) In general.-Section 924(c)(1)(C) of title 18, United States Code, is amended, in the matter preceding clause (i), by striking second or subsequent conviction under this subsection and inserting violation of this subsection that occurs after a prior conviction under this subsection has become final.

(b) Applicability to pending cases.-This section, and the amendments made by this section, shall apply to any offense that was committed before the date of enactment of this Act, if a sentence for the offense has not been imposed as of such date of enactment.

SEC. 404. Application of Fair Sentencing Act.

(a) Definition of covered offense.-In this section, the term covered offense means a violation of a Federal criminal statute, the statutory penalties for which were modified by section 2 or 3 of the Fair Sentencing Act of 2010 (Public Law 111-220; 124 Stat. 2372), that was committed before August 3, 2010.

(b) Defendants previously sentenced.-A court that imposed a sentence for a covered offense may, on motion of the defendant, the Director of the Bureau of Prisons, the attorney for the Government, or the court, impose a reduced sentence as if sections 2 and 3 of the Fair Sentencing Act of 2010 (Public Law 111-220; 124 Stat. 2372) were in effect at the time the covered offense was committed.

(c) Limitations.-No court shall entertain a motion made under this section to reduce a sentence if the sentence was previously imposed or previously reduced in accordance with the amendments made by sections 2 and 3 of the Fair Sentencing Act of 2010 (Public Law 111-220; 124 Stat. 2372) or if a previous motion made under this section to reduce the sentence was, after the date of enactment of this Act, denied after a complete review of the motion on the merits. Nothing in this section shall be construed to require a court to reduce any sentence pursuant to this section.

TITLE V Second Chance Act of 2007 reauthorization

SEC. 501. Short Title.

This title may be cited as the Second Chance Reauthorization Act of 2018. SEC. 502. Improvements to existing programs.

SEC. 502. Improvements To Existing Programs.

(a) Reauthorization of adult and juvenile offender State and local demonstration projects.-Section 2976 of title I of the Omnibus Crime Control and Safe Streets Act of 1968 (34 U.S.C. 10631) is amended-

(1) by striking subsection (a) and inserting the following:

"(a) Grant authorization.-The Attorney General shall make grants to States, local governments, territories, or Indian tribes, or any combination thereof (in this section referred to as an 'eligible entity'), in partnership with interested persons (including Federal corrections and supervision agencies), service providers, and nonprofit organizations for the purpose of strategic planning and implementation of adult and juvenile offender reentry projects.";

(2) in subsection (b)-

(A) in paragraph (3), by inserting or reentry courts, after community,;

(B) in paragraph (6), by striking and at the end;

(C) in paragraph (7), by striking the period at the end and inserting ; and; and

(D) by adding at the end the following:

"(8) promoting employment opportunities consistent with the Transitional Jobs strategy (as defined in section 4 of the Second Chance Act of 2007 **(34 U.S.C. 60502))**."; and

(3) by striking subsections (d), (e), and (f) and inserting the following:

"(d) Combined grant application; priority consideration.-

(1) IN GENERAL.-The Attorney General shall develop a procedure to allow applicants to submit a single application for a planning grant under subsection (e) and an implementation grant under subsection (f)."

(2) PRIORITY CONSIDERATION.-The Attorney General shall give priority consideration to grant applications under subsections (e) and (f) that include a commitment by the applicant to partner with a local evaluator to identify and analyze data that will-

(A) enable the grantee to target the intended offender population; and

(B) serve as a baseline for purposes of the evaluation.

(e) Planning grants.-

(1) IN GENERAL.-Except as provided in paragraph (3), the Attorney General may make a grant to an eligible entity of not more than $75,000 to develop a strategic, collaborative plan for an adult or juvenile offender reentry demonstration project as described in subsection (h) that includes-

(A) a budget and a budget justification;

(B) a description of the outcome measures that will be used to measure the effective- ness of the program in promoting public safety and public health;

(C) the activities proposed;

(D) a schedule for completion of the activities described in subparagraph (C); and

(E) a description of the personnel necessary to complete the activities described in sub- paragraph (C).

(2) MAXIMUM TOTAL GRANTS AND GEOGRAPHIC DIVERSITY.-

(A) MAXIMUM AMOUNT.-The Attorney General may not make initial planning grants and implementation grants to 1 eligible entity in a total amount that is more than a $1,000,000.

(B) GEOGRAPHIC DIVERSITY.-The Attorney General shall make every effort to ensure equitable geographic distribution of grants under this section and take into consideration the needs of underserved populations, including rural and tribal communities.

(3) PERIOD OF GRANT.-A planning grant made under this subsection shall be for a period of not longer than 1 year, beginning on the first day of the month in which the planning grant is made.

(f) Implementation grants.-

(1) APPLICATIONS.-An eligible entity desiring an implementation grant under this subsection shall submit to the Attorney General an application that-

(A) contains a reentry strategic plan as described in subsection (h), which describes the long-term strategy and incorporates a detailed implementation schedule, including the plans of the applicant to fund the program after Federal funding is discontinued;

(B) identifies the local government role and the role of governmental agencies and nonprofit organizations that will be coordinated by, and that will collaborate on, the offender reentry strategy of the applicant, and certifies the involvement of such agencies and organizations;

(C) describes the evidence-based methodology and outcome measures that will be used to evaluate the program funded with a grant under this subsection, and specifically explains how such measurements will provide valid measures of the impact of that pro- gram; and

(D) describes how the project could be broadly replicated if demonstrated to be effective.

(2) REQUIREMENTS.- The Attorney General may make a grant to an applicant under this subsection only if the application-

(A) reflects explicit support of the chief executive officer, or their designee, of the State, unit of local government, territory, or Indian tribe applying for a grant under this subsection;

(B) provides discussion of the role of Federal corrections, State corrections departments, community corrections agencies, juvenile justice systems, and tribal or local jail systems in ensuring successful reentry of offenders into their communities;

(C) provides evidence of collaboration with State, local, or tribal government agencies overseeing health, housing, child welfare, education, substance abuse, victims services, and employment services, and with local law enforcement agencies;

(D) provides a plan for analysis of the statutory, regulatory, rules-based, and practice- based hurdles to reintegration of offenders into the community;

(E) includes the use of a State, local, territorial, or tribal task force, described in sub- section (i), to carry out the activities funded under the grant;

(F) provides a plan for continued collaboration with a local evaluator as necessary to meeting the requirements under subsection (h); and

(G) demonstrates that the applicant participated in the planning grant process or engaged in comparable planning for the reentry project.

(3) PRIORITY CONSIDERATIONS.-The Attorney General shall give priority to grant applications under this subsection that best-

(A) focus initiative on geographic areas with a disproportionate population of offenders released from prisons, jails, and juvenile facilities;

(B) include-

(i) input from nonprofit organizations, in any case where relevant input is available and appropriate to the grant application;

(ii) consultation with crime victims and offenders who are released from prisons, jails, and juvenile facilities;

(iii) coordination with families of offenders;

(iv) input, where appropriate, from the juvenile justice coordinating council of the region;

(v) input, where appropriate, from the reentry coordinating council of the region; or

(vi) input, where appropriate, from other interested persons;

(C) demonstrate effective case assessment and management abilities in order to pro- vide comprehensive and continuous reentry, including-

(i) planning for prerelease transitional housing and community release that begins upon admission for juveniles and jail inmates, and, as appropriate, for prison inmates, depending on the length of the sentence;

(ii) establishing prerelease planning procedures to ensure that the eligibility of an offender for Federal, tribal, or State benefits upon release is established prior to release, subject to any limitations in law, and to ensure that offenders obtain all necessary referrals for reentry services, including assistance identifying and securing suitable housing; or

(iii) delivery of continuous and appropriate mental health services, drug treatment, medical care, job training and placement, educational services, vocational services, and any other service or support needed for reentry;

(D) review the process by which the applicant adjudicates violations of parole, probation, or supervision following release from prison, jail, or a juvenile facility, taking into account public safety and the use of graduated, community-based sanctions for minor and technical violations of parole, probation, or supervision (specifically those violations that are not otherwise, and independently, a violation of law);

(E) provide for an independent evaluation of reentry programs that include, to the maximum extent possible, random assignment and controlled studies to determine the effectiveness of such programs;

(F) target moderate and high-risk offenders for reentry programs through validated assessment tools; or

(G) target offenders with histories of homelessness, substance abuse, or mental illness, including a prerelease assessment of the housing status of the offender and behavioral health needs of the offender with clear coordination with mental health, substance abuse, and homelessness services systems to achieve stable and permanent housing out- comes with appropriate support service.

(4) PERIOD OF GRANT.-A grant made under this subsection shall be effective for a 2-year period-

(A) beginning on the date on which the planning grant awarded under subsection (e) concludes; or

(B) in the case of an implementation grant awarded to an eligible entity that did not receive a planning grant, beginning on the date on which the implementation grant is awarded.;

(4) in subsection (h)-

(A) by redesignating paragraphs (2) and (3) as paragraphs (3) and (4), respectively; and

(B) by striking paragraph (1) and inserting the following:

(1) IN GENERAL.- As a condition of receiving financial assistance under subsection (f), each application shall develop a comprehensive reentry strategic plan that-

(A) contains a plan to assess inmate reentry needs and measurable annual and 3-year performance outcomes;

(B) uses, to the maximum extent possible, randomly assigned and controlled studies, or rigorous quasi-experimental studies with matched comparison groups, to determine the effectiveness of the program funded with a grant under subsection (f); and

(C) includes as a goal of the plan to reduce the rate of recidivism for offenders released from prison, jail or a juvenile facility with funds made available under subsection (f).

(2) LOCAL EVALUATOR.-A partnership with a local evaluator described in subsection (d)(2) shall require the local evaluator to use the baseline data and target population characteristics developed under a subsection (e) planning grant to derive a target goal for recidivism reduction during the 3-year period beginning on the date of implementation of the program.;

(5) in subsection (i)(1)-

(A) in the matter preceding subparagraph (A), by striking under this section and inserting under subsection (f); and

(B) in subparagraph (B), by striking subsection (e)(4) and inserting subsection (f)(2) (D);

(6) "in subsection (j)-

(A) in paragraph (1), by inserting for an implementation grant under subsection (f) after applicant;

(B) in paragraph (2)-

      (i) in subparagraph (E), by inserting , where appropriate after support; and

      (ii) by striking subparagraphs (F), (G), and (H), and inserting the following:

      (F) increased number of staff trained to administer reentry services;

      (G) increased proportion of individuals served by the program among those eligible to receive services;

      (H) increased number of individuals receiving risk screening needs assessment, and case planning services;

      (I) increased enrollment in, and completion of treatment services, including substance abuse and mental health services among those assessed as needing such services;

      (J) increased enrollment in and degrees earned from educational programs, including high school, GED, vocational training, and college education;

      (K) increased number of individuals obtaining and retaining employment;

      (L) increased number of individuals obtaining and maintaining housing;

      (M) increased self-reports of successful community living, including stability of living situation and positive family relationships;

      (N) reduction in drug and alcohol use; and

      (O) reduction in recidivism rates for individuals receiving reentry services after release, as compared to either baseline recidivism rates in the jurisdiction of the grantee or recidivism rates of the control or comparison group.";

(C) in paragraph (3), by striking facilities. and inserting facilities, including a cost- benefit analysis to determine the cost effectiveness of the reentry program.;

(D) in paragraph (4), by striking this section and inserting subsection (f); and

(E) in paragraph (5), by striking this section and inserting subsection (f);

(7) in subsection (k)(1), by striking this section each place the term appears and inserting subsection (f);

(8) in subsection (l)-

(A) in paragraph (2), by inserting beginning on the date on which the most recent implementation grant is made to the grantee under subsection (f) after 2-year period; and

(B) in paragraph (4), by striking over a 2-year period and inserting during the 2-year period described in paragraph (2);

(9) in subsection (o)(1), by striking appropriated and all that follows and inserting the following: appropriated $35,000,000 for each of fiscal years 2019 through 2023.; and

(10) by adding at the end the following:

"(p) Definition.-In this section, the term 'reentry court' means a program that-

(1) monitors juvenile and adult eligible offenders reentering the community;

(2) provides continual judicial supervision;

(3) provides juvenile and adult eligible offenders reentering the community with coordinated and comprehensive reentry services and programs, such as-

(A) drug and alcohol testing and assessment for treatment;

(B) assessment for substance abuse from a substance abuse professional who is approved by the State or Indian tribe and licensed by the appropriate entity to provide alcohol and drug addiction treatment, as appropriate;

(C) substance abuse treatment, including medication assisted treatment, from a provider that is approved by the State or Indian tribe, and licensed, if necessary, to provide medical and other health services;

(D) health (including mental health) services and assessment; (E) aftercare and case management services that-

(i) facilitate access to clinical care and related health services; and

(ii) coordinate with such clinical care and related health services; and

(F) any other services needed for reentry;

(4) convenes community impact panels, victim impact panels, or victim impact educational classes;

(5) provides and coordinates the delivery of community services to juvenile and adult eligible offenders, including-

(A) housing assistance;

(B) education;

(C) job training;

(D) conflict resolution skills training;

(E) batterer intervention programs; and

(F) other appropriate social services; and

(6) establishes and implements graduated sanctions and incentives..

(b) Grants for family-Based substance abuse treatment.- Part DD of title I of the Omni- bus Crime Control and Safe Streets Act of 1968 **(34 U.S.C. 10591 et seq.)** is amended-

(1) in section 2921 **(34 U.S.C. 10591)**, in the matter preceding paragraph (1), by inserting nonprofit organizations, before and Indian;

(2) in section 2923 **(34 U.S.C. 10593)**, by adding at the end the following:

(c) Priority considerations.-The Attorney General shall give priority consideration to grant applications for grants under section 2921 that are submitted by a nonprofit organization that demonstrates a relationship with State and local criminal justice agencies, including-

(1) within the judiciary and prosecutorial agencies; or

(2) with the local corrections agencies, which shall be documented by a written agreement that details the terms of access to facilities and participants and provides information on the history of the organization of working with correctional populations.; and

(3) by striking section 2926(a) and inserting the following:

(a) In general.-There are authorized to be appropriated to carry out this part $10,000,000 for each of fiscal years 2019 through 2023..

(c) Grant program To evaluate and improve educational methods at prisons, jails, and juvenile facilities.-Title I of the Omnibus Crime Control and Safe Streets Act of 1968 **(42 U.S.C. 3711 et seq.)** is amended-

(1) by striking the second part designated as part JJ, as added by the Second Chance Act of 2007 (Public Law 110-199; 122 Stat. 677), relating to grants to evaluate and improve educational methods at prisons, jails, and juvenile facilities;

(2) by adding at the end the following:

"PART NN-Grant program to evaluate and improve educational methods at prisons, jails, and juvenile facilities."

SEC. 3041. Grant program to evaluate and improve educational methods at prisons, jails, and juvenile facilities.

(a) Grant program authorized.-The Attorney General may carry out a grant program under which the Attorney General may make grants to States, units of local government, territories, Indian Tribes, and other public and private entities to-

(1) evaluate methods to improve academic and vocational education for offenders in prisons, jails, and juvenile facilities;

(2) identify, and make recommendations to the Attorney General regarding, best practices relating to academic and vocational education for offenders in prisons, jails, and juvenile facilities, based on the evaluation under paragraph (1);

(3) improve the academic and vocational education programs (including technology career training) available to offenders in prisons, jails, and juvenile facilities; and

(4) implement methods to improve academic and vocational education for offenders in prisons, jails, and juvenile facilities consistent with the best practices identified in sub- section (c).

(b) Application.-To be eligible for a grant under this part, a State or other entity described in subsection (a) shall submit to the Attorney General an application in such form and manner, at such time, and accompanied by such information as the Attorney General specifies.

(c) Best practices.-Not later than 180 days after the date of enactment of the Second Chance Reauthorization Act of 2018, the Attorney General shall identify and publish best practices relating to academic and vocational education for offenders in prisons, jails, and juvenile facilities. The best practices shall consider the evaluations performed and recommendations made under grants made under subsection (a) before the date of enactment of the Second Chance Reauthorization Act of 2018.

(d) Report.-Not later than 90 days after the last day of the final fiscal year of a grant under this part, each entity described in subsection (a) receiving such a grant shall submit to the Attorney General a detailed report of the progress made by the entity using such grant, to permit the Attorney General to evaluate and improve academic and vocational education methods carried out with grants under this part.; and

(3) in section 1001(a) of part J of title I of **the Omnibus Crime Control and Safe Streets Act of 1968 (34 U.S.C. 10261(a))**, by adding at the end the following:

"(28) There are authorized to be appropriated to carry out section 3031(a)(4) of part NN $5,000,000 for each of fiscal years 2019, 2020, 2021, 2022, and 2023."

(d) Careers training demonstration grants.-Section 115 of the Second Chance Act of 2007 **(34 U.S.C. 60511)** is amended-

(1) in the heading, by striking Technology careers and inserting Careers;

(2) in subsection (a)-

(A) by striking and Indian and inserting nonprofit organizations, and Indian; and

(B) by striking technology career training to prisoners and inserting career training, including subsidized employment, when part of a training program, to prisoners and reentering youth and adults;

(3) in subsection (b)-

(A) by striking technology careers training;

(B) by striking technology-based; and

(C) by inserting , as well as upon transition and reentry into the community after facility;

(4) by striking subsection (e);

(5) by redesignating subsections (c) and (d) as subsections (d) and (e), respectively;

(6) by inserting after subsection (b) the following:

(c) Priority consideration.-Priority consideration shall be given to any application under this section that-

(1) provides assessment of local demand for employees in the geographic areas to which offenders are likely to return;

(2) conducts individualized reentry career planning upon the start of incarceration or post-release employment planning for each offender served under the grant;

(3) demonstrates connections to employers within the local community; or

(4) tracks and monitors employment outcomes.; and

by adding at the end the following:

"(f) Authorization of appropriations.-There are authorized to be appropriated to carry out this section $10,000,000 for each of fiscal years 2019, 2020, 2021, 2022, and 2023."

(e) Offender reentry substance abuse and criminal justice collaboration program.-Section 201(f)(1) of the Second Chance Act of 2007 **(34 U.S.C. 60521(f)(1))** is amended to read as follows:

(1) IN GENERAL.-There are authorized to be appropriated to carry out this section $15,000,000 for each of fiscal years 2019 through 2023..

(f) Community-Based mentoring and transitional service grants to nonprofit organizations.-

(1) IN GENERAL.-Section 211 of the **Second Chance Act of 2007**

(34 U.S.C. 60531) is amended-

(A) in the header, by striking Mentoring grants to nonprofit organizations and inserting Community-based mentoring and transitional service grants to nonprofit organizations;

(B) in subsection (a), by striking mentoring and other;

(C) in subsection (b), by striking paragraph (2) and inserting the following:

(2) transitional services to assist in the reintegration of offenders into the community, including-

(A) educational, literacy, and vocational, services and the Transitional Jobs strategy;

(B) substance abuse treatment and services;

(C) coordinated supervision and services for offenders, including physical health care and comprehensive housing and mental health care;

(D) family services; and

(E) validated assessment tools to assess the risk factors of returning inmates; and..

in subsection (f), by striking this section and all that follows and inserting the following: this section $15,000,000 for each of fiscal years 2019 through 2023.

(2) TABLE OF CONTENTS AMENDMENT.-The table of contents in section 2 of the Second Chance Act of 2007 (Public Law 110-199; 122 Stat. 657) is amended by striking the item relating to section 211 and inserting the following:

"Sec. 211. Community-based mentoring and transitional service grants."

(g) Definitions.-

(1) IN GENERAL.-Section 4 of the Second Chance Act of 2007 **(34 U.S.C. 60502)** is amended to read as follows:

SEC. 4. Definitions. In this Act-

(1) the term 'exoneree' means an individual who-

(A) has been convicted of a Federal, tribal, or State offense that is punishable by a term of imprisonment of more than 1 year;

(B) has served a term of imprisonment for not less than 6 months in a Federal, tribal, or State prison or correctional facility as a result of the conviction described in subparagraph (A); and

(C) has been determined to be factually innocent of the offense described in subparagraph (A);

(2) the term 'Indian tribe' has the meaning given in section 901 of title I of the Omni- bus Crime Control and Safe Streets Act of 1968 **(34 U.S.C. 10251)**;

(3) the term 'offender' includes an exoneree; and

(4) the term 'Transitional Jobs strategy' means an employment strategy for youth and adults who are chronically unemployed or those that have barriers to employment that-

(A) is conducted by State, tribal, and local governments, State, tribal, and local work- force boards, and nonprofit organizations;

(B) provides time-limited employment using individual placements, team placements, and social enterprise placements, without displacing existing employees;

(C) pays wages in accordance with applicable law, but in no event less than the higher of the rate specified in section 6(a)(1) of the Fair Labor Standards Act of 1938 **(29 U.S.C. 206(a)(1))** or the applicable State or local minimum wage law, which are subsidized, in whole or in part, by public funds;

(D) combines time-limited employment with activities that

promote skill development, remove barriers to employment, and lead to unsubsidized employment such as a thorough orientation and individual assessment, job readiness and life skills training, case management and supportive services, adult education and training, child support-related services, job retention support and incentives, and other similar activities;

(E) places participants into unsubsidized employment; and

(F) provides job retention, re-employment services, and continuing and vocational edu- cation to ensure continuing participation in unsubsidized employment and identification of opportunities for advancement..

(2) TABLE OF CONTENTS AMENDMENT.-The table of contents in section 2 of the Second Chance Act of 2007 (Public Law 110-199; 122 Stat. 657) is amended by striking the item relating to section 4 and inserting the following:

Sec. 4. Definitions..

(h) Extension of the length of section 2976 grants.-Section 6(1) of the Second Chance Act of 2007 **(34 U.S.C. 60504(1))** is amended by inserting or under section 2976 of the Omnibus Crime Control and Safe Streets Act of 1968 **(34 U.S.C. 10631)** after and 212.

SEC. 503. Audit and accountability of grantees.

(a) Definitions. In this section -

(1) the term covered grant program means grants awarded under section 115, 201, or 211 of the Second Chance Act of 2007 **(34 U.S.C. 60511, 60521, and 60531)**, as amended by this title;

(2) the term covered grantee means a recipient of a grant from a covered grant pro- gram;

(3) the term nonprofit, when used with respect to an organization, means an organization that is described in section 501(c)(3) of the Internal Revenue Code of 1986, and is exempt from taxation under section 501(a) of such Code; and

(4) the term unresolved audit finding means an audit report finding in a final audit report of the Inspector General of the Department of Justice that a covered grantee has used grant funds awarded to that grantee under a covered grant program for an unauthorized expenditure or otherwise unallowable cost that is not closed or resolved during a 12-month period prior to the date on which the final audit report is issued.

(b) Audit requirement.-Beginning in fiscal year 2019, and annually thereafter, the Inspector General of the Department of Justice shall conduct audits of covered grantees to prevent waste, fraud, and abuse of funds awarded under covered grant programs.   The Inspector General shall determine the appropriate number of covered grantees to be audited each year.

(c) Mandatory exclusion.-A grantee that is found to have an unresolved audit finding under an audit conducted under subsection (b) may not receive grant funds under a covered grant program in the fiscal year following the fiscal year to which the finding relates.

(d) Reimbursement.-If a covered grantee is awarded funds under the covered grant program from which it received a grant award during the 1-fiscal-year period during which the covered grantee is ineligible for an allocation of grant funds under subsection (c), the Attorney General shall-

(1) deposit into the General Fund of the Treasury an amount that is equal to the amount of the grant funds that were improperly awarded to the covered grantee; and

(2) seek to recoup the costs of the repayment to the Fund from the covered grantee that was improperly awarded the grant funds.

(e) Priority of grant awards.-The Attorney General, in awarding grants under a covered grant program shall give priority to eligible entities that during the 2-year period pre- ceding the application for a grant have not been found to have an unresolved audit finding.

(f) Nonprofit requirements.-

(1) PROHIBITION.-A nonprofit organization that holds money in offshore accounts for the purpose of avoiding the tax described in section 511(a)

of the Internal Revenue Code of 1986, shall not be eligible to receive, directly or indirectly, any funds from a covered grant program.

(2) DISCLOSURE.-Each nonprofit organization that is a covered grantee shall disclose in its application for such a grant, as a condition of receipt of such a grant, the compensation of its officers, directors, and trustees. Such disclosure shall include a description of the criteria relied on to determine such compensation.

(g) Prohibition on lobbying activity.-

(1) IN GENERAL.-Amounts made available under a covered grant program may not be used by any covered grantee to-

(A) lobby any representative of the Department of Justice regarding the award of grant funding; or

(B) lobby any representative of the Federal Government or a State, local, or tribal government regarding the award of grant funding.

(2) PENALTY.-If the Attorney General determines that a covered grantee has violated paragraph (1), the Attorney General shall-

(A) require the covered grantee to repay the grant in full; and

(B) prohibit the covered grantee from receiving a grant under the covered grant pro- gram from which it received a grant award during at least the 5-year period beginning on the date of such violation.

SEC. 504. FEDERAL REENTRY IMPROVEMENTS.

(a) Responsible reintegration of offenders.-Section 212 of the Second Chance Act of 2007 (34 U.S.C. 60532) is repealed.

(b) Federal prisoner reentry initiative.-Section 231 of the Second Chance Act of 2007 (34 U.S.C. 60541) is amended-

(1) in subsection (g)-

(A) in paragraph (3), by striking carried out during fiscal years 2009 and 2010 and inserting carried out during fiscal years 2019 through 2023; and

(B) in paragraph (5)(A)(ii), by striking the greater of 10 years or;

(2) by striking subsection (h);

(3) by redesignating subsection (i) as subsection (h); and

(4) in subsection (h), as so redesignated, by striking 2009 and 2010 and inserting 2019 through 2023.

(c) Enhancing reporting requirements pertaining to community corrections.-Section 3624(c) of title 18, United States Code, is amended-

(1) in paragraph (5), in the second sentence, by inserting , and number of prisoners not being placed in community corrections facilities for each reason set forth before , and any other information; and

(2) in paragraph (6), by striking the Second Chance Act of 2007 and inserting the Second Chance Reauthorization Act of 2018.

(d) Termination of study on effectiveness of depot naltrexone for heroin addiction.

Section 244 of the Second Chance Act of 2007 **(34 U.S.C. 60554)** is repealed.

(e) Authorization of appropriations for research.-Section 245 of the Second Chance Act of 2007 **(34 U.S.C. 60555)** is amended-

(1) by striking 243, and 244 and inserting and 243; and

(2) by striking $10,000,000 for each of the fiscal years 2009 and 2010 and inserting $5,000,000 for each of the fiscal years 2019, 2020, 2021, 2022, and 2023.

(f) Federal prisoner recidivism reduction programming enhancement.-

(1) IN GENERAL.-Section 3621 of title 18, United States Code, as amended by section 102(a) of this Act, is amended-

(A) by redesignating subsection (g) as subsection (i); and

(B) by inserting after subsection (f) the following:

"(g) Partnerships To expand access to reentry programs proven To reduce recidivism.-

(1) DEFINITION.-The term 'demonstrated to reduce recidivism' means that the Director of Bureau of Prisons has determined that appropriate research has been conducted and has validated the effectiveness of the type of program on recidivism.

(2) ELIGIBILITY FOR RECIDIVISM REDUCTION PARTNERSHIP.-A faith-based or community-based nonprofit organization that provides mentoring or other programs that have been demonstrated to reduce recidivism is eligible to enter into a recidivism reduction partnership with a prison or community-based facility operated by the Bureau of Prisons.

(3) RECIDIVISM REDUCTION PARTNERSHIPS.-The Director of the Bureau of Prisons shall develop policies to require wardens of prisons and community-based facilities to enter into recidivism reduction partnerships with faith-based and community-based nonprofit organizations that are willing to provide, on a volunteer basis, programs described in paragraph (2).

(4) REPORTING REQUIREMENT.-The Director of the Bureau of Prisons shall submit to Congress an annual report on the last day of each fiscal year that-

(A) details, for each prison and community-based facility for the fiscal year just ended-

(i) the number of recidivism reduction partnerships under this section that were in effect;

(ii) the number of volunteers that provided recidivism reduction programming; and

(iii) the number of recidivism reduction programming hours provided; and

(B) explains any disparities between facilities in the numbers reported under subparagraph (A).

(2) EFFECTIVE DATE.-The amendments made by paragraph (1) shall take effect 180 days after the date of enactment of this Act."

(g) Repeals.-

(1) Section 2978 of title I of the Omnibus Crime Control and Safe Streets Act of 1968 **(34 U.S.C. 10633)** is repealed.

(2) Part CC of title I of the Omnibus Crime Control and Safe Streets Act of 1968 **(34 U.S.C. 10581 et seq.)** is repealed.

SEC. 505. Federal interagency reentry coordination.

(a) Reentry coordination.-The Attorney General, in consultation with the Secretary of Housing and Urban Development, the Secretary of Labor, the Secretary of Education, the Secretary of Health and Human Services, the Secretary of Veterans Affairs, the Secretary of Agriculture, and the heads of such other agencies of the Federal Government as the Attorney General considers appropriate, and in collaboration with interested persons, service providers, nonprofit organizations, and State, tribal, and local governments, shall coordinate on Federal programs, policies, and activities relating to the reentry of individuals returning from incarceration to the community, with an emphasis on evidence-based practices and protection against duplication of services.

(b) Report.-Not later than 2 years after the date of the enactment of this Act, the Attorney General, in consultation with the Secretaries listed in subsection (a), shall submit to Congress a report summarizing the achievements under subsection (a), and including recommendations for Congress that would further reduce barriers to successful reentry.

SEC. 506. CONFERENCE EXPENDITURES.

(a) Limitation.-No amounts authorized to be appropriated to the Department of Justice under this title, or any amendments made by this title, may be used by the Attorney General, or by any individual or organization awarded discretionary funds under this title, or any amendments made by this title, to host or support any expenditure for conferences that uses more than $20,000 in Department funds, unless the Deputy Attorney General or such Assistant Attorney Generals, Directors, or principal deputies as the Deputy Attorney General may designate, provides prior written authorization that the funds may be expended to host a conference. A conference that uses more than $20,000 in such funds, but less than an average of $500 in such funds for each attendee of the conference, shall not be subject to the limitations of this section.

(b) Written approval.-Written approval under subsection (a) shall include a written estimate of all costs associated with the conference, including the cost of all food and beverages, audiovisual equipment, honoraria for speakers, and any entertainment.

(c) Report.-The Deputy Attorney General shall submit an annual report to the Commit- tee on the Judiciary of the Senate and the Committee on the Judiciary of the House of Representatives on all approved conference expenditures referenced in this section.

SEC. 507. Evaluation of the Second Chance Act program.

SEC. 507. EVALUATION OF THE SECOND CHANCE ACT PROGRAM.

(a) Evaluation of the second chance act grant program.- Not later than 5 years after the date of enactment of this Act, the National Institute of Justice shall evaluate the effectiveness of grants used by the Department of Justice to support offender reentry and recidivism reduction programs at the State, local, Tribal, and Federal levels. The National Institute of Justice shall evaluate the following:

(1) The effectiveness of such programs in relation to their cost, including the extent to which the programs improve reentry outcomes, including employment, education, housing, reductions in recidivism, of participants in comparison to comparably situated individuals who did not participate in such programs and activities.

(2) The effectiveness of program structures and mechanisms for delivery of services.

(3) The impact of such programs on the communities and participants involved.

(4) The impact of such programs on related programs and activities.

(5) The extent to which such programs meet the needs of various demographic groups.

(6) The quality and effectiveness of technical assistance provided by the Department of Justice to grantees for implementing such programs.

(7) Such other factors as may be appropriate.

(b) Authorization of funds for evaluation.-Not more than 1 percent of any amounts authorized to be appropriated to carry out the Second Chance Act grant program shall be made available to the National Institute of Justice each year to evaluate the processes, implementation, outcomes, costs, and effectiveness of the Second Chance Act grant program in improving reentry and reducing recidivism. Such funding may be used to provide support to grantees for supplemental data collection, analysis, and coordination associated with evaluation activities.

(c) Techniques.-Evaluations conducted under this section shall use appropriate methodology and research designs. Impact evaluations conducted under this section shall include the use of intervention and control groups chosen by random assignment methods, to the extent possible.

(d) Metrics and Outcomes for Evaluation.-

(1) IN GENERAL.-Not later than 180 days after the date of enactment of this Act, the National Institute of Justice shall consult with relevant stakeholders and identify outcome measures, including employment, housing, education, and public safety, that are to be achieved by programs authorized under the Second Chance Act grant program and the metrics by which the achievement of such outcomes shall be determined.

(2) PUBLICATION.-Not later than 30 days after the date on

which the National Institute of Justice identifies metrics and outcomes under paragraph (1), the Attorney General shall publish such metrics and outcomes identified.

(e) Data collection.-As a condition of award under the Second Chance Act grant pro- gram (including a subaward under section 3021(b) of title I of the Omnibus Crime Control and Safe Streets Act of 1968 **(34 U.S.C. 10701(b)))**, grantees shall be required to collect and report to the Department of Justice data based upon the metrics identified under subsection (d). In accordance with applicable law, collection of individual-level data under a pledge of confidentiality shall be protected by the National Institute of Justice in accordance with such pledge.

(f) Data accessibility.-Not later than 5 years after the date of enactment of this Act, the National Institute of Justice shall-

(1) make data collected during the course of evaluation under this section available in de-identified form in such a manner that reasonably protects a pledge of confidentiality to participants under subsection (e); and

(2) make identifiable data collected during the course of evaluation under this section available to qualified researchers for future research and evaluation, in accordance with applicable law.

(g) Publication and reporting of evaluation findings.-The National Institute of Justice shall-

(1) not later than 365 days after the date on which the enrollment of participants in an impact evaluation is completed, publish an interim report on such evaluation;

(2) not later than 90 days after the date on which any evaluation is completed, publish and make publicly available such evaluation; and

(3) not later than 60 days after the completion date described in paragraph (2), submit a report to the Committee on the Judiciary of the House of Representatives and the Committee on the Judiciary of the Senate on such evaluation.

(h) Second Chance Act grant program defined.-In this section, the term Second Chance Act grant program means any grant program reauthorized under this title and the amendments made by this title.

SEC. 508. GAO REVIEW.

Not later than 3 years after the date of enactment of the First Step Act of 2018 the Comptroller General of the United States shall conduct a review of all of the grant awards made under this title and amendments made by this title that includes-

(1) an evaluation of the effectiveness of the reentry programs funded by grant awards under this title and amendments made by this title at reducing recidivism, including a determination of which reentry programs were most effective;

(2) recommendations on how to improve the effectiveness of reentry programs, including those for which prisoners may earn time credits under the First Step Act of 2018; and

(3) an evaluation of the effectiveness of mental health services, drug treatment, medical care, job training and placement, educational services, and vocational services programs funded under this title and amendments made by this title.

TITLE VI Miscellaneous criminal justice

SEC. 601. Placement of prisoners close to families.

Section 3621(b) of title 18, United States Code, is amended-

(1) by striking shall designate the place of the prisoner's imprisonment. and inserting shall designate the place of the prisoner's imprisonment, and shall, subject to bed availability, the prisoner's security designation, the prisoner's programmatic needs, the prisoner's mental and medical health needs, any request made by the prisoner related to faith-based needs, recommendations of the sentencing court, and other security concerns of the Bureau of Prisons, place the prisoner in a facility as close as practicable to the prisoner's primary residence, and to the extent practicable, in a facility within 500

driving miles of that residence. The Bureau shall, subject to consideration of the factors described in the preceding sentence and the prisoner's preference for staying at his or her current facility or being transferred, transfer prisoners to facilities that are closer to the prisoner's primary residence even if the prisoner is already in a facility within 500 driving miles of that residence.; and

(2) by adding at the end the following: Notwithstanding any other provision of law, a designation of a place of imprisonment under this subsection is not reviewable by any court..

SEC. 602. Home confinement for low-risk prisoners.

Section 3624(c)(2) of title 18, United States Code, is amended by adding at the end the following: The Bureau of Prisons shall, to the extent practicable, place prisoners with lower risk levels and lower needs on home confinement for the maximum amount of time permitted under this paragraph.

SEC. 603. Federal prisoner reentry initiative reauthorization; modification of imposed term of imprisonment.

(a) Federal prisoner reentry initiative reauthorization.-Section 231(g) of the Second Chance Act of 2007 **(34 U.S.C. 60541(g))** is amended-

(1) in paragraph (1)-

(A) by inserting and eligible terminally ill offenders after elderly offenders each place the term appears;

(B) in subparagraph (A), by striking a Bureau of Prisons facility and inserting Bureau of Prisons facilities;

(C) in subparagraph (B)-

(i) by striking the Bureau of Prisons facility and inserting Bureau of Prisons facilities; and

(ii) by inserting , upon written request from either the Bureau of Prisons or an eligible elderly offender or eligible terminally ill offender after to home detention; and

(D) in subparagraph (C), by striking the Bureau of Prisons facility and inserting Bureau of Prisons facilities;

(2) in paragraph (2), by inserting or eligible terminally ill offender after elderly offender;

(3) in paragraph (3), as amended by section 504(b)(1)(A) of this Act, by striking at least one Bureau of Prisons facility and inserting Bureau of Prisons facilities; and

(4) in paragraph (4)-

(A) by inserting or eligible terminally ill offender after each eligible elderly offender; and

(B) by inserting and eligible terminally ill offenders after eligible elderly offenders; and

(5) in paragraph (5)-

(A) in subparagraph (A)-

(i) in clause (i), striking 65 years of age and inserting 60 years of age; and

(ii) in clause (ii), as amended by section 504(b)(1)(B) of this Act, by striking 75 percent and inserting 2/3 ; and

(B) by adding at the end the following:

"(D) ELIGIBLE TERMINALLY ILL OFFENDER.-The term 'eligible terminally ill offender' means an offender in the custody of the Bureau of Prisons who-

(i) is serving a term of imprisonment based on conviction for an offense or offenses that do not include any crime

of violence (as defined in section 16(a) of title 18, United States Code), sex offense (as defined in section 111(5) of the Sex Offender Registration and Notification Act **(34 U.S.C. 20911(5)))**, offense described in section 2332b(g)(5)(B) of title 18, United States Code, or offense under chapter 37 of title 18, United States Code;

(ii) satisfies the criteria specified in clauses (iii) through (vii) of subparagraph (A); and

(iii) has been determined by a medical doctor approved by the Bureau of Prisons to be-

> (I) in need of care at a nursing home, intermediate care facility, or assisted living facility, as those terms are defined in section 232 of the National Housing Act **(12 U.S.C. 1715w)**; or

> (II) diagnosed with a terminal illness."

(b) Increasing the use and transparency of compassionate release.- Section 3582 of title 18, United States Code, is amended-

(1) in subsection (c)(1)(A), in the matter preceding clause (i), by inserting after Bureau of Prisons, the following: or upon motion of the defendant after the defendant has fully exhausted all administrative rights to appeal a failure of the Bureau of Prisons to bring a motion on the defendant's behalf or the lapse of 30 days from the receipt of such a request by the warden of the defendant's facility, whichever is earlier,;

(2) by redesignating subsection (d) as subsection (e); and

(3) by inserting after subsection (c) the following:

(d) Notification requirements.-

(1) TERMINAL ILLNESS DEFINED.-In this subsection, the term 'terminal illness' means a disease or condition with an end-of-life trajectory.

(2) NOTIFICATION.-The Bureau of Prisons shall, subject to any applicable confidentiality requirements-

    (A) in the case of a defendant diagnosed with a terminal illness-

        (i) not later than 72 hours after the diagnosis notify the defendant's attorney, partner, and family members of the defendant's condition and inform the defendant's attorney, partner, and family members that they may prepare and submit on the defendant's behalf a request for a sentence reduction pursuant to subsection (c)(1)(A);

        (ii) not later than 7 days after the date of the diagnosis, provide the defendant's partner and family members (including extended family) with an opportunity to visit the defendant in person;

        (iii) upon request from the defendant or his attorney, partner, or a family member, ensure that Bureau of Prisons employees assist the defendant in the preparation, drafting, and submission of a request for a sentence reduction pursuant to subsection (c)(1) (A); and

        (iv) not later than 14 days of receipt of a request for a sentence reduction submitted on the defendant's behalf by the defendant or the defendant's attorney, partner, or family member, process the request;

    (B) in the case of a defendant who is physically or mentally unable to submit a request for a sentence reduction pursuant to subsection (c)(1)(A)-

        (i) inform the defendant's attorney, partner, and family members that they may prepare and submit on the defendant's behalf a request for a sentence reduction pursuant to subsection (c)(1)(A);

        (ii) accept and process a request for sentence reduction that has been prepared and submitted on the defendant's behalf by the defendant's attorney, partner, or family member under clause (i); and

(iii) upon request from the defendant or his attorney, partner, or family member, ensure that Bureau of Prisons employees assist the defendant in the preparation, drafting, and submission of a request for a sentence reduction pursuant to subsection (c)(1) (A); and

(C) ensure that all Bureau of Prisons facilities regularly and visibly post, including in prisoner handbooks, staff training materials, and facility law libraries and medical and hospice facilities, and make available to prisoners upon demand, notice of-

(i) a defendant's ability to request a sentence reduction pursuant to subsection (c)(1) (A);

(ii) the procedures and timelines for initiating and resolving requests described in clause (i); and

(iii) the right to appeal a denial of a request described in clause (i) after all administrative rights to appeal within the Bureau of Prisons have been exhausted.

(3) ANNUAL REPORT.- Not later than 1 year after the date of enactment of this subsection, and once every year thereafter, the Director of the Bureau of Prisons shall submit to the Committee on the Judiciary of the Senate and the Committee on the Judiciary of the House of Representatives a report on requests for sentence reductions pursuant to subsection (c)(1)(A), which shall include a description of, for the previous year-

(A) the number of prisoners granted and denied sentence reductions, categorized by the criteria relied on as the grounds for a reduction in sentence;

(B) the number of requests initiated by or on behalf of prisoners, categorized by the criteria relied on as the grounds for a reduction in sentence;

(C) the number of requests that Bureau of Prisons employees assisted prisoners in drafting, preparing, or submitting, categorized by the criteria relied on as the grounds for a reduction in sentence, and the final decision made in each request;

(D) the number of requests that attorneys, partners, or family members submitted on a defendant's behalf, categorized by the criteria relied on as the grounds for a reduction in sentence, and the final decision made in each request;

(E) the number of requests approved by the Director of the Bureau of Prisons, categorized by the criteria relied on as the grounds for a reduction in sentence;

(F) the number of requests denied by the Director of the Bureau of Prisons and the rea- sons given for each denial, categorized by the criteria relied on as the grounds for a reduction in sentence;

(G) for each request, the time elapsed between the date the request was received by the warden and the final decision, categorized by the criteria relied on as the grounds for a reduction in sentence;

(H) for each request, the number of prisoners who died while their request was pending and, for each, the amount of time that had elapsed between the date the request was received by the Bureau of Prisons, categorized by the criteria relied on as the grounds for a reduction in sentence;

(I) the number of Bureau of Prisons notifications to attorneys, partners, and family members of their right to visit a terminally ill defendant as required under paragraph (2)(A)(ii) and, for each, whether a visit occurred and how much time elapsed between the notification and the visit;

(J) the number of visits to terminally ill prisoners that were denied by the Bureau of Prisons due to security or other concerns, and the reasons given for each denial; and

(K) the number of motions filed by defendants with the court after all administrative rights to appeal a denial of a sentence reduction had been exhausted, the outcome of each motion, and the time that had elapsed between the date the request was first received by the Bureau of Prisons and the date the defendant filed the motion with the court..

SEC. 604. Identification for returning citizens.

(a) Identification and release assistance for Federal prisoners.-Section 231(b) of the Second Chance Act of 2007 **(34 U.S.C. 60541(b))** is amended-

(1) in paragraph (1)-

(A) by striking (including and inserting prior to release from a term of imprisonment in a Federal prison or if the individual was not sentenced to a term of imprisonment in a Federal prison, prior to release from a sentence to a term in community confinement, including; and

(B) by striking or birth certificate) prior to release and inserting and a birth certificate; and

(2) by adding at the end the following:

"(4) DEFINITION.-In this subsection, the term 'community confinement' means residence in a community treatment center, halfway house, restitution center, mental health facility, alcohol or drug rehabilitation center, or other community facility."

(b) Duties of the Bureau of Prisons.-Section 4042(a) of title 18, United States Code, is amended-

(1) by redesignating paragraphs (D) and (E) as paragraphs (6) and (7), respectively;

(2) in paragraph (6) (as so redesignated)-

(A) in clause (i)-

(i) by striking Social Security Cards,; and

(ii) by striking and at the end;

(B) by redesignating clause (ii) as clause (iii);

(C) by inserting after clause (i) the following:

(ii) obtain identification, including a social security card, driver's license or other official photo identification, and a birth certificate; and;

(D) in clause (iii) (as so redesignated), by inserting after prior to release the following: from a sentence to a term of imprisonment in a Federal prison or if the individual was not sentenced to a term of imprisonment in a Federal prison, prior to release from a sentence to a term of community confinement; and

(E) by redesignating clauses (i), (ii), and (iii) (as so amended) as subparagraphs (A), (B), and (C), respectively, and adjusting the margins accordingly; and

(3) in paragraph (7) (as so redesignated), by redesignating clauses (i) through (vii) as subparagraphs (A) through (G), respectively, and adjusting the margins accordingly.

SEC. 605. Expanding inmate employment through Federal Prison Industries.

(a) New market authorizations.-Chapter 307 of title 18, United States Code, is amended by inserting after section 4129 the following:

(a) In general.-Except as provided in subsection (b), notwithstanding any other provision of law, Federal Prison Industries may sell products to-

(1) public entities for use in penal or correctional institutions;

(2) public entities for use in disaster relief or emergency response;

(3) the government of the District of Columbia; and

(4) any organization described in subsection (c)(3), (c)(4), or (d) of section 501 of the Internal Revenue Code of 1986 that is exempt from taxation under section 501(a) of such Code.

(b) Office furniture.-Federal Prison Industries may not sell office furniture to the organizations described in subsection (a)(4).

(c) Definitions.-In this section:

(1) The term 'office furniture' means any product or service offering intended to meet the furnishing needs of the workplace, including office, healthcare, educational, and hospitality environments.

(2) The term 'public entity' means a State, a subdivision of a State, an Indian tribe, and an agency or governmental corporation or business of any of the foregoing.

(3) The term 'State' means a State, the District of Columbia, the Commonwealth of Puerto Rico, Guam, American Samoa, the Northern Mariana Islands, and the United States Virgin Islands..

(b) Technical amendment.-The table of sections for chapter 307 of title 18, United States Code, is amended by inserting after the item relating to section 4129 the following:

4130. Additional markets.

(c) Deferred compensation.-Section 4126(c)(4) of title 18, United States Code, is amended by inserting after operations, the following: not less than 15 percent of such compensation for any inmate shall be reserved in the fund or a separate account and made available to assist the inmate with costs associated with release from prison;

(d) GAO report.-Beginning not later than 90 days after the date of enactment of this Act, the Comptroller General of the United States shall conduct an audit of Federal Prison Industries that includes the following:

(1) An evaluation of Federal Prison Industries's effectiveness in reducing recidivism compared to other rehabilitative programs in the prison system.

(2) An evaluation of the scope and size of the additional markets made available to Federal Prison Industries under this section and the total market value

that would be opened up to Federal Prison Industries for competition with private sector providers of products and services.

(3) An evaluation of whether the following factors create an unfair competitive environment between Federal Prison Industries and private sector providers of products and services which would be exacerbated by further expansion:

(A) Federal Prison Industries's status as a mandatory source of supply for Federal agencies and the requirement that the buying agency must obtain a waiver in order to make a competitive purchase from the private sector if the item to be acquired is listed on the schedule of products and services published by Federal Prison Industries.

(B) Federal Prison Industries's ability to determine that the price to be paid by Federal Agencies is fair and reasonable, rather than such a determination being made by the buying agency.

(C) An examination of the extent to which Federal Prison Industries is bound by the requirements of the generally applicable Federal Acquisition Regulation pertaining to the conformity of the delivered product with the specified design and performance specifications and adherence to the delivery schedule required by the Federal agency, based on the transactions being categorized as interagency transfers.

(D) An examination of the extent to which Federal Prison Industries avoids transactions that are little more than pass through transactions where the work provided by inmates does not create meaningful value or meaningful work opportunities for inmates.

(E) The extent to which Federal Prison Industries must comply with the same worker protection, workplace safety and similar regulations applicable to, and enforceable against, Federal contractors.

(F) The wages Federal Prison Industries pays to inmates, taking into account inmate productivity and other factors such as security concerns associated with having a facility in a prison.

(G) The effect of any additional cost advantages Federal Prison

Industries has over private sector providers of goods and services, including-

> (i) the costs absorbed by the Bureau of Prisons such as inmate medical care and infra- structure expenses including real estate and utilities; and

> (ii) its exemption from Federal and State income taxes and property taxes.

(4) An evaluation of the extent to which the customers of Federal Prison Industries are satisfied with quality, price, and timely delivery of the products and services provided it provides, including summaries of other independent assessments such as reports of agency inspectors general, if applicable.

SEC. 606. DE-ESCALATION TRAINING.

Beginning not later than 1 year after the date of enactment of this Act, the Director of the Bureau of Prisons shall incorporate into training programs provided to officers and employees of the Bureau of Prisons (including officers and employees of an organization with which the Bureau of Prisons has a contract to provide services relating to imprisonment) specialized and comprehensive training in procedures to-

(1) de-escalate encounters between a law enforcement officer or an officer or employee of the Bureau of Prisons, and a civilian or a prisoner (as such term is defined in section 3635 of title 18, United States Code, as added by section 101(a) of this Act); and

(2) identify and appropriately respond to incidents that involve the unique needs of individuals who have a mental illness or cognitive deficit.

SEC. 607. Evidence-Based treatment for opioid and heroin abuse.

(a) Report on evidence-based treatment for opioid and heroin abuse.-Not later than 90 days after the date of enactment of this Act, the Director of the Bureau of Prisons shall submit to the Committees on the Judiciary and the Committees on Appropriations of the Senate and of the House of Representatives a report assessing the availability of and the capacity of the Bureau of Prisons to treat heroin and opioid abuse through evidence- based programs, including medication-assisted treatment where appropriate. In preparing the report, the Director shall consider medication-assisted treatment as a strategy to assist in treatment where appropriate and not as a replacement for holistic and other drug-free approaches. The report shall include a description of plans to expand access to evidence-based treatment for heroin and opioid abuse for prisoners, including access to medication-assisted treatment in appropriate cases. Following submission, the Director shall take steps to implement these plans.

(b) Report on the availability of medication-Assisted treatment for opioid and heroin abuse, and implementation thereof.-Not later than 120 days after the date of enactment of this Act, the Director of the Administrative Office of the United States Courts shall submit to the Committees on the Judiciary and the Committees on Appropriations of the Senate and of the House of Representatives a report assessing the availability of and capacity for the provision of medication assisted treatment for opioid and heroin abuse by treatment service providers serving prisoners who are serving a term of supervised release, and including a description of plans to expand access to medication-assisted treatment for heroin and opioid abuse whenever appropriate among prisoners under supervised release. Following submission, the Director will take steps to implement these plans.

SEC. 608. PILOT PROGRAMS.

(a) In general.- The Bureau of Prisons shall establish each of the following pilot programs for 5 years, in at least 20 facilities:

(1) MENTORSHIP FOR YOUTH.-A program to pair youth with volunteers from faith- based or community organizations, which may include formerly incarcerated offenders, that have relevant experience or expertise in mentoring, and a willingness to serve as a mentor in such a capacity.

(2) SERVICE TO ABANDONED, RESCUED, OR OTHERWISE VULNERABLE ANIMALS.-A program to equip prisoners with the skills to provide training and therapy to animals seized by Federal law enforcement under asset forfeiture authority and to organizations that provide shelter and similar services to abandoned, rescued, or otherwise vulnerable animals.

(b) Reporting requirement.-Not later than 1 year after the conclusion of the pilot pro- grams, the Attorney General shall report to Congress on the results of the pilot pro- grams under this section. Such report shall include cost savings, numbers of participants, and information about recidivism rates among participants.

(c) Definition.-In this title, the term youth means a prisoner (as such term is defined in section 3635 of title 18, United States Code, as added by section 101(a) of this Act) who was 21 years of age or younger at the time of the commission or alleged commission of the criminal offense for which the individual is being prosecuted or serving a term of imprisonment, as the case may be.

SEC. 609. Ensuring supervision of released sexually dangerous persons.

(a) Probation officers.-Section 3603 of title 18, United States Code, is amended in para- graph (8)(A) by striking or 4246 and inserting , 4246, or 4248.

(b) Pretrial services officers.-Section 3154 of title 18, United States Code, is amended in paragraph (12)(A) by striking or 4246 and inserting , 4246, or 4248.

SEC. 610. DATA COLLECTION.

(a) National Prisoner Statistics Program.-Beginning not later than 1 year after the date of enactment of this Act, and annually thereafter, pursuant to the authority under section 302 of the Omnibus Crime Control and Safe Streets Act of 1968 (42 U.S.C. 3732), the Director of the Bureau of Justice Statistics, with information that shall be provided by the Director of the Bureau of Prisons, shall include in the National Prisoner Statistics Program the following:

(1) The number of prisoners (as such term is defined in section 3635 of title 18, United States Code, as added by section 101(a) of this Act) who are veterans of the Armed Forces of the United States.

(2) The number of prisoners who have been placed in solitary confinement at any time during the previous year.

(3) The number of female prisoners known by the Bureau of Prisons to be pregnant, as well as the outcomes of such pregnancies, including information on pregnancies that result in live birth, stillbirth, miscarriage, abortion, ectopic pregnancy, maternal death, neonatal death, and preterm birth.

(4) The number of prisoners who volunteered to participate in a substance abuse treatment program, and the number of prisoners who have participated in such a program.

(5) The number of prisoners provided medication-assisted treatment with medication approved by the Food and Drug Administration while in custody in order to treat sub- stance use disorder.

(6) The number of prisoners who were receiving medication-assisted treatment with medication approved by the Food and Drug Administration prior to the commencement of their term of imprisonment.

(7) The number of prisoners who are the parent or guardian of a minor child.

(8) The number of prisoners who are single, married, or otherwise in a committed relationship.

(9) The number of prisoners who have not achieved a GED, high school diploma, or equivalent prior to entering prison.

(10) The number of prisoners who, during the previous year, received their GED or other equivalent certificate while incarcerated.

(11) The numbers of prisoners for whom English is a second language.

(12) The number of incidents, during the previous year, in which restraints were used on a female prisoner during pregnancy, labor, or postpartum recovery, as well as information relating to the type of restraints used, and the circumstances under which each incident occurred.

(13) The vacancy rate for medical and healthcare staff positions, and average length of such a vacancy.

(14) The number of facilities that operated, at any time during the previous year, with- out at least 1 clinical nurse, certified paramedic, or licensed physician on site.

(15) The number of facilities that during the previous year were accredited by the American Correctional Association.

(16) The number and type of recidivism reduction partnerships described in section 3621(h)(5) of title 18, United States Code, as added by section 102(a) of this Act, entered into by each facility.

(17) The number of facilities with remote learning capabilities.

(18) The number of facilities that offer prisoners video conferencing.

(19) Any changes in costs related to legal phone calls and visits following implementation of section 3632(d)(1) of title 18, United States Code, as added by section 101(a) of this Act.

(20) The number of aliens in prison during the previous year.

(21) For each Bureau of Prisons facility, the total number of violations that resulted in reductions in rewards, incentives, or time credits, the number of such violations for each category of violation, and the demographic breakdown of the prisoners who have received such reductions.

(22) The number of assaults on Bureau of Prisons staff by prisoners and the number of criminal prosecutions of prisoners for assaulting Bureau of Prisons staff.

(23) The capacity of each recidivism reduction program and productive activity to accommodate eligible inmates at each Bureau of Prisons facility.

(24) The number of volunteers who were certified to volunteer in a Bureau of Prisons facility, broken down by level (level I and level II), and by each Bureau of Prisons facility.

(25) The number of prisoners enrolled in recidivism reduction programs and productive activities at each Bureau of Prisons facility, broken down by risk level and by program, and the number of those enrolled prisoners who successfully completed each program.

(26) The breakdown of prisoners classified at each risk level by demographic characteristics, including age, sex, race, and the length of the sentence imposed.

(b) Report to Judiciary committees.-Beginning not later than 1 year after the date of enactment of this Act, and annually thereafter for a period of 7 years, the Director of the Bureau of Justice Statistics shall submit a report containing the information described in paragraphs (1) through (26) of subsection (a) to the Committee on the Judiciary of the Senate and the Committee on the Judiciary of the House of Representatives.

SEC. 611. HEALTHCARE PRODUCTS.

(a) Availability.-The Director of the Bureau of Prisons shall make the healthcare products described in subsection (c) available to prisoners for free, in a quantity that is appropriate to the healthcare needs of each prisoner.

(b) Quality products.-The Director shall ensure that the healthcare products provided under this section conform with applicable industry standards.

(c) Products.-The healthcare products described in this subsection are tampons and sanitary napkins.

SEC. 612. Adult and juvenile collaboration programs.

Section 2991 of title I of the Omnibus Crime Control and Safe Streets Act of 1968 (34 U.S.C. 10651) is amended-

(1) in subsection (b)(4)-

(A) by striking subparagraph (D); and

(B) by redesignating subparagraph (E) as subparagraph (D);

(2) in subsection (e), by striking may use up to 3 percent and inserting shall use not less than 6 percent; and

(3) by amending subsection (g) to read as follows:

(g) Collaboration set aside.- The Attorney General shall use not less than 8 percent of funds appropriated to provide technical assistance to State and local governments receiving grants under this part to foster collaboration between such governments in furtherance of the purposes set forth in section 3 of the Mentally Ill Offender Treatment and Crime Reduction Act of 2004 **(34 U.S.C. 10651 note)**.

SEC. 613. JUVENILE SOLITARY CONFINEMENT.

(a) In general.-Chapter 403 of title 18, United States Code, is amended by adding at the end the following:

§ 5043. Juvenile solitary confinement

(a) Definitions.-In this section-

(1) the term 'covered juvenile' means-

(A) a juvenile who-

(i) is being proceeded against under this chapter for an alleged act of juvenile delinquency; or

(ii) has been adjudicated delinquent under this chapter; or

(B) a juvenile who is being proceeded against as an adult in a district court of the United States for an alleged criminal offense;

(2) the term 'juvenile facility' means any facility where covered juveniles are-

(A) committed pursuant to an adjudication of delinquency under this chapter; or

(B) detained prior to disposition or conviction; and

(3) the term 'room confinement' means the involuntary placement of a covered juvenile alone in a cell, room, or other area for any reason.

(b) Prohibition on room confinement in juvenile facilities.-

(1) IN GENERAL.-The use of room confinement at a juvenile facility for discipline, punishment, retaliation, or any reason other than as a temporary response to a covered juvenile's behavior that poses a serious and immediate risk of physical harm to any individual, including the covered juvenile, is prohibited.

(2) JUVENILES POSING RISK OF HARM.-

(A) REQUIREMENT TO USE LEAST RESTRICTIVE TECHNIQUES.-

(i) IN GENERAL.-Before a staff member of a juvenile facility places a covered juvenile in room confinement, the staff member shall attempt to use less restrictive techniques, including-

(I) talking with the covered juvenile in an attempt to de-escalate the situation; and

(II) permitting a qualified mental health professional to talk to the covered juvenile.

(ii) EXPLANATION.-If, after attempting to use less restrictive techniques as required under clause (i), a staff member of a juvenile facility decides to place a covered juvenile in room confinement, the staff member shall first-

(I) explain to the covered juvenile the reasons for the room confinement; and

(II) inform the covered juvenile that release from room confinement will occur-

(aa) immediately when the covered juvenile regains self control, as described in sub-paragraph (B)(i); or

(bb) not later than after the expiration of the time period described in subclause (I) or

(II) of subparagraph (B)(ii), as applicable.

(B) MAXIMUM PERIOD OF CONFINEMENT.-If a covered juvenile is placed in room confinement because the covered juvenile poses a serious and immediate risk of physical harm to himself or herself, or to others, the covered juvenile shall be released-

(i) immediately when the covered juvenile has sufficiently gained control so as to no longer engage in behavior that threatens serious and immediate risk of physical harm to himself or herself, or to others; or

(ii) if a covered juvenile does not sufficiently gain control as described in clause (i), not later than-

(I) 3 hours after being placed in room confinement, in the case of a covered juvenile who poses a serious and immediate risk of physical harm to others; or

(II) 30 minutes after being placed in room confinement, in the case of a covered juvenile who poses a serious and immediate risk of physical harm only to himself or herself.

(C) RISK OF HARM AFTER MAXIMUM PERIOD OF CONFINEMENT.- If, after the applicable maximum period of confinement under subclause (I) or (II) of subparagraph (B) (ii) has expired, a covered juvenile continues to pose a serious and immediate risk of physical harm described in that subclause-

(i) the covered juvenile shall be transferred to another juvenile facility or internal location where services can be provided to the covered juvenile without relying on room confinement; or

(ii) if a qualified mental health professional believes the level of crisis service needed is not currently available, a staff member of the juvenile facility shall initiate a referral to a location that can meet the needs of the covered juvenile.

(D) SPIRIT AND PURPOSE.-The use of consecutive periods of room confinement to evade the spirit and purpose of this subsection shall be prohibited..

(b) Technical and conforming amendment.-The table of sections for chapter 403 of title 18, United States Code, is amended by adding at the end the following:

"5043. Juvenile solitary confinement."

[THIS PAGE INTENTIONALLY LEFT BLANK]

Evidence-based Recidivism Reduction (EBRR) Programs and Productive Activities (PA)

The BOP assesses inmates for criminogenic needs and other needs that are associated with an increased risk of recidivism in the following areas: Anger/Hostility; Antisocial Peers; Cognitions; Dyslexia; Education; Family/Parenting; Finance; Poverty; Medical; Mental Health; Recreation/Leisure/Fitness; Substance Abuse; Trauma; and Work. The needs assessment system, inclusive of the screening and other assessment instruments and/or tools developed, is used to appropriately identify the individual needs of each inmate to assign appropriate evidence-based recidivism reduction programming (EBRRs) and productive activities.

Evidence-based Recidivism Reduction (EBRR) Programs

EBRR Name (short description)	Duration	Frequency	Hours[1]	Program Location(s)	Needs(s) Addressed
Bureau Literacy Program (Reading, math, and writing skills leading to high school equivalency)	Dependent on inmate progress	1.5 hours/day	240	All BOP institutions[2]	Dyslexia, Education
Occupational Education Programs (Vocational training and marketable skills in a wide variety of trades)	Varies	Varies	500	All BOP institutions	Work
Federal Prison Industries (Trade name UNICOR, a job skills program)	Indefinite Duration	Full or shared half time	500	57 factories and 2 farms located at 51 facilities	Work
National Parenting from Prison Program (Program focused on family engagement and parenting skills)	Phase 1: 4 weeks; Phase 2: 5 - 10 weeks	2 hours/week	40	All BOP institutions	Family/Parenting
BRAVE (CBT[3] for young males with first offense)	6 months	20 hours/week	500	Beckley; Victorville-Medium	Antisocial Peers, Cognitions
Challenge (CBT for high security males focused on substance use and mental illness intervention)	Minimum of 9 months	20 hours/week	500	At 17 high security facilities[4]	Cognitions, Mental Health, Substance Abuse
Female Integrated Treatment (CBT program for women addressing mental illness, trauma, substance use and vocational needs)	Varies based on individual need	20 hours/week	500	Danbury - female	Cognitions, Mental Health, Substance Abuse, Trauma, Work
Mental Health Step Down Program (CBT for SMI[5] inmates)	12-19 months	20 hours/week	500	Allenwood- High; Atlanta; Butner-Medium	Cognitions, Mental Health
Residential Drug Abuse Treatment Program (RDAP) (CBT for inmates with diagnosed substance use disorders)	9 months	20 hours/week	500	At 88 locations[6]	Cognitions, Substance Abuse

---

[1] Hours Awarded for Completion
[2] All BOP institutions means the program can be offered; scheduled offerings will be based on specific population needs.
[3] CBT – Cognitive Behavioral Therapy
[4] See BOP National Programs Catalog for specific locations
[5] SMI - Serious Mental Illness
[6] See BOP National Programs Catalog for specific locations

EBRR Name (short description)	Duration	Frequency	Hours[7]	Program Location(s)	Needs(s) Addressed
Resolve Program (Trauma treatment)	40 weeks	Varies	80	All female sites except satellites; Florence and Danbury - male	Cognitions, Mental Health, Trauma
STAGES Program (High intensity CBT for SMI and personality disorder inmates)	12-18 months	20 hours/week	500	Florence High; Terre Haute - Medium	Cognitions, Mental Health
Skills Program (CBT and educational residential programs for inmates with cognitive impairments)	12-18 months	20 hours/week	500	Danbury; Coleman-Medium	Cognitions, Mental Health
Life Connections Programs (Faith-based values and life skills program)	18 months	20 hours/week	500	Petersburg - Low; Leavenworth; Milan; Terre Haute - High; Carswell	Family/Parenting
Anger Management (CBT program to manage anger)	12 Sessions	1.5 hours/week	18	All BOP institutions	Anger/Hostility Cognitions
Assert Yourself for Female Offenders (CBI[8] and psychoeducational program that teaches women to be assertive)	8 weeks	1 hour/week	8	All female sites	Cognitions, Family/Parenting
Basic Cognitive Skills (Introductory program to CBT)	12-16 weeks	1 - 1.5 hours/week	24	All BOP institutions	Cognitions
Criminal Thinking (Rational behavioral therapy for addressing antisocial cognitions)	12-18 sessions	1.5 hours/week	27	All BOP institutions	Antisocial Peers, Cognitions
Emotional Self-Regulation (CBT for managing personal emotions)	8-12 sessions	1-2 hours/week	24	All BOP institutions	Cognitions, Mental Health
Illness Management and Recovery (CBT for SMI)	12-40 sessions	Up to 1.5 hours/week	60	All BOP institutions	Mental Health
Social Skills Training (SST) for Schizophrenia (CBT for SMI)	Varies	Varies	60	All BOP institutions	Cognitions, Mental Health
Threshold Program (Faith-based program focused on values and life skills)	6-9 months	1.5 - 2 hours/week	72	All BOP institutions	Family/Parenting

---

[7] Hours Awarded for Completion
[8] CBI - Cognitive Behavioral Intervention

~ 2 ~

Productive Activities (PA)

PA Name (short description)	Duration	Frequency	Hours	Program Location(s)	Needs(s) Addressed
English-as-a-Second Language	Depends on inmate progress	Minimum of 1.5 hours/day	500	All BOP institutions	Education, Work
Drug Education	Varies	Varies	15	All BOP institutions	Substance Abuse
Non-Residential Drug Abuse Treatment Program	3-6 months	1.5 - 2 hours/week	24	All BOP institutions	Cognitions, Substance Abuse
Sex Offender Treatment Program (Residential and Non-Residential)	9-12 months	12 hours/week	500	Carswell; Devens; Elkton; Englewood; Petersburg-Medium; Marianna; Marion; Seagoville; Tucson-High	Cognitions
Ultra Key 6: The Ultimate Keyboarding Tutor (Typing skills)	Varies	Self-paced	20	All BOP institutions	Education, Work
A Healthier Me in the BOP (Educational wellness program for women)	4 sessions	1.25 hours/week	5	All female sites	Recreation/Leisure/Fitness
A Matter of Balance (Helps build self-efficacy in strength and mobility)	8 sessions	2 hours/week	16	All BOP institutions	Recreation/Leisure/Fitness
AARP Foundation Finances 50+ (Financial literacy for older adults)	3 sessions	1.5 hours/week	5	All BOP institutions	Finance/Poverty
Access (Program to assist women overcoming domestic violence)	5 sessions	2 hours/week	10	All female sites	Cognitions, Mental Health, Trauma
Alcoholics Anonymous	Varies	Varies	50	All BOP institutions	Substance Abuse
Arthritis Foundation Walk with Ease	6 weeks	Varies	6	All BOP institutions	Medical, Recreation/Leisure/Fitness
Beyond Violence: A Prevention Program for Criminal-Justice Involved Women (Women focusing on anger management)	20 sessions	2 hours/week	40	All female sites	Anger/Hostility, Cognitions
Brain Health as You Age: You can Make a Difference! (Improved memory and decision-making)	Varies	Varies	5	All BOP institutions	Medical, Recreation/Leisure/Fitness
Brief CBT for Suicidal Individuals (Addresses suicidality)	Varies	Varies	20	All BOP institutions	Mental Health
CBT for Prison Gambling	Varies	Varies	20	All BOP institutions	Antisocial Peers, Cognitions
Circle of Strength (Support group that introduces CBI to women)	13 sessions	1.5 hours/week	20	All female sites	Cognitions, Mental Health
CBT for Eating Disorders	Varies	Varies	20	All BOP institution	Mental Health
CBT of Insomnia	4-8 Session	Varies	10	All BOP institutions	Mental Health
Cognitive Process Therapy (CBT to address trauma)	12 sessions	1.5 hours/week	18	All BOP institutions	Cognitions, Mental Health, Trauma

~ 3 ~

PA Name (short description)	Duration	Frequency	Hours	Program Location(s)	Needs(s) Addressed
Dialectical Behavior Therapy Skills Training (CBT for managing emotions and distress)	52 sessions	1.5 - 2 hours/week	104	All BOP institutions	Cognitions, Mental Health, Trauma
Embracing Interfaith Cooperations (Fosters interfaith understanding)	5 sessions	1-2 hours/week	10	All BOP institutions	Cognitions
Federal Prison Industries (FPI) Lean Basics Training (Business processing training class)	16 hours	Varies	16	51 FPI facilities	Work
Foundation (Reentry focused goal setting program for women)	10 sessions	1.5 hours/week	15	All female sites	Cognitions, Education, Mental Health, Work
Getting to Know Your Healthy Aging Body (Discusses changes over the lifespan)	12 sessions	1 hour/week	12	All BOP institutions	Medical , Recreation/Leisure/Fitness
Health and Wellness Throughout the Lifespan	3 sessions	.75 hours/week	3	All BOP institutions	Recreation/Leisure/Fitness
Healthy Steps for Older Adults (Reduce falls)	3 sessions	Varies	3	All BOP institutions	Medical, Recreation/Leisure/Fitness
Hooked on Phonics (Aids in combatting dyslexia)	Varies	1.5 hours/day	500	All BOP institutions	Dyslexia, Education, Work
Houses of Healing: A Prisoner's Guide to Inner Power and Freedom (Emotional literacy and understanding)	12 sessions	2 hours/week	24	All BOP institutions	Cognitions
Key Train for ACT WorkKeys (Building job-relevant skills)	Varies	Varies	50	All BOP institutions	Education, Work
Living a Healthy Life with Chronic Conditions	Varies	Varies	24	All BOP institutions	Medical, Recreation/Leisure/Fitness
Managing Your Diabetes	12 sessions	1 hour/week	12	All BOP institutions	Medical, Recreation/Leisure/Fitness
Mindfulness-Based Cognitive Therapy	8 sessions	2 hours/week	16	All BOP institutions	Mental Health
Money Smart for Older Adults	14 sessions	1-2 hours/week	28	All BOP institutions	Finance/Poverty
Narcotics Anonymous	Varies	Varies	50	All BOP institutions	Substance Abuse
National Diabetes Prevention Program	16 sessions	Varies	16	All BOP institutions	Medical, Recreation/Leisure/Fitness
PEER (Disabilities support group)	10 sessions	1 hour/week	10	All BOP institutions	Antisocial Peers
Pu'a Foundation Reentry Program (Program for women grounded in Hawaiian culture)	Varies	2 hours/week	20	FDC Honolulu	Family/Parenting, Trauma
Service Fit (Wellness group for veterans)	8 weeks	2 hours/week	16	All BOP institutions	Recreation/Leisure/Fitness
Sexual Self-Regulation (SSR) (CBT programs for sex offenders)	3-6 months	Varies	100	All BOP institutions	Cognitions

~ 4 ~

PA Name (short description)	Duration	Frequency	Hours	Program Location(s)	Needs(s) Addressed
Soldier On (Support group for veterans)	10 weeks	1-1.5 hours/week	15	All BOP institutions	Antisocial Peers, Trauma
Square One: Essentials for Women (Psychoeducation life skills for women)	8 sessions	1.5 hours/week	12	All female sites	Finance/Poverty, Mental Health, Recreation/Leisure/ Fitness
START Now (Program behavior disorders)	32 sessions	Varies	32	All BOP institutions (gendered curricula)	Anger/Hostility, Cognitions
Supported Employment (Matching SMI with jobs)	Varies	Varies	20	All BOP institutions	Education, Mental Health, Work
Talking with Your Doctor - Guide for Older Adults (Prepares for medical appointments)	Varies	Varies	5	All BOP institutions	Medical, Recreation/Leisure/ Fitness
Understanding Your Feelings: Shame and Low Self Esteem (Program for women)	7 sessions	1 hour/week	7	All female sites	Cognitions, Mental Health, Trauma
Victim Impact: Listen and Learn	13 Sessions	2 hours/week	26	All BOP institutions	Cognitions
Wellness Recovery Action Plan (Manage mental illness)	8 Sessions	2.5 hours/session	20	All BOP institutions	Mental Health
Women in the 21st Century Workplace (Occupational program for women)	10 sessions	1 hour/week	10	All female sites	Education, Work
Women's Relationships (Teaching women about healthy interpersonal dynamics)	5 sessions	1 hour/week	5	All female sites	Antisocial Peers, Cognitions, Family/Parenting

Directory of National Programs

Federal Bureau of Prisons

A practical guide highlighting reentry programs available in the Federal Bureau of Prisons.

5/18/2017

INTRODUCTION

Supporting a successful transition to the community is central to the mission of the Federal Bureau of Prisons (Bureau). The Bureau protects public safety by ensuring that federal inmates receive reentry programming to support their successful return to the community. National programs are the Bureau's premier reentry programs, designed to ensure that inmates have the skills necessary to succeed upon release. National programs are standardized across institutions, described in the Bureau's national policies, implemented with dedicated resources, and regularly reviewed for quality assurance. When appropriate, national programs are developed or modified to address the needs of specific populations within the Bureau. For example, a gender-responsive version of the Residential Drug Abuse Treatment Program has been created to specifically address the treatment needs of female inmates.

This practical guide was prepared to highlight the Bureau's national programs. Each program summary in this directory contains key information: a Program Description, Time Frame, Admission Criteria, Program Content, Empirical Support, Applicable Policies, and Institution Locations. Additional information about these programs can be obtained by accessing the referenced policies, which are available on the Bureau's public website: www.bop.gov. More specific inquiries about these programs should be directed to the responsible disciplines with the Bureau, as identified in the Table of Contents.

In addition to national programs, the Bureau maintains a catalog of evidence-based and promising model programs to address a wide range of reentry needs. Programs contained in this catalog are implemented at the local level with existing resources. These supplemental program offerings vary based on available resources and the needs of each institution's inmate population. Each institution's Reentry Affairs Coordinator maintains a list of the model programs that is currently available at his/her institution.

Disclaimer: The Bureau provides this directory as a means of describing programs offered throughout the agency. This list contains information which is accurate as of November 2016, but programming offered at various institutions is subject to change over time. The Bureau attempts to follow all judicial recommendations regarding place of incarceration; however, many factors are considered when making a designation decision and the Bureau is not always able to accommodate a judicial recommendation.

Table of Contents

Bureau Literacy Program

Program Description	The Literacy Program is designed to help inmates develop foundational knowledge and skill in reading, math, and written expression, and to prepare inmates to get a General Educational Development (GED) credential. Completion of the Literacy Program is often only the first step towards adequate preparation for successful post-release reintegration into society.
Time Frame	Depending on student needs, students participate in literacy classes for a varied length of time. Literacy classes are scheduled Monday through Friday. Each literacy class session meets a minimum of 1 1/2 hours per day. With few exceptions, inmates without a confirmed GED or high school diploma are required to enroll and participate in the Literacy Program for a minimum of 240 instructional hours or until they achieve a GED credential.
Admission Criteria	All inmates without a GED credential or a high school diploma are enrolled in literacy classes in Bureau correctional facilities. The following inmates are not required to attend the Literacy Program; (1) pretrial inmates; (2) inmates committed for purpose of study and observation under the provisions of 18 U.S.C. 4205(c), 4241(d), or, effective November 1, 1987, 18 U.S.C. 3552(b); (3) sentenced deportable aliens; and (4) inmates determined by staff to be temporarily unable to participate in the Literacy Program due to special circumstances beyond their control (e.g., due to a medical condition, transfer on writ, on a waiting list for initial placement). However, these inmates are required to participate when the special circumstances are no longer applicable.
Program Content	Program content focuses on developing foundational knowledge and skill in reading, math, and written expression, and to prepare inmates to get a GED credential. Inmates withdrawing from literacy programs prior to obtaining a GED will be restricted to the lowest pay and have an inability to vest or earn the maximum amount of Good Conduct Time. Occupational training programs generally require a GED/High School Diploma or concurrent enrollment in a Literacy Program.
Empirical Support	Research has shown that passing the GED Test increases earnings for some dropouts, but labor market payoffs take time (Murnane, Willett, & Tyler, 2000; Tyler, 2004; Tyler & Berk, 2008; Tyler, Murnane, & Willett, 2000, 2003). GED credentials provide a pathway into postsecondary education, and finishing even a short term program offers important economic benefits to GED credential recipients (Patterson, Zhang, Song & Guison-Dowdy, 2010).
Applicable Policies	5350.28 Literacy Program (GED Standard) 5300.21 Education Training and Leisure Time Program Standards 5353.01 Occupational Education Programs
Institution Locations	All Bureau facilities offer the Literacy Program.

English-as-a-Second Language Program

Program Description	The English-as-a-Second Language (ESL) Program is designed to help limited English proficient inmates improve their English until they function at the equivalency of the eighth grade level in listening and reading comprehension.
Time Frame	Depending on English skills and motivation, inmates participate in the ESL program for a varied length of time. ESL classes are scheduled Monday through Friday. Each class session meets a minimum of 1 ½ hours per day. With few exceptions, limited English proficient inmates are required to participate in the ESL program until they function at the eighth grade level as measured by standardized reading and listening assessment tests.
Admission Criteria	All limited English proficient inmates in the Bureau's correctional facilities are required to participate in the ESL Program. The following inmates are exempt from the mandatory ESL participation requirement: (1) pretrial inmates; (2) inmates committed for the purpose of study and observation under the provisions of 18 U.S.C. 4205(c) or, effective November 1, 1987, 18 U.S.C. 3552 (b); (3) sentenced aliens with a deportation detainer; and (4) other inmates whom, for documented good cause, the Warden may excuse from attending the ESL program. Such inmates, however, shall be required to participate when the special circumstances are no longer applicable. Although exempted from mandatory ESL participation requirement, all limited proficient English speaking inmates are strongly encouraged to participate in the ESL Program.
Program Content	Program content primarily focuses on developing functional English listening and reading comprehension skills such as locating and utilizing resources (e.g., libraries, public transportation, drug stores, grocery stores, employment opportunities).
Empirical Support	Research has shown that individuals who are literate only in a language other than English are more likely to have non-continuous employment and earn less than those literate in English (Greenberg, Macas, Rhodes, & Chan, 2001). Data from the 2000 U.S. Census on immigrant earnings revealed a positive relation between earnings and English skill ability (Chiswick & Miller, 2002). An analysis of higher quality research studies has shown, on average, inmates who participated in correctional education programs (to include ESL instruction) had a 43% lower recidivism rate than those inmates who did not participate (Davis et al., 2014). The same research study also demonstrated correctional education is cost effective (i.e., a savings of $5 on re-incarceration costs for every $1 spent on correctional education).
Applicable Policies	5300.21 Education Training and Leisure Time Program Standards 5350.24 English-as-a-Second Language Program (ESL)
Institution Locations	All Bureau facilities offer the ESL Program.

Federal Prison Industries Program

Program Description	The mission of Federal Prison Industries, (FPI) Inc. is to protect society and reduce crime by preparing inmates for successful reentry through job training. FPI (also known by its trade name UNICOR) is a critical component of the Bureau's comprehensive efforts to improve inmate reentry. By providing inmates the skills needed to join the workforce upon release, FPI reduces recidivism and helps curb the rising costs of corrections. FPI was established in 1934 by statute and executive order to provide opportunities for training and work experience to federal inmates (18 U.S.C. § 4121, et seq.). FPI does not rely on tax dollars for support; its operations are completely self-sustaining. FPI is overseen by a Presidentially-appointed Board of Directors. It is one of the Bureau's most critical programs in support of reentry and recidivism reduction.
Time Frame	Employment opportunities are dependent upon institutional needs, FPI requirements, and the inmate employment waiting list.
Admission Criteria	Inmate workers are ordinarily hired through waiting lists. A renewed emphasis has been placed on the use of job share and half-time workers. This will allow for an increase in the number of inmates who benefit from participating in the FPI program. FPI has placed emphasis on prioritizing inmates on the waiting list within two years of release for available FPI positions, with the aim these inmates should be hired at least six months prior to release. FPI has also placed an emphasis on prioritizing inmates on the waiting list who are military veterans, as well as those with financial responsibilities.
Program Content	FPI is, first and foremost, a correctional program. Its impetus is helping inmates acquire the skills necessary to successfully make the transition from prison to law-abiding, tax paying, productive members of society. The production of items and provision of services are necessary by-products of those efforts, as FPI does not receive any appropriated funds for operation.
Empirical Support	Rigorous research, as outlined in the Post-Release Employment Project (PREP Study), demonstrates participation in prison industries and vocational training programs has a positive effect on post-release employment and recidivism. The research revealed inmates who worked in prison industries were 24% less likely to recidivate than non-program participants and 14% more likely to be gainfully employed. These programs had an even greater positive impact on minority inmates who are at a greater risk of recidivism.
Applicable Policies	8120.02 Work Programs for Inmates – FPI 1600.10 Environmental Management Systems 5180.05 Central Inmate Monitoring System 5251.06 Work and Performance Pay Program, Inmate 5290.14 Admission and Orientation Program 5353.01 Occupational Education Programs 5350.28 Literacy Program (GED Standard) 5380.08 Financial Responsibility Program, Inmate 8000.01 UNICOR Corporate Policy and Procedures
	The Federal Prison Industries Program is available at the following facilities:

Institution Locations	Mid-Atlantic Region	North Central Region	Northeast Region
	FCI Ashland, KY-Low FCI Beckley, WV-Medium FCC Butner, NC-Complex FCI Cumberland, MD-Medium FCI Gilmer, WV-Medium FMC Lexington, KY-Adm. FCI Manchester, KY-Medium FCI Memphis, TN-Medium FCC Petersburg, VA-Complex	FCI Englewood, CO-Low FCI Greenville, IL-Medium USP Leavenworth, KS-Medium USP Marion, IL-Medium FCI Milan, MI-Low FCI Sandstone, MN-Low FCC Terre Haute, IN-Complex FCI Waseca, MN-Low (F)	FCC Allenwood, PA-Complex FCI Elkton, OH-Low FCI Fairton, NJ-Medium FCI Fort Dix, NJ-Low USP Lewisburg, PA-High FCI Schuylkill, PA-Medium
	South Central Region	**Southeast Region**	**Western Region**
	FCI Bastrop, TX-Low FCC Beaumont, TX-Complex FPC Bryan, TX-Minimum (F) FCI El Reno, OK-Medium FCC Forrest City, AR-Complex FCI La Tuna, TX-Low FCC Oakdale, LA- Complex FCC Pollock, LA- Complex FCI Seagoville, TX-Low FCI Texarkana, TX-Low	USP Atlanta, GA-Medium FCC Coleman, FL-Complex FCI Edgefield, SC-Medium FCI Jesup, GA-Medium FCI Marianna, FL-Medium FCI Miami, FL-Low FPC Montgomery, AL-Minimum FPC Pensacola, FL-Minimum FCI Talladega, AL- Medium FCI Tallahassee, FL-Low (F) FCC Yazoo City, MS-Complex	USP Atwater, CA-High FCI Dublin, CA-Low (F) FCC Lompoc, CA-Complex FCI Phoenix, AZ-Medium FCI Safford, AZ-Low FCI Sheridan, OR-Medium FCI Terminal Island, CA - Low FCC Tucson, AZ-Complex FCC Victorville, CA-Complex
	(F) = Female Program		

Occupational Education Programs

Program Description	The Occupational Education Program is designed to help inmates acquire marketable skills in a wide variety of trades. Programs which vary from institution to institution are provided by either career civil-service vocational training instructors or through contracts with colleges and technical schools. Many institutions also provide registered apprenticeships through the United States Department of Labor's Office of Apprenticeship. The current Inmate Occupational Training Directory, outlining the specifics for programs offered at each institution is accessible via: http://www.bop.gov/inmates/custody_and_care/docs/inmate_occupational_training_directory.pdf
Time Frame	Program length varies with the provider and the complexity of the program. Upon completion of a marketable occupational education program, inmates may earn an AA, AS, AAS degree and/or an industry recognized certification. Apprenticeship programs are usually 2,000+ hours and may take three to four years to complete.
Admission Criteria	All inmates are eligible to participate in an institution's occupational education program. The inmate's unit team, in consultation with the Education Department, determines if a particular course of study is suited to the inmate's needs. Occupational education programs typically require an inmate to have a GED or high school diploma or concurrent enrollment in the Literacy Program. Inmates under orders of deportation, exclusion, or removal may participate in an institution's occupational education program if institution resources permit after meeting the needs of other eligible inmates.
Program Content	Program content focuses on developing the skills necessary for entry-level employment in a given trade.
Empirical Support	Evidence shows a relationship between correctional education program participation before release and lower odds of recidivating after release (Davis et al., 2014; Saylor and Gaes, 1996; Aos, Phipps, Barnoski and Lieb, 2001). In a study conducted in Maryland, Minnesota and Ohio, correctional education participants had lower recidivism rates in the categories of re-arrest, re-conviction, and re-incarceration (Steurer, Smith and Tracy, 2001). There is some evidence that in-prison vocational education is effective in improving the likelihood of post-release employment (Davis et al., 2014).
Applicable Policies	5353.01 Occupational Education Programs 5300.21 Education, Training and Leisure Time Program Standards
Institution Locations	All Bureau facilities are mandated to offer Occupational Training with the following exceptions: metropolitan correctional centers, metropolitan/federal detention centers, the Federal Transfer Center, satellite camps, and the administrative maximum facility.

Parenting Program

Program Description	The Parenting Program provides inmates information and counseling through directed classes on how to enhance their relationship with their children even while incarcerated. All parenting programs include a classroom component and relationship building visitation activities. In addition, social services outreach contacts are often established to facilitate the provision of services to the inmate parent, visiting custodial parent, and children.
Time Frame	Inmates may participate in the Parenting Program at any point during their sentence. The duration of the program varies by institution-to-institution.
Admission Criteria	All inmates are afforded the opportunity to participate in the Parenting Program.
Program Content	The Parenting Program varies in length, depth, and content from institution-to-institution. Providers of Parenting Program components may include educational staff, as well as volunteers from a community group and/or a social service organization. However, the program's curriculum is recommended to address parenting skills, skills for family support, family literacy education, substance abuse education, and prenatal care information for expectant mothers. Content may be supplemented by curriculum contained in the Model Programs Catalog.
Empirical Support	Research has shown parenting programs for incarcerated parents can improve their self-esteem, parenting attitudes, and institutional adjustment.
Applicable Policies	5355.03 Parenting Program Standards 5267.09 Visiting Regulations 5300.20 Volunteer Services 5300.21 Education Training and Leisure Time Program Standards
Institution Locations	All Bureau facilities offer the Parenting Program.

Bureau Rehabilitation and Values Enhancement Program

Program Description	The Bureau Rehabilitation and Values Enhancement (BRAVE) Program is a cognitive-behavioral, residential treatment program for young males, serving their first federal sentence. Programming is delivered within a modified therapeutic community environment; inmates participate in interactive groups and attend community meetings. The BRAVE Program is designed to facilitate favorable institutional adjustment and reduce incidents of misconduct. In addition, the program encourages inmates to interact positively with staff members and take advantage of opportunities to engage in self-improvement activities throughout their incarceration.
Time Frame	The BRAVE Program is a six-month program. Inmates participate in treatment groups for four hours per day, Monday through Friday. As the BRAVE Program is designed to facilitate a favorable initial adjustment to incarceration, inmates are assigned to the program at the beginning of their sentence.
Admission Criteria	Program admission criteria are as follows: medium security male inmate, 32 years of age or younger, a sentence of 60 months or more, and new to the federal system.
Program Content	Program content focuses on developing interpersonal skills, behaving pro-socially in a prison environment, challenging antisocial attitudes and criminality, developing problem solving skills, and planning for release.
Empirical Support	Research found BRAVE Program participants had a misconduct rate lower than a comparison group and BRAVE Program graduates also had a lower misconduct rate. The BRAVE Program utilizes cognitive behavioral treatment within a modified therapeutic community; these interventions have been found to be effective with an incarcerated population in the reduction of recidivism.
Applicable Policies	5330.11 CN-1 Psychology Treatment Programs
Institution Locations	The BRAVE Program is located at the following facilities: FCI Beckley, WV-Medium FCI Victorville, CA-Medium

Challenge Program

Program Description	The Challenge Program is a cognitive-behavioral, residential treatment program developed for male inmates in penitentiary settings. The Challenge Program provides treatment to high security inmates with substance abuse problems and/or mental illnesses. Programming is delivered within a modified therapeutic community environment; inmates participate in interactive groups and attend community meetings. In addition to treating substance use disorders and mental illnesses, the program addresses criminality, via cognitive-behavioral challenges to criminal thinking errors. The Challenge Program is available in most high security institutions.
Time Frame	Inmates may participate in the program at any point during their sentence; however, they must have at least 18 months remaining on their sentence. The duration of the program varies based on inmate need, with a minimum duration of nine months.
Admission Criteria	A high security inmate must meet one of the following criteria to be eligible to participate in the Challenge Program: a history of substance abuse/dependence or a major mental illness as evidenced by a current diagnosis of a psychotic disorder, mood disorder, anxiety disorder, or personality disorder.
Program Content	The Challenge Program focuses on the reduction of antisocial peer associations; promotion of positive relationships; increased self-control and problem solving skills; and development of pro-social behaviors. The program places a special emphasis on violence prevention. In addition, there are separate supplemental protocols for inmates with substance use disorders and inmates with serious mental illnesses.
Empirical Support	Interventions used in the Challenge Program (i.e., cognitive-behavioral protocols and a modified therapeutic community model) have been demonstrated to be effective in other treatment programs, such as the Bureau's Residential Drug Abuse Program and BRAVE Program. Specifically, they have been noted to reduce misconduct, substance abuse/dependence, and recidivism. The mental health interventions selected for the Challenge Program also have strong empirical support and appear in multiple evidence-based programs (EBPs) registries.
Applicable Policies	5330.11 CN-1 Psychology Treatment Programs

Institution Locations

The Challenge Program is available at the following facilities:

Mid-Atlantic Region	North Central Region	Northeast Region
USP Big Sandy, KY-High USP Hazelton, WV-High USP Lee, VA-High USP McCreary, KY-High	USP Terre Haute, IN-High	USP Allenwood, PA-High USP Canaan, PA-High

Southeast Region	South Central Region	Western Region
USP Coleman I, FL-High USP Coleman II, FL-High	USP Beaumont, TX-High USP Pollock, LA-High	USP Atwater, CA-High USP Tucson, AZ-High

Drug Abuse Education

Program Description	Drug Abuse Education is designed to encourage inmates with a history of drug use to review the consequences of their choice to use drugs and the physical, social, and psychological impacts of this choice. Drug Abuse Education is designed to motivate appropriate inmates to participate in drug abuse treatment, as needed; Drug Abuse Education is not drug treatment.
Time Frame	Drug Abuse Education is a 12-15 hour educational course. Class lengths and times are varied to meet the scheduling needs of each institution. Since the goal of Drug Abuse Education is to motivate inmates to participate in treatment, they are given the opportunity to participate in the course at the beginning of their sentence, ordinarily within the first 12 months.
Admission Criteria	Inmates are required to participate in Drug Abuse Education if any of the following criteria are met: their substance use contributed to the instant offense; their substance use resulted in a supervised release violation; a significant substance use history is noted; or a judicial recommendation for substance abuse treatment is noted. Additionally, any inmate may volunteer to take the course.
Program Content	Participants in Drug Abuse Education receive information on what distinguishes drug use, abuse, and addiction. Participants in the course also review their individual drug use histories, explore evidence of the nexus between drug use and crime, and identify negative consequences of continued drug abuse.
Empirical Support	Research has demonstrated psycho-educational techniques are effective motivational strategies, particularly in moving individuals toward seriously considering a significant life change.
Applicable Policies	5330.11 CN-1 Psychology Treatment Programs
Institution Locations	All Bureau facilities offer the Drug Abuse Education Program.

Mental Health Step Down Unit Program

Program Description	The Mental Health Step Down Unit Program is a residential treatment program offering an intermediate level of care for inmates with serious mental illnesses. The program is specifically designed to serve inmates who do not require inpatient treatment, but lack the skills to function in a general population prison setting. The program uses an integrative model that includes an emphasis on a modified therapeutic community, cognitive-behavioral therapies, and skills training. The goal of the Mental Health Step Down Unit Program is to provide evidence-based treatment to seriously mentally ill inmates in order to maximize their ability to function and minimize relapse and the need for inpatient hospitalization.
Time Frame	The Mental Health Step Down Unit Program is typically conducted over 12-18 months. Inmates may participate in the program at any point in their sentence. Formal programming is facilitated half-days, five days a week with the remaining half-day dedicated to an institution work assignment or other programming, as participants are able.
Admission Criteria	Inmates with serious mental illnesses, who would benefit from intensive residential treatment, are considered for the program. Inmates with a primary diagnosis of Borderline Personality Disorder are referred to the STAGES Program, as opposed to the Mental Health Step Down Unit Program. Program participants must volunteer for the program and must not be acutely mentally ill (i.e., they must not meet criteria for inpatient mental health treatment).
Program Content	Mental Health Step Down Unit Programs operate as modified therapeutic communities and utilize cognitive-behavioral treatments, cognitive rehabilitation, and skills training. Criminal thinking is addressed through the identification of criminal thinking errors and engagement in pro-social interactions with staff and peers. The programs work closely with Psychiatry Services to ensure participants receive appropriate medication and have the opportunity to build a positive relationship with the treating psychiatrist. Program content is designed to promote successful reentry into society at the conclusion of their term of incarceration, and program staff collaborate with community partners to facilitate reentry.
Empirical Support	The mental health interventions selected for this program have strong empirical support and appear in multiple evidence-based programs (EBPs) registries.
Applicable Policies	5330.11 CN-1 Psychology Treatment Programs
Institution Locations	Mental Health Step Down Unit Programs are available at the following facilities: USP Allenwood, PA-High (Secure) USP Atlanta, GA-Medium (Secure) FCI Butner, NC-Medium

Nonresidential Drug Abuse Program

Program Description	The Nonresidential Drug Abuse Program is a flexible, moderate intensity cognitive-behavioral treatment program. The program is designed to meet the needs of a variety of inmates including inmates who are waiting to enter the Residential Drug Abuse Program (RDAP); inmates who do not meet admission criteria for the RDAP, but who wish to benefit from less intensive drug abuse treatment services; and inmates who have been referred by other Psychology Services or institution staff for drug abuse treatment.
Time Frame	The Nonresidential Drug Abuse Program is comprised of 90-120 minute weekly group treatment sessions, for a minimum of 12 weeks and a maximum of 24 weeks. Treatment staff may offer treatment beyond the 12 week minimum based upon the treatment needs of the inmate and supplemental treatment services available at the facility.
Admission Criteria	An inmate must have a history of drug abuse as evidenced by self-report, Presentence Investigation Report (PSR) documentation, or incident reports for use of alcohol or drugs to be eligible to participate in the program.
Program Content	The Bureau's treatment of substance abuse includes a variety of clinical activities organized to treat complex psychological and behavioral problems. The activities are unified through the use of Cognitive Behavioral Therapy (CBT), which was selected as the theoretical model because of its proven effectiveness with the inmate population.
Empirical Support	The Nonresidential Drug Abuse Program utilizes cognitive-behavioral interventions, which have been proven to be effective in the treatment of substance use disorders. The group treatment format used in this program also offers empirically supported benefits from pro-social peer interaction among participants.
Applicable Policies	5330.11 CN-1 Psychology Treatment Programs
Institution Locations	All Bureau facilities offer the Nonresidential Drug Abuse Program.

Residential Drug Abuse Program

Program Description	The Residential Drug Abuse Program (RDAP) provides intensive cognitive-behavioral, residential drug abuse treatment. Programming is delivered within a modified therapeutic community environment; inmates participate in interactive groups and attend community meetings. The RDAP is currently available to Spanish speaking inmates at two facilities. In addition, Dual Diagnosis RDAPs provide specialized treatment services for the inmate with co-occurring substance abuse and mental illness and/or medical problems. Inmates who successfully complete the RDAP and meet other criteria (e.g., sufficient time remaining on their sentence, no precluding offense convictions) may be eligible for up to a 12 month sentence reduction.
Time Frame	The RDAP consists of a minimum of 500 hours of treatment programming delivered over the course of 9 to 12 months. In order to facilitate a successful transition to the community, most inmates participating in the RDAP have between 22 and 42 months remaining on their sentence when they begin the program.
Admission Criteria	In order to gain admission to the RDAP an inmate must meet all of the following admission criteria: US citizen; the presence of a verifiable substance use disorder within the 12 months prior to their arrest for the instant offense(s); able to participate in all three phases of the program, including transitional treatment in the Residential Reentry Center/home confinement; and a signed agreement acknowledging program responsibility.
Program Content	Program content focuses on reducing the likelihood of substance abuse through cognitive-behavioral interventions and relapse prevention strategies. The program also focuses on challenging antisocial attitudes and criminality. In addition, the program facilitates the development of interpersonal skills and pro-social behavior.
Empirical Support	In coordination with the National Institute on Drug Abuse (NIDA), the Bureau conducted a rigorous three-year outcome study of the RDAP, which was published in 2000. The study revealed that male participants were 16% less likely to recidivate and 15% less likely to relapse than similarly situated inmates who do not participate in residential drug abuse treatment for up to 3 years after release. The analysis also found that female inmates who participate in RDAP are 18% less likely to recidivate than similarly situated female inmates who do not participate in treatment.
Applicable Policies	5330.11 CN-1 Psychology Treatment Programs 5331.02 CN-1 Early Release Procedures Under U.S.C. 3621(e)

Institution Locations	The RDAP is available at the following facilities:		
	Mid-Atlantic Region	**North Central Region**	**Northeast Region**
	FPC Alderson, WV-Minimum (2, F) FCI Beckley, WV-Medium SCP Beckley, WV-Minimum USP Big Sandy, KY-High FCI Butner, NC-Medium (2) FCI Cumberland, MD-Medium SCP Cumberland, MD-Minimum SFF Hazelton, WV-Low (F) FMC Lexington, KY-Low FMC Lexington, KY-Low (D) FCI Memphis, TN-Medium FCI Morgantown, WV-Minimum (2) FCI Petersburg, VA-Low FCI Petersburg, VA-Medium	FPC Duluth, MN-Minimum FCI Englewood, CO-Low FCI Florence, CO-Medium SCP Florence, CO-Minimum SCP Greenville, IL-Minimum (F) SCP Leavenworth, KS-Minimum USP Leavenworth, KS-Medium USP Marion, IL-Medium FCI Milan, MI-Low FCI Oxford, WI-Medium SCP Pekin, IL-Minimum FCI Sandstone, MN-Low USMCFP Springfield, MO-Adm. (D) FCI Terre Haute, IN-Medium FCI Waseca, MN-Low (F) FPC Yankton, SD-Minimum (2)	FCI Allenwood, PA-Low FCI Allenwood, PA-Medium FCI Berlin, NH-Medium USP Canaan, PA-High FCI Danbury, CT-Low FSL Danbury, CT-Low (F) (Activating) FCI Elkton, OH-Low FCI Fairton, NJ-Medium FCI Fort Dix, NJ-Low (2) SCP Lewisburg, PA-Minimum SCP McKean, PA-Minimum FCI Schuylkill, PA-Medium
	South Central Region	**Southeast Region**	**Western Region**
	FCI Bastrop, TX-Low FCI Beaumont, TX-Low FCI Beaumont, TX-Medium SCP Beaumont, TX-Minimum USP Beaumont, TX-High FPC Bryan, TX-Minimum (F) FMC Carswell, TX-Adm. (F, D) FMC Carswell, TX-Adm. (F, S) FCI El Reno, OK-Medium FCI Forrest City, AR-Low FCI Forrest City, AR-Medium FMC Fort Worth, TX-Low FCI La Tuna, TX-Low FCI Seagoville, TX-Low (2) SCP Texarkana, TX-Minimum	FCI Coleman, FL-Low USP Coleman, FL-High SCP Edgefield, SC-Minimum FCI Jesup, GA-Medium FCI Marianna, FL-Medium SCP Miami, FL-Minimum FCI Miami, FL-Low (S, 2) FPC Montgomery, AL-Minimum (2) FPC Pensacola, FL-Minimum SCP Talladega, AL- Minimum FCI Tallahassee, FL-Low (F) FCI Yazoo City, MS-Low	FCI Dublin, CA-Low (2, F) FCI Herlong, CA-Medium FCI Lompoc, CA-Low FCI Phoenix, AZ-Medium SCP Phoenix, AZ-Minimum (F) FCI Safford, AZ-Low FCI Sheridan, OR-Medium SCP Sheridan, OR-Minimum (2) FCI Terminal Island, CA – Low FCI Terminal Island, CA – Low (D)
	(D) = Dual Diagnosis Program (F) = Female Program (S) = Spanish Program (2) = 2 Programs at the Facility		

Resolve Program

Program Description	The Resolve Program is a cognitive-behavioral program designed to address the trauma related mental health needs of inmates. Specifically, the program seeks to decrease the incidence of trauma related psychological disorders and improve inmates' level of functioning. In addition, the program aims to increase the effectiveness of other treatments, such as drug treatment and healthcare. The program uses a standardized treatment protocol consisting of three components: an initial psycho-educational workshop (Trauma in Life); a brief, skills based treatment group (Seeking Safety); and Dialectical Behavioral Therapy (DBT), Cognitive Processing Therapy (CPT), and/or a Skills Maintenance Group which are intensive, cognitive-behavioral treatment groups to address persistent psychological and interpersonal difficulties. The Resolve Program is currently available in many female institutions and a limited number of male institutions.
Time Frame	In most instances, inmates are expected to participate in the Resolve Program during their first 12 months of incarceration. The full Resolve Program protocol takes approximately 40 weeks to complete; however, scheduling conflicts may extend the length of the program. Inmates also have the option of continuing to participate in the Skills Maintenance Group indefinitely to continue practicing healthy coping skills.
Admission Criteria	The Resolve Program is for inmates with a mental health diagnosis due to trauma. While the Trauma in Life Workshop is the first stage of the Resolve Program, other inmates without a history of trauma may participate in this workshop if institution resources permit.
Program Content	The program content focuses on the development of personal resilience, effective coping skills, emotional self-regulation, and healthy interpersonal relationships. These skills are attained through the use of educational, cognitive, behavioral, and problem-solving focused interventions. The program materials are modified to be gender responsive to male and female populations.
Empirical Support	Empirical support for the interventions utilized in the Resolve Program is well-established. Seeking Safety, CPT, and DBT appear in multiple evidence-based programs (EBP) registries. These protocols are also used in the Veterans Administration, the country's largest provider of trauma-related treatment.
Applicable Policies	5330.11 CN-1 Psychology Treatment Programs

Institution Locations	The Resolve Program is available at the following facilities:		
	Mid-Atlantic Region	**North Central Region**	**Northeast Region**
	FPC Alderson, WV-Minimum (F) SFF Hazelton, WV-Low (F) SCP Lexington, KY-Minimum (F)	ADX Florence, CO-Maximum (M) SCP Greenville, IL-Minimum (F) FCI Waseca, MN-Low (F)	FCI Danbury, CT-Low (M) SCP Danbury, CT-Minimum (F) FSL Danbury, CT-Low (F) (Activating)
	South Central Region	**Southeast Region**	**Western Region**
	FPC Bryan, TX-Minimum (F) FMC Carswell, TX-Adm. (F)	FCI Aliceville, AL-Low (F) SCP Coleman, FL-Minimum (F) SCP Marianna, FL-Minimum (F) FCI Tallahassee, FL-Low (F)	FCI Dublin, CA-Low (F) SCP Victorville, CA-Minimum (F)
	(F) Female Program (M) = Male Program		

Sex Offender Treatment Program - Nonresidential

Program Description	The Sex Offender Treatment Program – Nonresidential (SOTP-NR) is a moderate intensity program designed for low to moderate risk sexual offenders. The program consists of cognitive-behaviorally based psychotherapy groups, totaling 4-6 hours per week.
Time Frame	Inmates are ordinarily placed in the SOTP-NR during the last 36 months of their sentence and, prioritized by release date. The typical duration of the SOTP-NR is 9-12 months.
Admission Criteria	Most participants in the SOTP-NR have a history of a single sex crime; many are first time inmates serving a sentence for an Internet Sex Offense. The program is voluntary. Prior to placement in the SOTP-NR, prospective participants are screened with a risk assessment instrument to ensure their offense history is commensurate with moderate intensity treatment.
Program Content	The SOTP-NR is designed to target dynamic risk factors associated with re-offense in sex offenders, as demonstrated by empirical research. These factors include: sexual self-regulation deficits and sexual deviancy; criminal thinking and behavior patterns; intimacy skills deficits; and, emotional self-regulation deficits. The program employs cognitive-behavioral techniques, with a primary emphasis on skills acquisition and practice.
Empirical Support	The SOTP-NR is designed to conform to the characteristics of sex offender treatment programs with proven effectiveness in reducing re-offense as demonstrated by outcome research. These characteristics include: 1) stratification of treatment into separate tracks for high and low/ moderate risk inmates; 2) targeting empirically demonstrated dynamic risk factors; and 3) training and oversight to ensure fidelity with the program model.
Applicable Policies	5324.10 Sex Offender Programs

Institution Locations

The SOTP-NR is available at the following facilities:

Mid-Atlantic Region	North Central Region	Northeast Region
FCI Petersburg, VA-Medium	FCI Englewood, CO-Low USP Marion, IL-Medium	FCI Elkton, OH-Low

South Central Region	Southeast Region	Western Region
FMC Carswell, TX-Adm. (F) FCI Seagoville, TX-Low	FCI Marianna, FL-Medium	USP Tucson, AZ-High

(F) = Female Program

Sex Offender Treatment Program - Residential

Program Description	The Sex Offender Treatment Program - Residential (SOTP-R) is a high intensity program designed for high risk sexual offenders. The program consists of cognitive-behaviorally based psychotherapy groups, totaling 10-12 hours per week, on a residential treatment unit employing a modified therapeutic community model.
Time Frame	Inmates are ordinarily placed in the SOTP-R during the last 36 months of their sentence, prioritized by release date. The typical duration of the SOTP-R is 12-18 months.
Admission Criteria	Participants in the SOTP-R have a history of multiple sex crimes, extensive non-sexual criminal histories, and/or a high level of sexual deviancy or hypersexuality. The program is voluntary. Prior to placement in the SOTP-R, prospective participants are screened with a risk assessment instrument to ensure their offense history is commensurate with high intensity treatment.
Program Content	The SOTP-R is designed to target dynamic risk factors associated with re-offense in sex offenders, as demonstrated by empirical research. These factors include: sexual self-regulation deficits and sexual deviancy; criminal thinking and behavior patterns; intimacy skills deficits; and emotional self-regulation deficits. The program employs cognitive-behavioral techniques, with a primary emphasis on skills acquisition and practice. The modified therapeutic community model is employed to address pro-offending attitudes and values.
Empirical Support	The SOTP-R is designed to conform to the characteristics of sex offender treatment programs with a proven effectiveness in reducing re-offense as demonstrated by outcome research. These characteristics include: 1) stratification of treatment into separate tracks for high and low/moderate risk inmates; 2) targeting empirically demonstrated dynamic risk factors; and 3) training and oversight to ensure fidelity with the program model.
Applicable Policies	5324.10 Sex Offender Programs
Institution Locations	The SOTP-R is available at the following facilities: FMC Devens, MA-Adm. USP Marion, IL-Medium

Skills Program

Program Description	The Skills Program is a residential treatment program designed to improve the institutional adjustment of inmates with intellectual disabilities and social deficiencies. The program uses an integrative model which includes a modified therapeutic community, cognitive-behavioral therapies, and skills training. The goal of the program is to increase the academic achievement and adaptive behavior of cognitively impaired inmates, thereby improving their institutional adjustment and likelihood for successful community reentry.
Time Frame	The Skills Program is conducted over 12-18 months. Participation in the program during the initial phase of an inmate's incarceration is recommended; however, inmates may participate in the program at a later time. Formal programming is facilitated half-days, five days a week with the remaining half-day dedicated to an institution work assignment or receiving tutorial assistance.
Admission Criteria	Inmates with significant functional impairment due to intellectual disabilities, neurological deficits, and/or remarkable social skills deficits are considered for the program. Participants must be appropriate for housing in a low or medium security institution. Inmates must volunteer for the program.
Program Content	The Skills Program operates as a modified therapeutic community and utilizes cognitive-behavioral treatments, cognitive rehabilitation, and skills training. The program employs a multi-disciplinary treatment approach aimed at teaching participants basic educational and social skills. Criminal thinking is addressed through the identification of criminal thinking errors and engagement in pro-social interactions with staff and peers. Program content is designed to promote successful reentry into society at the conclusion of their term of incarceration. Program staff collaborate with community partners to facilitate reentry.
Empirical Support	The cognitive-behavioral, cognitive rehabilitation, skills training, and modified therapeutic community interventions selected for this program have sound empirical support and consistently appear in evidence-based programs (EBPs) registries.
Applicable Policies	5330.11 CN-1 Psychology Treatment Programs
Institution Locations	The Skills Program is available at the following facilities: FCI Coleman, FL-Medium FCI Danbury, CT-Low

Steps Toward Awareness, Growth, and Emotional Strength Program

Program Description	The Steps Toward Awareness, Growth, and Emotional Strength (STAGES) Program is a residential treatment program for inmates with serious mental illnesses and a primary diagnosis of Borderline Personality Disorder. The program uses an integrative model which includes a modified therapeutic community, cognitive behavioral therapies, and skills training. The program is designed to increase the time between disruptive behaviors, foster living within the general population or community setting, and increase pro-social skills.
Time Frame	The STAGES Program is typically conducted over 12-18 months. Inmates may participate in the program at any time during their sentence. Formal programming is facilitated half-days, five days a week with the remaining half-day dedicated to an institution work assignment or other programming.
Admission Criteria	Inmates referred to the STAGES Program have a primary diagnosis of Borderline Personality Disorder and a history of unfavorable institutional adjustment linked to this disorder. Examples of unfavorable institutional adjustment include multiple incident reports, suicide watches, and/or extended placement in restrictive housing. Inmates designated to the STAGES Program must volunteer for treatment and be willing to actively engage in the treatment process. Willingness to engage in the treatment is assessed through a brief course of pre-treatment in which the inmate learns basic skills at the referring institution.
Program Content	The program curriculum is derived from Dialectical Behavior Therapy (DBT) and takes place in a modified therapeutic community. There is also an emphasis on basic cognitive-behavioral skills consistent with other Bureau treatment programs. For example, criminal thinking is addressed through the identification of criminal thinking errors and engagement in pro-social interactions with staff and peers. Program content is designed to prepare inmates for transition to less restrictive prison settings and promote successful reentry into society at the conclusion of their term of incarceration. Program staff collaborate with community partners to facilitate reentry.
Empirical Support	DBT is an evidence-based practice for the treatment of Borderline Personality Disorder, with strong empirical support. In addition, the cognitive-behavioral interventions and modified therapeutic community model employed in the program are well supported in the professional literature. These interventions appear in a number of evidence-based programs (EBPs) registries.
Applicable Policies	5330.11 CN-1 Psychology Treatment Programs
Institution Locations	The STAGES Program is available at the following facilities: USP Florence, CO-High (Secure) FCI Terre Haute, IN-Medium

Life Connections Program

Program Description	The Life Connections Program (LCP) is a residential faith-based program offered to inmates of all faith traditions, including for those who do not hold to a religious preference. This program is available to inmates at low, medium, and high security facilities. The goal of LCP is to provide opportunities for the development and maturation of the participants' commitment to normative values and responsibilities, resulting in overall changed behavior and better institutional adjustments. In addition, the participants receive life skills and practical tools and strategies to assist them in transitioning back to society once released from federal custody.
Time Frame	The LCP is an 18 month program in which participants attend classes and meetings, Monday through Friday afternoons for approximately four hours per day, as well as evening mentoring sessions and seminars. In addition, the participants participate in their respective faith services and chapel programs during the evening and weekend hours.
Admission Criteria	Program admission criteria are as follows: • Low security male inmates within 24 to 36 months of their projected release date. • Medium security male inmates with 24 months or more prior to their projected release date. • High security male inmates with 30 months or more prior to their projected release date. • Low security female inmates with 30 months or more prior to their projected release date. • Must not have a written deportation order. • Must not be on Financial Responsibility Program (FRP) Refuse status. • Must have met English-as-a-Second Language (ESL) and GED obligations. • Must receive recommendation from relevant staff (Chaplain, Unit Team, and Associate Warden) and approval from the Warden.
Program Content	The objectives of the program are to foster personal growth and responsibility, and to right the relationships among their victim(s), community, and inmate, using secular outcome-based objectives. The program facilitates the practice of one's personal belief system, whether secular or religious, to bring reconciliation and restoration, and to take responsibility for their criminal behavior. In addition, community organizations and volunteers at the inmates' release destinations serve as mentors to assist and support the participants upon their release.
Empirical Support	The LCP materials and workbooks are based on interactive journaling which was listed on SAMHSA's National Registry of Evidence-based Programs and Practices (NREPP).
Applicable Policies	Operations Memorandum 003-2013 Life Connections Program

Institution Locations	The LCP is available at the following facilities:		
	Mid-Atlantic Region	North Central Region	South Centra Region
	FCI Petersburg, VA-Low	USP Leavenworth, KS-Medium FCI Milan, MI-Low USP Terre Haute, IN-High	FMC Carswell, TX-Adm. (F)
	(F) = Female Program		

Inmate Occupational Training Directory

Region: All
Institution: All
DOL Category: All
DOL Specific Category: All
Months Duration: All
Pre-Requisite: All
Specific Cert/Degree: All
Credit Type CEUs: All

Credit Type College: All
Instructional Source: All
Certificate/Degree Source: All
Apprenticeship: All
Green Component: All
Public Works: All
FPI Component: All

Report Key: CEUs - Continuing Education Units
Appr - Apprenticeship
DOL - Department of Labor
VT - Vocational Training

125

Institution: ALDERSON FPC

Program / Location	Occupation		Requirements	Certification / Employer	
Air Conditioning/Refrigeration Location: Camp	Installation, Maintenance, and Repair - Heating, Air Conditioning, and Refrigeration Mechanics and Installers - Apprenticeship	36	High School Diploma or GED - employed by HVAC at the facility for 60 days, 6 months clear conduct	BOP Employee Department of Labor Certificate HVAC worker	0 / 0
Automotive Mechanic Location: Camp	Installation, Maintenance, and Repair - Automotive Service Technicians and Mechanics - Apprenticeship	18	High School Diploma or GED - 6 months clear conduct	BOP Employee Department of Labor Certificate Automotive Mechanic	0 / 0
Cook Location: Camp	Food Preparation and Serving - Cooks - Apprenticeship	30	High School Diploma or GED - employed by Food Service for 60 days, 6 months clear conduct	BOP Employee Department of Labor Certificate Cook	0 / 0
Cosmetology Location: Camp	Personal Care and Service - Barbers, Hairdressers, and Cosmetologists - Occ Ed Class	18	High School Diploma or GED - 6 months clear conduct	Independent Contractor Industry-Recognized Certificate Cosmetologist	0 / 65
Customer Service Representative Location: Camp	Office and Administrative Support - Customer Service Representatives - Occ Ed Class	12	High School Diploma or GED - 6 months clear conduct	Accredited Post Secondary Institution Post-Secondary (College) Certificate Only Customer Service Representative	0 / 15

Program / Location	Occupational Area	Months	Eligibility	Certification / Employer	Ratio
Electrician Location: Camp	Construction and Extraction - Electricians - Apprenticeship	18	High School Diploma or GED - employed by Electric Shop for 60 days, 6 months clear conduct	BOP Employee Department of Labor Certificate Electrician	0 / 0
Horticulture Location: Camp	Farming, Fishing, and Forestry - Agricultural Workers - Occ Ed Class	6	High School Diploma or GED - 6 months clear conduct	Independent Contractor Post-Secondary (College) Certificate Only Greenhouse Worker	0 / 43
Landscaping Location: Camp	Building and Grounds Cleaning - Grounds Maintenance Workers - Apprenticeship	18	High School Diploma or GED - 6 months clear conduct	BOP Employee Department of Labor Certificate Landscaper	0 / 0
Medical Insurance and Billing Clerk Location: Camp	Office and Administrative Support - Financial Clerks - Occ Ed Class	24	High School Diploma or GED - 6months clear conduct	Accredited Post Secondary Institution Post-Secondary (College) Certificate Only Medical Insurance and Billing Clerk	0 / 30
Medical Transcriptionist Location: Camp	Office and Administrative Support - General Office Clerks - Occ Ed Class	18	High School Diploma or GED - 6 months clear conduct	Accredited Post Secondary Institution Post-Secondary (College) Certificate Only Medical Machine Transcriptionist	0 / 18

Institution: ALDERSON FPC   **(Cont'd)**

Program	Occupation	#	Requirements	Certification	Ratio
Plumber Location: Camp	Installation, Maintenance, and Repair - General Maintenance and Repair Workers - Apprenticeship	27	High School Diploma or GED - employed by Plumbing Shop for 60 days, 6 months clear conduct	BOP Employee Department of Labor Certificate Plumber	0 / 0
Receptionist Location: Camp	Office and Administrative Support - Receptionists - Occ Ed Class	18	High School Diploma or GED - 6 months clear conduct	Accredited Post Secondary Institution Post-Secondary (College) Certificate Only Receptionist	0 / 21
Teacher Assistant Location: Camp	Education, Training, and Library - Teacher Assistants - Apprenticeship	18	High School Diploma or GED - employed in Education as an aide for 60 days, 6 months clear conduct	BOP Employee Department of Labor Certificate Teacher Assistant	0 / 0
VT Masonry Location: Camp	Construction and Extraction - Brickmasons, Blockmasons, and Stonemasons - Occ Ed Class	5	High School Diploma or GED - 6 months clear conduct	BOP Employee Industry-Recognized Certificate Mason	0 / 0
Welder Location: Camp	Production - Welders, Cutters, Solderers, and Brazers - Apprenticeship	48	High School Diploma or GED - employed by Welding Shop for 60 days, 6 months clear conduct	BOP Employee Department of Labor Certificate Welder	0 / 0

Institution: ALICEVILLE FCI

Apprenticeship - Carpenter	Construction and Extraction	41	High School Diploma or GED	BOP Employee
Location: Main	- Carpenters			BOP Certificate & Department of Labor Certificate
	- Apprenticeship			Carpenter Maintenance
				0 / 0
Apprenticeship - Electrician	Construction and Extraction	41	High School Diploma or GED	BOP Employee
Location: Main	- Electricians			BOP Certificate & Department of Labor Certificate
	- Apprenticeship			Electrician
				0 / 0
Apprenticeship - HVAC	Installation, Maintenance, and Repair	41	High School Diploma or GED	BOP Employee
Location: Main	- Heating, Air Conditioning, and Refrigeration Mechanics and Installers			BOP Certificate & Department of Labor Certificate
	- Apprenticeship			HVAC-Entry Level
				0 / 0
Apprenticeship - Plumbing	Installation, Maintenance, and Repair	44	High School Diploma or GED	BOP Employee
Location: Main	- General Maintenance and Repair Workers			BOP Certificate & Department of Labor Certificate
	- Apprenticeship			Plumber
				0 / 0
VT Carpentry	Construction and Extraction	6	High School Diploma or GED	BOP Employee
Location: Main	- Carpenters			Vocational/Technical School Certificate Only
	- Occ Ed Class			Carpenter
				0 / 0

Institution: ALICEVILLE FCI   (Cont'd)

VT Computer Skills - MS Office Location: Main	Office and Administrative Support - Desktop Publishers - Occ Ed Class	4	High School Diploma or GED	BOP Employee BOP Certificate Only Clerk	0 / 0
VT Computer Skills - MS Office Location: Camp	Office and Administrative Support - Desktop Publishers - Occ Ed Class	4	High School Diploma or GED	BOP Employee BOP Certificate Only Clerk	0 / 0
VT Electrical Location: Main	Construction and Extraction - Electricians - Occ Ed Class	6	High School Diploma or GED	Accredited Vocational/Technical School Vocational/Technical School Certificate Only Electrician Tech	0 / 0

Institution: ALLENWOOD LOW FCI

Program	Occupation		Education Requirement	Credentials	
Cook Apprenticeship Location: Main	Food Preparation and Serving - Cooks - Apprenticeship	24	Concurrent GED Enrollment -	BOP Employee BOP Certificate & Department of Labor Certificate Cook	0 / 0
Culinary Arts Location: Main	Food Preparation and Serving - Food Preparation Workers - Occ Ed Class	6	High School Diploma or GED -	BOP Employee BOP Certificate & Industry Recognized Certificate Food Preparation Worker	0 / 0
Housekeeping Apprentice Location: Main	Building and Grounds Cleaning - Grounds Maintenance Workers - Apprenticeship	24	High School Diploma or GED	BOP Employee BOP Certificate & Department of Labor Certificate Housekeeping Worker	0 / 0
VT Computer--IC3--Internet Computing Core Certification Location: Main	Office and Administrative Support - General Office Clerks - Occ Ed Class	6	Concurrent GED Enrollment -	BOP Employee BOP Certificate & Industry Recognized Certificate General Office Clerk	0 / 0

Institution: ALLENWOOD MED FCI

Program / Location	Occupation			Credential	
Fishery Worker Apprentice Location: Main	Farming, Fishing, and Forestry - Fishers and Related Fishing Workers - Apprenticeship	24	Concurrent GED Enrollment	-	BOP Employee BOP Certificate & Department of Labor Certificate Fishery Worker	0 / 0
Housekeeping Apprentice Location: Main	Building and Grounds Cleaning - Janitors and Building Cleaners - Apprenticeship	24	Concurrent GED Enrollment	-	BOP Employee BOP Certificate & Department of Labor Certificate Housekeeping Worker	0 / 0
QA Tech Apprenticeship Location: Main	Production - Quality Control Inspectors - Apprenticeship	24	Concurrent GED Enrollment	-	BOP Employee BOP Certificate & Department of Labor Certificate Quality Assurance Technician	0 / 0
VT Aquaculture Science Location: Main	Farming, Fishing, and Forestry - Fishers and Related Fishing Workers - Occ Ed Class	6	Concurrent GED Enrollment	-	BOP Employee BOP Certificate Only Fishery Worker	0 / 0
VT Carpentry Location: Main	Construction and Extraction - Carpenters - Occ Ed Class	24	High School Diploma or GED	-	BOP Employee BOP Certificate & Industry Recognized Certificate Carpenter	0 / 0

Institution: ALLENWOOD MED FCI   (Cont'd)

VT Computer--IC3--Internet Computing Core Certification Location: Main	Office and Administrative Support - General Office Clerks - Occ Ed Class	6	Concurrent GED Enrollment -	BOP Employee BOP Certificate & Industry Recognized Certificate Office Clerk	0 / 0
VT Computer--IC3--Internet Computing Core Certification Location: PCU	Office and Administrative Support - General Office Clerks - Occ Ed Class	6	Concurrent GED Enrollment -	BOP Employee BOP Certificate & Industry Recognized Certificate Office Clerk	0 / 0
VT ELECTRIC Location: Main	Installation, Maintenance, and Repair - Heating, Air Conditioning, and Refrigeration Mechanics and Installers - Occ Ed Class	10	High School Diploma or GED -	BOP Employee BOP Certificate & Industry Recognized Certificate Electric - Entry Level	0 / 0

Institution: ALLENWOOD USP

Program / Location		Hours	Education Requirement	0 / 0	Certification / Outcome
Cook Apprenticeship Location: Main	Food Preparation and Serving - Chefs and Head Cooks - Apprenticeship	48	High School Diploma or GED	0 / 0	BOP Employee BOP Certificate & Department of Labor Certificate Cook/Chef
Quality Control Technician Location: Main	Production - Quality Control Inspectors - Apprenticeship	30	High School Diploma or GED	0 / 0	BOP Employee BOP Certificate & Department of Labor Certificate Quality Control Technician
Upholsterer Location: Main	Production - Upholsterers - Apprenticeship	30	High School Diploma or GED	0 / 0	BOP Employee BOP Certificate & Department of Labor Certificate Upholsterer
VT Computer--IC3--Internet Computing Core Certification Location: Main	Office and Administrative Support - General Office Clerks - Occ Ed Class	6	Concurrent GED Enrollment -	0 / 0	BOP Employee BOP Certificate & Industry Recognized Certificate Office Clerk

Institution: ASHLAND FCI

Program		Capacity	Pre-Requisites	Credentials	Enrolled / Waitlist
Auto Body Program Location: Main	Installation, Maintenance, and Repair - Automotive Body and Glass Repairers - Occ Ed Class	9	No Pre-Requisites Required	BOP Employee BOP Certificate Only Auto Body Repairer	0 / 0
Baker Apprenticeship Location: Main	Food Preparation and Serving - Cooks - Apprenticeship	36	Concurrent GED Enrollment -	BOP Employee BOP Certificate & Department of Labor Certificate Baker	0 / 0
Baker Apprenticeship Location: Camp	Food Preparation and Serving - Cooks - Apprenticeship	36	Concurrent GED Enrollment -	BOP Employee BOP Certificate & Department of Labor Certificate Baker	0 / 0
Car Care Program Location: Main	Installation, Maintenance, and Repair - Automotive Service Technicians and Mechanics - Occ Ed Class	2	No Pre-Requisites Required	BOP Employee BOP Certificate Only Automotive Technician	0 / 0
Cook Apprenticeship Location: Main	Food Preparation and Serving - Cooks - Apprenticeship	24	Concurrent GED Enrollment -	BOP Employee BOP Certificate & Department of Labor Certificate Cook	0 / 0

135

Institution: ASHLAND FCI   (Cont'd)

Cook Apprenticeship	Food Preparation and Serving	24	Concurrent GED Enrollment	BOP Employee	0 / 0
Location: Camp	- Cooks		-	BOP Certificate & Department of Labor Certificate	
	- Apprenticeship			Cook	
Dental Assistant Apprenticeship	Production	18	High School Diploma or GED	BOP Employee	0 / 0
Location: Main	- Dental Laboratory Technicians			BOP Certificate & Department of Labor Certificate	
	- Apprenticeship			Dental Assistant	
Maintenance Electrician Apprenticeship	Installation, Maintenance, and Repair	48	High School Diploma or GED	BOP Employee	0 / 0
Location: Main	- Electrical and Electronics Installers and Repairers			BOP Certificate & Department of Labor Certificate	
	- Apprenticeship			Maintenance Electrician	
Master Gardener Program	Farming, Fishing, and Forestry	7	High School Diploma or GED	Accredited Post Secondary Institution	0 / 0
Location: Camp	- Agricultural Workers		-	BOP Certificate & Industry Recognized Certificate	
	- Occ Ed Class			Master Gardener	
Welder Apprenticeship	Production	36	High School Diploma or GED	BOP Employee	0 / 0
Location: Main	- Welders, Cutters, Solderers, and Brazers			BOP Certificate & Department of Labor Certificate	
	- Apprenticeship			Welder	

Institution: ASHLAND FCI (Cont'd)

Welding Program		10	High School Diploma or GED	BOP Employee	0 / 0
Location: Main	Production			BOP Certificate & Industry Recognized Certificate	
	- Welders, Cutters, Solderers, and Brazers				
	- Occ Ed Class			Welder	

Institution: ATLANTA USP

VT Electrical Location: Main	Construction and Extraction - Electricians - Occ Ed Class	18	High School Diploma or GED	Accredited Vocational/Technical School Vocational/Technical School Certificate Only Electricians' tech	40 / 0
Custodial Maintenance Location: Main	Building and Grounds Cleaning - Janitors and Building Cleaners - Occ Ed Class	9	High School Diploma or GED	Accredited Post Secondary Institution Post-Secondary (College) Certificate & Industry Recognized Certificate Custodial Maintenance Tech	0 / 24
Custodial Maintenance Location: Camp	Building and Grounds Cleaning - Janitors and Building Cleaners - Occ Ed Class	9	High School Diploma or GED	Accredited Post Secondary Institution Post-Secondary (College) Certificate Only Custodial Maintenance	0 / 24
VT Electrical Location: Camp	Construction and Extraction - Electricians - Occ Ed Class	18	High School Diploma or GED	Accredited Vocational/Technical School Both Vo-Tech School and Industry-Recognized Certificates Electrical Tech	40 / 0

Institution: ATLANTA USP   (Cont'd)

VT HVAC Location: Main	Installation, Maintenance, and Repair - Heating, Air Conditioning, and Refrigeration Mechanics and Installers - Occ Ed Class	24	High School Diploma or GED	Accredited Vocational/Technical School Industry-Recognized Certificate HVAC Tech	60 / 0

Institution: ATWATER USP

Program	Occupation	Duration	Requirements	Certification	
Electrician Apprentice Location: Camp	Construction and Extraction - Electricians - Apprenticeship	48	High School Diploma or GED - Employment in Facilities Electric Shop	BOP Employee Department of Labor Certificate Electrician	0 / 0
Electrician Apprenticeship Location: Main	Construction and Extraction - Electricians - Apprenticeship	48	High School Diploma or GED - Employment as Electric Shop Worker	BOP Employee Department of Labor Certificate Electrician	0 / 0
Food Service--Cook Location: Main	Food Preparation and Serving - Cooks - Apprenticeship	24	High School Diploma or GED - Employment as Food Service Food Prep Worker	BOP Employee Department of Labor Certificate Cook	0 / 0
Food Service--Cook Location: Camp	Food Preparation and Serving - Food Preparation Workers - Apprenticeship	24	High School Diploma or GED - Employment as Food Service Food Prep Worker	BOP Employee Department of Labor Certificate Cook	0 / 0
HVAC Apprentice Location: Camp	Installation, Maintenance, and Repair - Heating, Air Conditioning, and Refrigeration Mechanics and Installers - Apprenticeship	36	High School Diploma or GED - Employment in Facilities HVAC Shop	BOP Employee Department of Labor Certificate HVAC Apprentice	0 / 0

Institution: ATWATER USP   **(Cont'd)**

HVAC Apprentice Location: Main	Installation, Maintenance, and Repair - Heating, Air Conditioning, and Refrigeration Mechanics and Installers - Apprenticeship	36	High School Diploma or GED - Employment as HVAC Worker	BOP Employee Department of Labor Certificate HVAC Worker	0 / 0
Landscape Technician Location: Camp	Farming, Fishing, and Forestry - Agricultural Workers - Apprenticeship	12	High School Diploma or GED - Employment in Facilities Landscape Work Detail	BOP Employee Department of Labor Certificate Tree/Plant Care Worker	0 / 0
Stationary Engineer Location: Camp	Installation, Maintenance, and Repair - Industrial Machinery Mechanics and Maintenance Workers - Apprenticeship	48	High School Diploma or GED	BOP Employee Department of Labor Certificate Stationary Engineer Apprentice	0 / 0
Teacher's Aide Location: Camp	Education, Training, and Library - Teacher Assistants - Apprenticeship	24	High School Diploma or GED - Employment as Education Tutor	BOP Employee Department of Labor Certificate Teacher's Aide	0 / 0
Teacher's Aide Apprenticeship Location: Main	Education, Training, and Library - Teacher Assistants - Apprenticeship	24	High School Diploma or GED - Employment as Education Tutor	BOP Employee Department of Labor Certificate Teacher's Aide	0 / 0

Institution: ATWATER USP   (Cont'd)

Program / Location	Occupation		Requirements	Certification	
VT Building Trades/Landscaping Location: Main	Construction and Extraction - Construction Laborers and Helpers - Occ Ed Class	5	High School Diploma or GED - Clear conduct > 1 year	BOP Employee BOP Certificate Only Construction Laborer	0 / 0
VT Computer Skills - Illustrator Location: Main	Office and Administrative Support - Desktop Publishers - Occ Ed Class	3	High School Diploma or GED - Clear conduct 1 yr/No computer restrictions	BOP Employee BOP Certificate Only Illustrator	0 / 0
VT Computer Skills - MS Office Location: Main	Office and Administrative Support - Desktop Publishers - Occ Ed Class	3	High School Diploma or GED - Clear Conduct 1 Year/ No computer restrictions	BOP Employee BOP Certificate Only Clerk	0 / 0

Institution: BASTROP FCI

Program	Location	Occupational Area		Pre-Requisites	Certification	Enrollment
Baker	Location: Main	Food Preparation and Serving - Cooks - Apprenticeship	36	No Pre-Requisites Required	BOP Employee BOP Certificate & Department of Labor Certificate Baker	0 / 0
Building Trades	Location: Main	Construction and Extraction - Construction Laborers and Helpers - Occ Ed Class	6	Concurrent GED Enrollment	BOP Employee Post-Secondary (College) Certificate & Industry Recognized Certificate Construction Laborer	34 / 0
Carpenter	Location: Main	Construction and Extraction - Carpenters - Apprenticeship	48	No Pre-Requisites Required	BOP Employee Department of Labor Certificate Carpenter	0 / 0
Cook	Location: Main	Food Preparation and Serving - Cooks - Apprenticeship	36	No Pre-Requisites Required	BOP Employee BOP Certificate & Department of Labor Certificate Cook	0 / 0
Culinary Arts	Location: Main	Food Preparation and Serving - Cooks - Occ Ed Class	6	High School Diploma or GED - w/in 2 years of release	Accredited Post Secondary Institution Post-Secondary (College) Certificate & Industry Recognized Certificate Cook	70 / 0

Institution: BASTROP FCI   (Cont'd)

Program / Location	Occupation	Hours	Pre-Requisites	Certifications	
Dental Assistant Location: Main	Production - Dental Laboratory Technicians - Apprenticeship	12	No Pre-Requisites Required	BOP Employee BOP Certificate & Department of Labor Certificate Dental Assistant	0 / 0
Electrician Location: Main	Construction and Extraction - Electricians - Apprenticeship	48	No Pre-Requisites Required	BOP Employee Department of Labor Certificate Electrician	0 / 0
Electrician Maintenance Location: Main	Construction and Extraction - Electricians - Apprenticeship	48	No Pre-Requisites Required	BOP Employee Department of Labor Certificate Maintenance Electrician	0 / 0
Heating and A/C Installer and Servicer Location: Main	Installation, Maintenance, and Repair - Heating, Air Conditioning, and Refrigeration Mechanics and Installers - Apprenticeship	48	No Pre-Requisites Required	BOP Employee Department of Labor Certificate HVAC Installer/ Repairer	0 / 0
Heating and A/C Installer Servicer Location: Camp	Installation, Maintenance, and Repair - Heating, Air Conditioning, and Refrigeration Mechanics and Installers - Apprenticeship	48	No Pre-Requisites Required	BOP Employee Department of Labor Certificate HVAC installer/ servicer	0 / 0

Institution: BASTROP FCI   (Cont'd)

Program / Location	Occupation	Months	Pre-Requisites	Certificates	Ratio
Horticulture Location: Main	Building and Grounds Cleaning - Grounds Maintenance Workers - Occ Ed Class	6	High School Diploma or GED	BOP Employee Post-Secondary (College) Certificate & Industry Recognized Certificate Landscaper / Pesticide Applicator Certificate	34 / 0
Maintenance Repairer Location: Main	Construction and Extraction - Construction and Building Inspectors - Apprenticeship	24	No Pre-Requisites Required	BOP Employee BOP Certificate & Department of Labor Certificate Maintenance Repairer	0 / 0
Painter Location: Main	Construction and Extraction - Painters, Construction and Maintenance - Apprenticeship	36	No Pre-Requisites Required	BOP Employee Department of Labor Certificate Painter	0 / 0
Plumber Location: Main	Construction and Extraction - Plumbers, Pipefitters, and Steamfitters - Apprenticeship	48	No Pre-Requisites Required	BOP Employee Department of Labor Certificate Painter	0 / 0
Quality Control Technician Location: Main	Production - Quality Control Inspectors - Apprenticeship	12	No Pre-Requisites Required	BOP Employee BOP Certificate & Department of Labor Certificate Quality Control Technician	0 / 0

Institution: BASTROP FCI   **(Cont'd)**

Stationary Engineer	Construction and Extraction	48	No Pre-Requisites Required	BOP Employee	0 / 0
Location: Main	- Boilermakers			BOP Certificate & Department of Labor Certificate	
	- Apprenticeship			Stationary Engineer	
Welder, Combination	Production	24	No Pre-Requisites Required	BOP Employee	0 / 0
Location: Camp	- Welders, Cutters, Solderers, and Brazers			BOP Certificate & Department of Labor Certificate	
	- Apprenticeship			Combination Welder	
Welder, combination	Production	24	No Pre-Requisites Required	BOP Employee	0 / 0
Location: Main	- Welders, Cutters, Solderers, and Brazers			BOP Certificate & Department of Labor Certificate	
	- Apprenticeship			Combination Welder	

Institution: BEAUMONT LOW FCI

Program	Occupation Area	Enrollment	Education Requirement	Credential / Institution	Ratio
Advanced Microcomputer Applications Location: Main	Office and Administrative Support - Secretaries and Administrative Assistants - Occ Ed Class	6	High School Diploma or GED	Accredited Post Secondary Institution Post-Secondary (College) Certificate Only Secretary or Administrative Assistant	0 / 14
Basic Diesel Location: Main	Installation, Maintenance, and Repair - Diesel Service Technicians and Mechanics - Occ Ed Class	4	High School Diploma or GED	Accredited Post Secondary Institution Post-Secondary (College) Certificate & Industry Recognized Certificate Diesel Service Technician or Mechanic	0 / 0
Building Trades Location: Main	Construction and Extraction - Carpenters - Occ Ed Class	4	High School Diploma or GED	Accredited Post Secondary Institution Post-Secondary (College) Certificate Only Carpenter	0 / 0
Carpentry Apprenticeship Location: Main	Construction and Extraction - Carpenters - Apprenticeship	60	High School Diploma or GED	BOP Employee Department of Labor Certificate Carpenter	0 / 0

Institution: BEAUMONT LOW FCI (Cont'd)

Culinary Arts Location: Main	Food Preparation and Serving - Food Preparation Workers - Occ Ed Class	6	High School Diploma or GED	Accredited Post Secondary Institution Post-Secondary (College) Certificate Only Food Preparation Worker	0 / 0
Electrician Apprenticeship Location: Main	Installation, Maintenance, and Repair - Electrical and Electronics Installers and Repairers - Apprenticeship	48	High School Diploma or GED	BOP Employee Department of Labor Certificate Electrician	0 / 0
Heating, Ventilation, and Air-Conditioning Location: Main	Installation, Maintenance, and Repair - Heating, Air Conditioning, and Refrigeration Mechanics and Installers - Occ Ed Class	6	High School Diploma or GED	Accredited Post Secondary Institution Post-Secondary (College) Certificate & Industry Recognized Certificate HVAC Mechanic or Technician	0 / 0
HVAC Apprenticeship Location: Main	Installation, Maintenance, and Repair - Heating, Air Conditioning, and Refrigeration Mechanics and Installers - Apprenticeship	48	High School Diploma or GED	BOP Employee Department of Labor Certificate HVAC Repairer or Installer	0 / 0

Institution: BEAUMONT LOW FCI   (Cont'd)

Industrial Sewing Location: Main	Production - Sewers and Tailors - Occ Ed Class	4	High School Diploma or GED	Accredited Post Secondary Institution Post-Secondary (College) Certificate Only Sewers or Tailors	0 / 0
Major Appliance Location: Main	Installation, Maintenance, and Repair - Home Appliance Repairers - Occ Ed Class	4	High School Diploma or GED	Accredited Post Secondary Institution Post-Secondary (College) Certificate Only Home Appliance Repairer	0 / 0
Microcomputer Applications Location: Main	Office and Administrative Support - Secretaries and Administrative Assistants - Occ Ed Class	6	High School Diploma or GED	Accredited Post Secondary Institution Post-Secondary (College) Certificate Only Secretary or Administrative Assistant	0 / 14
Painter Apprenticeship Location: Main	Construction and Extraction - Painters, Construction and Maintenance - Apprenticeship	36	High School Diploma or GED	BOP Employee Department of Labor Certificate Painter	0 / 0
Plumber Apprenticeship Location: Main	Construction and Extraction - Plumbers, Pipefitters, and Steamfitters - Apprenticeship	36	High School Diploma or GED	BOP Employee Department of Labor Certificate Plumber	0 / 0

Institution: BEAUMONT MED FCI

Program	Related Occupation	#	Education	Credential	
Advanced Heating, Ventilation, and Air-Conditioning – Advanced HVAC Location: Main	Installation, Maintenance, and Repair - Heating, Air Conditioning, and Refrigeration Mechanics and Installers - Occ Ed Class	4	High School Diploma or GED	Accredited Post Secondary Institution Post-Secondary (College) Certificate Only HVAC Mechanic or Installer	0 / 0
Advanced Microcomputer Applications Location: Main	Office and Administrative Support - Secretaries and Administrative Assistants - Occ Ed Class	6	High School Diploma or GED	Accredited Post Secondary Institution Post-Secondary (College) Certificate Only Secretary or Administrative Assistant	0 / 14
Building Trades Location: Main	Construction and Extraction - Carpenters - Occ Ed Class	4	High School Diploma or GED	Accredited Post Secondary Institution Post-Secondary (College) Certificate Only Carpenter	0 / 0
Carpenter Apprenticeship Location: Main	Construction and Extraction - Carpenters - Apprenticeship	48	High School Diploma or GED	BOP Employee Department of Labor Certificate Carpenter	0 / 0
Culinary Arts Location: Main	Food Preparation and Serving - Food Preparation Workers - Occ Ed Class	6	High School Diploma or GED	Accredited Post Secondary Institution Post-Secondary (College) Certificate Only Food Preparation Worker	0 / 0

Institution: BEAUMONT MED FCI (Cont'd)

Electrician Apprenticeship Location: Main	Installation, Maintenance, and Repair - Electrical and Electronics Installers and Repairers - Apprenticeship	48	High School Diploma or GED	BOP Employee Department of Labor Certificate Electrician	0 / 0
Heating, Ventilation, and Air-Conditioning - HVAC Location: Main	Installation, Maintenance, and Repair - Heating, Air Conditioning, and Refrigeration Mechanics and Installers - Occ Ed Class	6	High School Diploma or GED	Accredited Post Secondary Institution Post-Secondary (College) Certificate Only HVAC Mechanic or Installer	0 / 0
HVAC Apprenticeship Location: Main	Installation, Maintenance, and Repair - Heating, Air Conditioning, and Refrigeration Mechanics and Installers - Apprenticeship	36	High School Diploma or GED	BOP Employee Department of Labor Certificate HVAC Installer or Repairer	0 / 0
Major Appliance Location: Main	Installation, Maintenance, and Repair - General Maintenance and Repair Workers - Occ Ed Class	4	High School Diploma or GED	Accredited Post Secondary Institution Post-Secondary (College) Certificate Only Home Appliance Repairer	0 / 0

151

Institution: BEAUMONT MED FCI   (Cont'd)

Program	Area		Hours	Requirement	Certification	
Microcomputer Applications Location: Main	Office and Administrative Support - Secretaries and Administrative Assistants - Occ Ed Class		6	High School Diploma or GED	Accredited Post Secondary Institution Post-Secondary (College) Certificate Only Secretary or Administrative Assistant	0 / 14
Painter Apprenticeship Location: Main	Construction and Extraction - Painters, Construction and Maintenance - Apprenticeship		36	High School Diploma or GED	BOP Employee Department of Labor Certificate Painter	0 / 0
Plumber Apprenticeship Location: Main	Construction and Extraction - Plumbers, Pipefitters, and Steamfitters - Apprenticeship		48	High School Diploma or GED	BOP Employee Department of Labor Certificate Plumber	0 / 0
Small Business Management Location: Main	Office and Administrative Support - General Office Clerks - Occ Ed Class		6	High School Diploma or GED	Accredited Post Secondary Institution Post-Secondary (College) Certificate Only Office Manager	0 / 0
Teacher Aide Location: Main	Education, Training, and Library - Teacher Assistants - Apprenticeship		24	High School Diploma or GED	BOP Employee Department of Labor Certificate Teacher Aide	0 / 0

152

Institution: BEAUMONT USP

Advanced Microcomputer Applications Location: Main	Office and Administrative Support - Secretaries and Administrative Assistants - Occ Ed Class	6	High School Diploma or GED	Accredited Post Secondary Institution Post-Secondary (College) Certificate Only Secretary or Administrative Assistant	0 / 0
Basic Diesel Repair Location: Camp	Installation, Maintenance, and Repair - Diesel Service Technicians and Mechanics - Occ Ed Class	4	High School Diploma or GED	Accredited Post Secondary Institution Post-Secondary (College) Certificate Only Diesel Service Technician	0 / 0
Commercial Driver License Location: Camp	Sales - Wholesale and Manufacturing Sales Representatives - Occ Ed Class	3	High School Diploma or GED	Accredited Post Secondary Institution Post-Secondary (College) Certificate Only Delivery Truck Driver	0 / 0
Culinary Arts Location: Main	Food Preparation and Serving - Food Preparation Workers - Occ Ed Class	6	High School Diploma or GED	Accredited Post Secondary Institution Post-Secondary (College) Certificate Only Food Preparation Worker	0 / 0

153

Institution: BEAUMONT USP   (Cont'd)

Program / Location	Program Details		Education	Credential	
Culinary Arts Location: Camp	Food Preparation and Serving - Food Preparation Workers - Occ Ed Class	6	High School Diploma or GED	Accredited Post Secondary Institution Post-Secondary (College) Certificate Only Food Preparation Worker	0 / 0
Electrician Apprenticeship Location: Camp	Installation, Maintenance, and Repair - Electrical and Electronics Installers and Repairers - Apprenticeship	48	High School Diploma or GED	BOP Employee Department of Labor Certificate Electrical Installer or Repairer	0 / 0
Electrician Apprenticeship Location: Main	Construction and Extraction - Electricians - Apprenticeship	48	High School Diploma or GED	BOP Employee Department of Labor Certificate Electrician	0 / 0
HVAC Apprenticeship Location: Main	Installation, Maintenance, and Repair - Heating, Air Conditioning, and Refrigeration Mechanics and Installers - Apprenticeship	48	High School Diploma or GED	BOP Employee Department of Labor Certificate HVAC Repairer	0 / 0
HVAC Apprenticeship Location: Camp	Installation, Maintenance, and Repair - Heating, Air Conditioning, and Refrigeration Mechanics and Installers - Apprenticeship	48	High School Diploma or GED	BOP Employee Department of Labor Certificate HVAC Repairer	0 / 0

Institution: BEAUMONT USP (Cont'd)

Microcomputer Applications Location: Main	Office and Administrative Support - Secretaries and Administrative Assistants - Occ Ed Class	6	High School Diploma or GED	Accredited Post Secondary Institution Post-Secondary (College) Certificate Only Secretary or Administrative Assistant	0 / 0
Painter Apprenticeship Location: Camp	Construction and Extraction - Painters, Construction and Maintenance - Apprenticeship	36	High School Diploma or GED	BOP Employee Department of Labor Certificate Painter	0 / 0
Painter Apprenticeship Location: Main	Construction and Extraction - Painters, Construction and Maintenance - Apprenticeship	36	High School Diploma or GED	BOP Employee Department of Labor Certificate Painter	0 / 0
Plumber Apprenticeship Location: Camp	Construction and Extraction - Plumbers, Pipefitters, and Steamfitters - Apprenticeship	48	High School Diploma or GED	BOP Employee Department of Labor Certificate Plumber	0 / 0
Plumber Apprenticeship Location: Main	Construction and Extraction - Plumbers, Pipefitters, and Steamfitters - Apprenticeship	48	High School Diploma or GED	BOP Employee Department of Labor Certificate Plumber	0 / 0

Institution: BEAUMONT USP   **(Cont'd)**

Small Business Management	Business and Financial	6	High School Diploma or GED	Accredited Post Secondary Institution	0 / 0
Location: Main	- Accountants and Auditors			Post-Secondary (College) Certificate Only	
	- Occ Ed Class			Bookkeeper	
Welding	Production	4	High School Diploma or GED	Accredited Post Secondary Institution	0 / 0
Location: Main	- Welders, Cutters, Solderers, and Brazers			Post-Secondary (College) Certificate Only	
	- Occ Ed Class			Welder Assistant	

Institution: BECKLEY FCI

Program / Location	Occupation		Education	Provider	Credential	Job Title	Ratio
AOE Business Retail Management Location: Main	Sales - Retail Sales Workers - Occ Ed Class	12	High School Diploma or GED	Accredited Post Secondary Institution	Post-Secondary (College) Certificate Only	Sales Representative/Manager	0 / 24
AOE Customer Service Location: Main	Sales - Wholesale and Manufacturing Sales Representatives - Occ Ed Class	12	High School Diploma or GED	Accredited Post Secondary Institution	Post-Secondary (College) Certificate Only	Sales Representatives	0 / 15
Appliance Repair & Refrigeration Location: Main	Installation, Maintenance, and Repair - General Maintenance and Repair Workers - Occ Ed Class	6	High School Diploma or GED	Independent Contractor	Post-Secondary (College) Certificate & Industry Recognized Certificate	Installation, Maintenance & Repair Workers	0 / 15
Appliance Repair & Refrigeration Location: Camp	Installation, Maintenance, and Repair - General Maintenance and Repair Workers - Occ Ed Class	6	High School Diploma or GED	Independent Contractor	Post-Secondary (College) Certificate Only	Installation, Maintenance & Repair Workers	0 / 15
Blueprint Reading Location: Main	Construction and Extraction - Construction Laborers and Helpers - Occ Ed Class	3	High School Diploma or GED	BOP Employee	Vocational/Technical School Certificate Only	Construction Helper	0 / 0

Institution: BECKLEY FCI (Cont'd)

Program / Location	Occ Class		Education	Employer / Certificate / Job Title	Ratio
Carpentry Location: Main	Construction and Extraction - Construction Laborers and Helpers - Occ Ed Class	6	High School Diploma or GED	BOP Employee Both Vo-Tech School and Industry-Recognized Certificates Carpenter	0 / 0
HVAC Location: Main	Installation, Maintenance, and Repair - Heating, Air Conditioning, and Refrigeration Mechanics and Installers - Occ Ed Class	6	High School Diploma or GED	Independent Contractor Post-Secondary (College) Certificate & Industry Recognized Certificate HVAC Technician	0 / 15
HVAC Location: Camp	Installation, Maintenance, and Repair - Heating, Air Conditioning, and Refrigeration Mechanics and Installers - Occ Ed Class	6	High School Diploma or GED	Independent Contractor Post-Secondary (College) Certificate Only HVAC Technician	0 / 15
Masonry Location: Main	Construction and Extraction - Brickmasons, Blockmasons, and Stonemasons - Occ Ed Class	5	High School Diploma or GED	BOP Employee Vocational/Technical School Certificate Only Block mason	0 / 15
Residential Wiring Location: Main	Construction and Extraction - Electricians - Occ Ed Class	3	High School Diploma or GED	BOP Employee Both Vo-Tech School and Industry-Recognized Certificates Electrician Helper	0 / 12

Institution: BECKLEY FCI   **(Cont'd)**

Residential Wiring	Construction and Extraction	3	High School Diploma or GED	BOP Employee	0 / 0
Location: Camp	- Electricians			Both Vo-Tech School and Industry-Recognized Certificates	
	- Occ Ed Class			Electrician Helper	

Institution: BENNETTSVILLE FCI

Program		Enrollment	Requirement	Certification/Outcome	
Automotive	Installation, Maintenance, and Repair	12	High School Diploma or GED	Independent Contractor	40 / 0
Location: Main	- Automotive Service Technicians and Mechanics		- NCCER Core class	BOP Certificate & Industry Recognized Certificate	
	- Occ Ed Class			Automotive Chassis Technician/Automotive Powertrain Tech.	
Microsoft 2010	Office and Administrative Support	5	High School Diploma or GED	BOP Employee	50 / 0
Location: Main	- General Office Clerks			Post-Secondary (College) Certificate Only	
	- Occ Ed Class			Office Clerk/Receptionist/Data Entry Clerk/Office Assistant	
NCCER Core	Construction and Extraction	4	High School Diploma or GED	BOP Employee	0 / 0
Location: Main	- Construction Laborers and Helpers			Industry-Recognized Certificate	
	- Occ Ed Class			Construction Laborer	
NCCER Electrical	Installation, Maintenance, and Repair	4	High School Diploma or GED	BOP Employee	0 / 0
Location: Main	- Electrical and Electronics Installers and Repairers		- NCCER Core class	BOP Certificate & Industry Recognized Certificate	
	- Occ Ed Class			Electrician	

Institution: BENNETTSVILLE FCI   (Cont'd)

Program	Location	Count	Education Requirement	Related Class	Certifications	Ratio
NCCER HVAC	Location: Main	4	High School Diploma or GED	Installation, Maintenance, and Repair - Heating, Air Conditioning, and Refrigeration Mechanics and Installers - Occ Ed Class	BOP Employee BOP Certificate & Industry Recognized Certificate HVAC Installer, HVAC Technician	0 / 0
			- NCCER Core class			
NCCER-Your Role in the Green Environment	Location: Main	4	High School Diploma or GED	Installation, Maintenance, and Repair - General Maintenance and Repair Workers - Occ Ed Class	BOP Employee BOP Certificate & Industry Recognized Certificate Recycler, Solar/Turbine Installer, Weatherization Tech.	0 / 0
			- NCCER Core class			
Welding	Location: Main	6	High School Diploma or GED	Production - Welders, Cutters, Solderers, and Brazers - Occ Ed Class	Accredited Vocational/Technical School Post-Secondary (College) Certificate & Industry Recognized Certificate Welder	50 / 0
			- NCCER Core class			
Welding	Location: Camp	6	High School Diploma or GED	Production - Welders, Cutters, Solderers, and Brazers - Occ Ed Class	Accredited Vocational/Technical School Post-Secondary (College) Certificate & Industry Recognized Certificate Welder	50 / 0
			- NCCER Core Class			

161

Institution: BERLIN FCI

VT Administrative Assistant Location: Main	Office and Administrative Support - Secretaries and Administrative Assistants - Occ Ed Class	3	High School Diploma or GED - Six Months Clear Conduct and Six Months Remaining On Sentence	BOP Employee BOP Certificate Only Secretaries and Administrative Assistant	0 / 0
VT Carpentry Location: Main	Construction and Extraction - Construction Laborers and Helpers - Occ Ed Class	4	High School Diploma or GED - Six Months Clear Conduct and Six Months Remaining on Sentence	BOP Employee BOP Certificate Only Carpenter/Laborer	0 / 0
VT Culinary Arts Location: Main	Food Preparation and Serving - Food Preparation Workers - Occ Ed Class	2	High School Diploma or GED - Six Months Clear Conduct and Six Months Remaining On Sentence	BOP Employee BOP Certificate Only Cook	0 / 0
VT Electrical Residential & Commercial Location: Main	Installation, Maintenance, and Repair - Electrical and Electronics Installers and Repairers - Occ Ed Class	2	High School Diploma or GED - Six Months Clear Conduct and Six Months Remaining On Sentence	BOP Employee BOP Certificate Only Electrical Technician	0 / 0
VT Janitorial Maintenance Location: Main	Building and Grounds Cleaning - Janitors and Building Cleaners - Occ Ed Class	4	High School Diploma or GED - Six Months Clear Conduct and Six Months Sentence Remaining	BOP Employee BOP Certificate Only Janitor/Custodian	0 / 0

162

Institution: BERLIN FCI   **(Cont'd)**

VT Weatherization Location: Camp	Installation, Maintenance, and Repair - Electrical and Electronics Installers and Repairers - Occ Ed Class	2	High School Diploma or GED - Six Months Clear Conduct and Six Months Remaining On Sentence	BOP Employee BOP Certificate Only Weatherization Technician	3 / 0

Institution: BIG SANDY USP

Data Entry Operator	Office and Administrative Support	4	High School Diploma or GED	BOP Employee
Location: Main	- Secretaries and Administrative Assistants			BOP Certificate Only
				Administrative Assistant
	- Occ Ed Class			0 / 0
Major Appliance Repair	Installation, Maintenance, and Repair	4	High School Diploma or GED	BOP Employee
Location: Main	- Home Appliance Repairers			BOP Certificate Only
				Appliance Repair Technician
	- Occ Ed Class			0 / 0
Receptionist	Office and Administrative Support	4	High School Diploma or GED	BOP Employee
Location: Main	- Receptionists			BOP Certificate Only
				Receptionist
	- Occ Ed Class			0 / 0

Institution: BIG SPRING FCI

Building Trades Location: Main	Construction and Extraction - Carpenters - Occ Ed Class	4	Concurrent GED Enrollment - Medically clear and able to wear safety shoes	Accredited Post Secondary Institution Post-Secondary (College) Certificate Only Carpenter	35 / 0
Commercial Maintenance Location: Main	Installation, Maintenance, and Repair - General Maintenance and Repair Workers - Occ Ed Class	4	Concurrent GED Enrollment - Medically clear and able to wear safety shoes	Accredited Post Secondary Institution Post-Secondary (College) Certificate Only Commercial Maintenance Worker	36 / 0
Computer Skills/Desktop Publishing Location: Main	Office and Administrative Support - General Office Clerks - Occ Ed Class	6	Concurrent GED Enrollment	Accredited Post Secondary Institution Post-Secondary (College) Certificate Only Computer Operators/Desktop Publishers	40 / 0
Electrical Trades Location: Main	Construction and Extraction - Electricians - Occ Ed Class	4	Concurrent GED Enrollment - Medically clear and wear safety shoes	Accredited Post Secondary Institution Post-Secondary (College) Certificate Only Electrician Helper	36 / 0

Institution: BIG SPRING FCI   (Cont'd)

Food Service Management Location: Main	Food Preparation and Serving - Food Preparation Workers - Occ Ed Class	4	Concurrent GED Enrollment - Medically clear for Food Service, wear safety shoes	Accredited Post Secondary Institution Post-Secondary (College) Certificate & Industry Recognized Certificate Cooks, Cafeteria and Institution workers	36 / 0
Green Insulation Technology Location: Main	Construction and Extraction - Insulation Workers - Occ Ed Class	4	Concurrent GED Enrollment - Medically clear and able to wear safety shoes	Accredited Post Secondary Institution Post-Secondary (College) Certificate Only Green Construction Laborers	36 / 0
Heating, Air Conditioning and Refrigeration Location: Main	Installation, Maintenance, and Repair - Heating, Air Conditioning, and Refrigeration Mechanics and Installers - Occ Ed Class	7	Concurrent GED Enrollment - Medically clear and able to wear safety shoes	Accredited Post Secondary Institution Post-Secondary (College) Certificate & Industry Recognized Certificate Heating, Ventilation and Air Conditioning Mechanics and Installers	60 / 0
High Reliability Soldering Location: Main	Production - Welders, Cutters, Solderers, and Brazers - Occ Ed Class	4	Concurrent GED Enrollment - See small objects and wear safety shoes	Accredited Post Secondary Institution Post-Secondary (College) Certificate & Industry Recognized Certificate Soldering Technician	40 / 0

Institution: BIG SPRING FCI (Cont'd)

Masonry Trades Location: Main	Construction and Extraction - Brickmasons, Blockmasons, and Stonemasons - Occ Ed Class	4	Concurrent GED Enrollment - Medically clear, able to wear safety shoes and lift 50 pounds	Accredited Post Secondary Institution Post-Secondary (College) Certificate Only Brick masons and Block masons	36 / 0
Plumbing Trades Location: Main	Construction and Extraction - Plumbers, Pipefitters, and Steamfitters - Occ Ed Class	4	Concurrent GED Enrollment - Medically clear and able to wear safety shoes	Accredited Post Secondary Institution Post-Secondary (College) Certificate Only Plumber	36 / 0
VT Horticulture Location: Camp	Education, Training, and Library - Career and Technical Education Teachers - Occ Ed Class	4	Concurrent GED Enrollment - Medically clear and able to wear safety shoes.	Accredited Post Secondary Institution Post-Secondary (College) Certificate Only Landscaping and Grounds keeping Workers	36 / 0
Wind Energy Technician Location: Main	Installation, Maintenance, and Repair - Industrial Machinery Mechanics and Maintenance Workers - Occ Ed Class	4	Concurrent GED Enrollment - Work in Heights exceeding 50 foot, wear safety shoes and lift 50 lbs.	Accredited Post Secondary Institution Post-Secondary (College) Certificate Only Wind Turbine Service Technicians	36 / 0

Institution: BRYAN FPC

Program / Location	Occupation		Requirement	Credential	
Accounting Technology Location: Camp	Business and Financial - Accountants and Auditors - Occ Ed Class	12	High School Diploma or GED	Accredited Vocational/Technical School Post-Secondary (College) Certificate Only Entry level Accountant	36 / 0
Administrative Assistant Specialist Location: Camp	Office and Administrative Support - Bookkeeping, Accounting, and Auditing Clerks - Occ Ed Class	12	High School Diploma or GED	Accredited Post Secondary Institution A.A, A.S., or A.A.S. Diploma Clerk, Receptionist or Secretary	0 / 36
Cosmetologist Location: Camp	Personal Care and Service - Barbers, Hairdressers, and Cosmetologists - Occ Ed Class	12	High School Diploma or GED	Accredited Post Secondary Institution Post-Secondary (College) Certificate Only Cosmetologist	0 / 36
Heating, Ventilation and Air Conditioning (HVAC) Location: Camp	Installation, Maintenance, and Repair - Heating, Air Conditioning, and Refrigeration Mechanics and Installers - Occ Ed Class	6	High School Diploma or GED	Accredited Vocational/Technical School Vocational/Technical School Certificate Only HVAC mechanic	0 / 15

Institution: BRYAN FPC   (Cont'd)

Horticulture Location: Camp	Production - Food Processing Operators - Occ Ed Class	4	High School Diploma or GED	Accredited Post Secondary Institution Vocational/Technical School Certificate Only Horticulture Technician	36 / 0
Medical Transcription and Coding Specialist Location: Camp	Office and Administrative Support - Bill and Account Collectors - Occ Ed Class	12	High School Diploma or GED	Accredited Post Secondary Institution Post-Secondary (College) Certificate Only Medical Office Positions	0 / 36
Small Business Management Location: Camp	Business and Financial - Purchasing Managers, Buyers, and Purchasing Agents - Occ Ed Class	12	High School Diploma or GED	Accredited Post Secondary Institution A.A, A.S., or A.A.S. Diploma Manager	0 / 36

Institution: BUTNER FMC

Program / Location	Occupation	#	Prerequisite	Provider	Certification	Related Occupation	Enrolled / Completed
Biomedical Technician Location: Main	Installation, Maintenance, and Repair - Medical Equipment Repairers - Apprenticeship	48	High School Diploma or GED	BOP Employee	BOP Certificate & Department of Labor Certificate	Medical Equipment Maintenance & Repairers	0 / 0
Commercial Cleaning Location: Main	Building and Grounds Cleaning - Janitors and Building Cleaners - Apprenticeship	12	No Pre-Requisites Required	BOP Employee	BOP Certificate & Department of Labor Certificate	Custodial Maintenance	0 / 0
Health and Sanitation Location: Main	Building and Grounds Cleaning - Janitors and Building Cleaners - Apprenticeship	24	High School Diploma or GED	BOP Employee	BOP Certificate & Department of Labor Certificate	Janitor, Health and Sanitation Worker,	0 / 0
Horticulture Location: Main	Building and Grounds Cleaning - Grounds Maintenance Workers - Occ Ed Class	4	High School Diploma or GED	BOP Employee	BOP Certificate & Industry Recognized Certificate	Landscaping	0 / 0
Logistics Location: Main	Business and Financial - Logisticians - Occ Ed Class	4	High School Diploma or GED	Accredited Post Secondary Institution	Post-Secondary (College) Certificate Only	Logistician, Cargo and Freight Agent, Freight Forwarder	0 / 0

Institution: BUTNER LOW FCI

Commercial Cleaning	Building and Grounds Cleaning	12	No Pre-Requisites Required	BOP Employee	0 / 0
Location: Main	- Janitors and Building Cleaners			BOP Certificate & Department of Labor Certificate	
	- Apprenticeship			Custodial Maintenance	
Electrical	Construction and Extraction	4	High School Diploma or GED	Accredited Post Secondary Institution	12 / 0
Location: Main	- Electricians			Post-Secondary (College) Certificate Only	
	- Occ Ed Class			Helpers-Electrician	
Hospitality	Food Preparation and Serving	4	High School Diploma or GED	Accredited Post Secondary Institution	18 / 0
Location: Main	- Food and Beverage Serving and Related Workers			Post-Secondary (College) Certificate Only	
	- Occ Ed Class			Hospitality Worker	
HVAC - 1	Installation, Maintenance, and Repair	18	High School Diploma or GED	BOP Employee	0 / 0
Location: Main	- Heating, Air Conditioning, and Refrigeration Mechanics and Installers			BOP Certificate & Industry Recognized Certificate	
	- Occ Ed Class			HVAC-Mechanics, HVC-Installers/Technicians	

171

Institution: BUTNER LOW FCI   **(Cont'd)**

Program / Location	Occupation	#	Requirement	Outcomes	Ratio
HVAC - 2 Location: Main	Installation, Maintenance, and Repair - Heating, Air Conditioning, and Refrigeration Mechanics and Installers - Occ Ed Class	12	High School Diploma or GED	BOP Employee BOP Certificate & Industry Recognized Certificate HVAC Repairers/Installers	0 / 0
HVAC Apprenticeship Location: Main	Installation, Maintenance, and Repair - Heating, Air Conditioning, and Refrigeration Mechanics and Installers - Apprenticeship	36	High School Diploma or GED	BOP Employee BOP Certificate & Department of Labor Certificate HVAC Mechanics and Technicians	0 / 0
HVAC-1 Location: Main	Installation, Maintenance, and Repair - Heating, Air Conditioning, and Refrigeration Mechanics and Installers - Occ Ed Class	4	High School Diploma or GED	BOP Employee BOP Certificate & Industry Recognized Certificate HVAC-Mechanics, HVC-Installers/Technicians	0 / 0
Logistics Location: Main	Business and Financial - Logisticians - Occ Ed Class	4	High School Diploma or GED	Accredited Post Secondary Institution Post-Secondary (College) Certificate Only Warehouse Worker	12 / 0

172

Institution: BUTNER MED I FCI

Program / Location	Occupation		Requirement	Outcome	Ratio
Carpentry Location: Main	Construction and Extraction - Carpenters - Occ Ed Class	4	High School Diploma or GED	BOP Employee BOP Certificate & Industry Recognized Certificate Carpenter	0 / 0
Electrical Location: Main	Construction and Extraction - Electricians - Occ Ed Class	4	High School Diploma or GED	Accredited Post Secondary Institution Post-Secondary (College) Certificate Only Helpers-Electrician	0 / 0
Horticulture 1 - Grounds Maintenance Location: Camp	Building and Grounds Cleaning - Grounds Maintenance Workers - Occ Ed Class	4	High School Diploma or GED	BOP Employee BOP Certificate & Industry Recognized Certificate Ground Maintenance Workers, Nursery Workers	0 / 0
Landscaping Location: Camp	Building and Grounds Cleaning - Grounds Maintenance Workers - Apprenticeship	24	High School Diploma or GED	BOP Employee BOP Certificate & Department of Labor Certificate Landscaper, Grounds Maintenance Workers	0 / 0
Logistics Location: Main	Business and Financial - Logisticians - Occ Ed Class	4	High School Diploma or GED	Accredited Post Secondary Institution Post-Secondary (College) Certificate Only Logistician, Warehouse Worker, Material Handler	0 / 0

Institution: BUTNER MED I FCI   (Cont'd)

Logistics Coordinator	Business and Financial	18	High School Diploma or GED	BOP Employee	0 / 0
Location: Camp	- Logisticians			BOP Certificate & Department of Labor Certificate	
	- Apprenticeship			Logistics Coordinator	

Institution: BUTNER MED II FCI

Program / Location		Count	Pre-Requisites	Credentials / Outcomes	0 / 0
Automotive Electrical Location: Main	Installation, Maintenance, and Repair - Automotive Body and Glass Repairers - Occ Ed Class	8	High School Diploma or GED	Accredited Post Secondary Institution Post-Secondary (College) Certificate Only Mechanics, Automotive Body Repairs	0 / 0
Commercial Cleaning Location: Main	Building and Grounds Cleaning - Janitors and Building Cleaners - Apprenticeship	12	No Pre-Requisites Required	BOP Employee BOP Certificate & Department of Labor Certificate Custodial Maintenance	0 / 0
Culinary Arts Location: Main	Food Preparation and Serving - Food Preparation Workers - Occ Ed Class	4	High School Diploma or GED	Accredited Post Secondary Institution Post-Secondary (College) Certificate Only Cooks, Food Service Preparers, Head Cooks, Waiters/Waitresses	0 / 0
Drive Train Location: Main	Installation, Maintenance, and Repair - Automotive Service Technicians and Mechanics - Occ Ed Class	2	High School Diploma or GED	Accredited Post Secondary Institution Post-Secondary (College) Certificate Only Mechanics, Automotive Service Technicians	0 / 0

Institution: BUTNER MED II FCI (Cont'd)

Engine Repair	Installation, Maintenance, and Repair	2	High School Diploma or GED	Accredited Post Secondary Institution	0 / 0
Location: Main	- Automotive Service Technicians and Mechanics			Post-Secondary (College) Certificate Only	
	- Occ Ed Class			Mechanic, Service Technician	
Under Carriage	Installation, Maintenance, and Repair	2	High School Diploma or GED	Accredited Post Secondary Institution	0 / 0
Location: Main	- Automotive Body and Glass Repairers			Post-Secondary (College) Certificate Only	
	- Occ Ed Class			Automotive Body Repairers, Mechanics, Automotive Service Technicians	

Institution: CANAAN USP

Program	Location		Education	Credential	
Culinary Arts	Location: Main	Food Preparation and Serving - Chefs and Head Cooks - Occ Ed Class	2	High School Diploma or GED	BOP Employee BOP Certificate Only Chef/Food Service Worker	0 / 0
Electrical	Location: Main	Building and Grounds Cleaning - Grounds Maintenance Workers - Apprenticeship	48	High School Diploma or GED	BOP Employee BOP Certificate & Department of Labor Certificate Electrician	0 / 0
Electrical	Location: Camp	Building and Grounds Cleaning - Grounds Maintenance Workers - Apprenticeship	48	High School Diploma or GED	BOP Employee BOP Certificate & Department of Labor Certificate Electrician	0 / 0
HVAC	Location: Main	Building and Grounds Cleaning - Grounds Maintenance Workers - Apprenticeship	48	High School Diploma or GED	BOP Employee BOP Certificate & Department of Labor Certificate HVAC Technician	0 / 0
Plumbing	Location: Main	Building and Grounds Cleaning - Grounds Maintenance Workers - Apprenticeship	48	High School Diploma or GED	BOP Employee BOP Certificate & Department of Labor Certificate Plumber	0 / 0
VT Horticulture	Location: Main	Farming, Fishing, and Forestry - Agricultural Workers - Occ Ed Class	3	High School Diploma or GED	BOP Employee BOP Certificate Only Horticulturist	0 / 0

Institution: CANAAN USP (Cont'd)

VT Horticulture	Farming, Fishing, and Forestry	3	High School Diploma or GED	BOP Employee	0 / 0
Location: Camp	- Agricultural Workers			BOP Certificate Only	
	- Occ Ed Class			Horticulturist	

Institution: CARSWELL FMC

Program / Location	Occupation	Months	Requirement	Credential	
Cosmetology Location: Main	Personal Care and Service - Barbers, Hairdressers, and Cosmetologists - Occ Ed Class	12	High School Diploma or GED	BOP Employee Industry-Recognized Certificate Cosmetologist and Cosmetology Instructor	0 / 0
Culinary Arts Location: Main	Food Preparation and Serving - Chefs and Head Cooks - Occ Ed Class	6	High School Diploma or GED - Clear Conduct, Medically Cleared, Mental Health Cleared, No RDAP Wait, No LCP Wait, Must have time remaining on sentence to complete the program.	Accredited Post Secondary Institution Post-Secondary (College) Certificate & Industry Recognized Certificate Chef, Cook, Other Food Service Related Services	0 / 36
Dental Assistant Location: Main	Production - Dental Laboratory Technicians - Apprenticeship	12	High School Diploma or GED	BOP Employee BOP Certificate & Department of Labor Certificate Dental Assistant	0 / 0
Electrician Location: Main	Installation, Maintenance, and Repair - Electrical and Electronics Installers and Repairers - Apprenticeship	48	High School Diploma or GED	BOP Employee BOP Certificate & Department of Labor Certificate Electrician	0 / 0

Program	Occupation	#	Requirements	Credential	
Horticulture Master Gardener Program Location: Camp	Farming, Fishing, and Forestry - Agricultural Workers - Occ Ed Class	4	High School Diploma or GED - Clear Conduct, No RDAP Wait, No LCP Wait, Medically Cleared, Mental Health Cleared, Ample time on sentence to complete program	Accredited Post Secondary Institution Post-Secondary (College) Certificate & Industry Recognized Certificate Master Gardener/Horticulture Technician	0 / 0
HVAC Location: Main	Installation, Maintenance, and Repair - Heating, Air Conditioning, and Refrigeration Mechanics and Installers - Apprenticeship	36	High School Diploma or GED	BOP Employee BOP Certificate & Department of Labor Certificate Heating and Air Conditioning Specialist	0 / 0
Landscape Management Technician Location: Main	Building and Grounds Cleaning - Grounds Maintenance Workers - Apprenticeship	12	High School Diploma or GED	BOP Employee BOP Certificate & Department of Labor Certificate Landscape Technician	0 / 0
Maintenance Repairer, Build Location: Main	Installation, Maintenance, and Repair - General Maintenance and Repair Workers - Apprenticeship	24	High School Diploma or GED	BOP Employee BOP Certificate & Department of Labor Certificate Facilities Maintenance	0 / 0

Institution: CARSWELL FMC (Cont'd)

Nurse Assistant Location: Main	Community and Social Service - Social and Human Service Assistants - Apprenticeship	12	High School Diploma or GED	BOP Employee BOP Certificate & Department of Labor Certificate Nursing Assistant	0 / 0
Physical Therapy Aide Location: Main	Community and Social Service - Rehabilitation Counselors - Apprenticeship	24	High School Diploma or GED	BOP Employee BOP Certificate & Department of Labor Certificate Physical Therapy Aide	0 / 0
Plumber Location: Main	Construction and Extraction - Plumbers, Pipefitters, and Steamfitters - Apprenticeship	48	High School Diploma or GED	BOP Employee BOP Certificate & Department of Labor Certificate Plumbing Assistant	0 / 0
Power Plant Operator Location: Camp	Production - Power Plant Operators, Distributors, and Dispatchers - Apprenticeship	36	High School Diploma or GED	BOP Employee BOP Certificate & Department of Labor Certificate Power Plant Technician	0 / 0
Small Engine Mechanic Location: Main	Installation, Maintenance, and Repair - Small Engine Mechanics - Apprenticeship	36	High School Diploma or GED	BOP Employee BOP Certificate & Department of Labor Certificate Small Mechanic Repair	0 / 0

Institution: CARSWELL FMC   **(Cont'd)**

Teacher Aide I	Education, Training, and Library	24	High School Diploma or GED	BOP Employee	0 / 0
Location: Main	- Teacher Assistants			BOP Certificate & Department of Labor Certificate	
	- Apprenticeship			Teacher Assistant	
Teacher Aide I	Education, Training, and Library	24	High School Diploma or GED	BOP Employee	0 / 0
Location: Camp	- Teacher Assistants			BOP Certificate & Department of Labor Certificate	
	- Apprenticeship			Teacher Assistant	
Undercar Specialist	Installation, Maintenance, and Repair	36	High School Diploma or GED	BOP Employee	0 / 0
Location: Camp	- Diesel Service Technicians and Mechanics			BOP Certificate & Department of Labor Certificate	
	- Occ Ed Class			Mechanic	
Welder	Production	36	High School Diploma or GED	BOP Employee	0 / 0
Location: Camp	- Welders, Cutters, Solderers, and Brazers			BOP Certificate & Department of Labor Certificate	
	- Apprenticeship			Welder	

182

Institution: COLEMAN I USP

Program	Occupation / Details	Months	Prerequisites	Certifications	Enrolled / Completed
Cook Location: Main	Food Preparation and Serving - Cooks - Apprenticeship	24	High School Diploma or GED	BOP Employee Department of Labor Certificate Cook	0 / 0
Culinary Arts Location: Main	Food Preparation and Serving - Cooks - Occ Ed Class	6	High School Diploma or GED - typically 7-18 months remaining on sentence	Accredited Post Secondary Institution Industry-Recognized Certificate Cook	0 / 0
Custodial Maintenance Location: Main	Building and Grounds Cleaning - Janitors and Building Cleaners - Occ Ed Class	6	High School Diploma or GED	BOP Employee BOP Certificate Only Janitor and Building Cleaner	0 / 0
Electrician Location: Main	Installation, Maintenance, and Repair - Electrical and Electronics Installers and Repairers - Apprenticeship	48	No Pre-Requisites Required	BOP Employee Department of Labor Certificate Electrician	0 / 0
HVAC Location: Main	Installation, Maintenance, and Repair - Heating, Air Conditioning, and Refrigeration Mechanics and Installers - Apprenticeship	36	No Pre-Requisites Required	BOP Employee Department of Labor Certificate HVAC mechanic and installer	0 / 0

Institution: COLEMAN I USP (Cont'd)

MS Office	Office and Administrative Support	4	High School Diploma or GED	BOP Employee	0 / 0
Location: Main	- Information Clerks			BOP Certificate Only	
	- Occ Ed Class			data entry/information clerk	
Plumber	Construction and Extraction	48	No Pre-Requisites Required	BOP Employee	0 / 0
Location: Main	- Plumbers, Pipefitters, and Steamfitters			Department of Labor Certificate	
	- Apprenticeship			Plumber	

Institution: COLEMAN II USP

Program / Location	Occupational Area	Months	Prerequisites	Certifications	
Cook - Any Industry Location: Main	Food Preparation and Serving - Cooks - Apprenticeship	24	No Pre-Requisites Required	BOP Employee Department of Labor Certificate Cook - Any Industry	0 / 0
Cook - Hotel and Restaurant Location: Main	Food Preparation and Serving - Cooks - Apprenticeship	36	No Pre-Requisites Required	BOP Employee Department of Labor Certificate Cook - Hotel and Restaurant	0 / 0
Culinary Arts Location: Main	Food Preparation and Serving - Cooks - Occ Ed Class	6	High School Diploma or GED - typically 7-18 months remaining on sentence	Accredited Post Secondary Institution Industry-Recognized Certificate Cook	0 / 0
Custodial Maintenance Location: Main	Building and Grounds Cleaning - Janitors and Building Cleaners - Occ Ed Class	6	High School Diploma or GED	BOP Employee BOP Certificate Only Janitor and Building Cleaner	0 / 0
Electrical Location: Main	Installation, Maintenance, and Repair - Electrical and Electronics Installers and Repairers - Occ Ed Class	4	High School Diploma or GED	BOP Employee BOP Certificate Only electrical and electronic installer and repairer	0 / 0
Electrician Location: Main	Installation, Maintenance, and Repair - Electrical and Electronics Installers and Repairers - Apprenticeship	48	No Pre-Requisites Required	BOP Employee Department of Labor Certificate Electrician	0 / 0

Program / Location	Occupation		Prereq	Certifications	
Fundamentals of Maintenance Location: Main	Installation, Maintenance, and Repair - General Maintenance and Repair Workers - Occ Ed Class	4	High School Diploma or GED	BOP Employee BOP Certificate Only general maintenance and repair worker	0 / 0
HVAC Location: Main	Installation, Maintenance, and Repair - Heating, Air Conditioning, and Refrigeration Mechanics and Installers - Apprenticeship	36	No Pre-Requisites Required	BOP Employee Department of Labor Certificate HVAC mechanic and installer	0 / 0
HVAC Location: Main	Installation, Maintenance, and Repair - Heating, Air Conditioning, and Refrigeration Mechanics and Installers - Occ Ed Class	4	High School Diploma or GED	BOP Employee BOP Certificate Only HVAC technician	0 / 0
MS Office Location: Main	Office and Administrative Support - Information Clerks - Occ Ed Class	4	High School Diploma or GED	BOP Employee BOP Certificate Only Data Entry/Information Clerk	0 / 0
Plumber Location: Main	Construction and Extraction - Plumbers, Pipefitters, and Steamfitters - Apprenticeship	48	No Pre-Requisites Required	BOP Employee Department of Labor Certificate Plumber	0 / 0

Institution: COLEMAN LOW FCI

Program / Location	Occupation / Class		Prerequisites	Certifications	
Cook - Any Industry Location: Main	Food Preparation and Serving - Cooks - Apprenticeship	24	No Pre-Requisites Required	BOP Employee Department of Labor Certificate Cook - Any Industry	0 / 0
Cook - Hotel and Restaurant Location: Main	Food Preparation and Serving - Cooks - Apprenticeship	36	No Pre-Requisites Required	BOP Employee Department of Labor Certificate Cook - Hotel and Restaurant	0 / 0
Culinary Arts Location: Main	Food Preparation and Serving - Cooks - Occ Ed Class	6	High School Diploma or GED - typically 7-18 months remaining on sentence	Accredited Post Secondary Institution Industry-Recognized Certificate Cook	0 / 0
Custodial Maintenance Location: Main	Building and Grounds Cleaning - Janitors and Building Cleaners - Occ Ed Class	4	High School Diploma or GED	BOP Employee BOP Certificate Only Janitor and Building Cleaner	0 / 0
Dental Assistant Location: Main	Production - Dental Laboratory Technicians - Apprenticeship	12	No Pre-Requisites Required	BOP Employee Department of Labor Certificate Dental Assistant	0 / 0
Electrical Location: Main	Installation, Maintenance, and Repair - Electrical and Electronics Installers and Repairers - Occ Ed Class	4	High School Diploma or GED	BOP Employee BOP Certificate Only Electrical and Electronics Installer and Repairer	0 / 0

Institution: COLEMAN LOW FCI   (Cont'd)

Program / Location	Course		Pre-Requisites	Certification	Enrolled/Completed
Electrician Location: Main	Installation, Maintenance, and Repair - Electrical and Electronics Installers and Repairers - Apprenticeship	48	No Pre-Requisites Required	BOP Employee Department of Labor Certificate Electrician	0 / 0
Horticulture/Landscape Location: Main	Building and Grounds Cleaning - Grounds Maintenance Workers - Occ Ed Class	4	High School Diploma or GED	Accredited Post Secondary Institution Industry-Recognized Certificate Landscaping and Grounds keeping Worker	0 / 0
HVAC Location: Main	Installation, Maintenance, and Repair - Heating, Air Conditioning, and Refrigeration Mechanics and Installers - Occ Ed Class	4	High School Diploma or GED	BOP Employee BOP Certificate Only HVAC technician	0 / 0
HVAC Location: Main	Installation, Maintenance, and Repair - Heating, Air Conditioning, and Refrigeration Mechanics and Installers - Apprenticeship	36	No Pre-Requisites Required	BOP Employee Department of Labor Certificate HVAC mechanic and installer	0 / 0

188

Institution: COLEMAN LOW FCI (Cont'd)

Landscape Tech Location: Main	Building and Grounds Cleaning - Grounds Maintenance Workers - Apprenticeship	12	High School Diploma or GED	BOP Employee Department of Labor Certificate Landscape Technician	0 / 0
Plumber Location: Main	Construction and Extraction - Plumbers, Pipefitters, and Steamfitters - Apprenticeship	48	No Pre-Requisites Required	BOP Employee Department of Labor Certificate Plumber	0 / 0

Institution: COLEMAN MED FCI

Program / Location	Category	Months	Pre-Requisites	Certification	
Cook - Any Industry Location: Camp	Food Preparation and Serving - Cooks - Apprenticeship	24	No Pre-Requisites Required	BOP Employee Department of Labor Certificate Cook - Any Industry	0 / 0
Cook - Any Industry Location: Main	Food Preparation and Serving - Cooks - Apprenticeship	24	No Pre-Requisites Required	BOP Employee Department of Labor Certificate Cook - Any Industry	0 / 0
Cook - Hotel and Restaurant Location: Main	Food Preparation and Serving - Cooks - Apprenticeship	36	No Pre-Requisites Required	BOP Employee Department of Labor Certificate Cook - Hotel and Restaurant	0 / 0
Cook- Hotel and Restaurant Location: Camp	Food Preparation and Serving - Cooks - Apprenticeship	36	No Pre-Requisites Required	BOP Employee Department of Labor Certificate Cook - Hotel and Restaurant	0 / 0
Cosmetology Location: Camp	Personal Care and Service - Barbers, Hairdressers, and Cosmetologists - Occ Ed Class	12	High School Diploma or GED - 18-24 months remaining on sentence	Independent Contractor State Certificate Cosmetologist	0 / 0
Culinary Arts Location: Main	Food Preparation and Serving - Cooks - Occ Ed Class	6	High School Diploma or GED - typically 7-18 months remaining on sentence	Accredited Post Secondary Institution Industry-Recognized Certificate Cook	0 / 0

Institution: COLEMAN MED FCI (Cont'd)

Program / Location	Occupation	Months	Prerequisites	Certificate	Ratio
Culinary Arts Location: Camp	Food Preparation and Serving - Cooks - Occ Ed Class	6	High School Diploma or GED - typically 7-18 months remaining on sentence	Accredited Post Secondary Institution Industry-Recognized Certificate Cook	0 / 0
Custodial Maintenance Location: Main	Building and Grounds Cleaning - Janitors and Building Cleaners - Occ Ed Class	6	High School Diploma or GED	BOP Employee BOP Certificate Only Janitor and Building Cleaner	0 / 0
Custodial Maintenance Location: Camp	Building and Grounds Cleaning - Janitors and Building Cleaners - Occ Ed Class	6	High School Diploma or GED	BOP Employee BOP Certificate Only Janitor and Building Cleaner	0 / 0
Dental Assistant Location: Main	Production - Dental Laboratory Technicians - Apprenticeship	12	No Pre-Requisites Required	BOP Employee Department of Labor Certificate Dental Assistant	0 / 0
Dental Assistant Location: Camp	Production - Dental Laboratory Technicians - Apprenticeship	12	No Pre-Requisites Required	BOP Employee Department of Labor Certificate Dental Assistant	0 / 0
Electrical Location: Main	Installation, Maintenance, and Repair - Electrical and Electronics Installers and Repairers - Occ Ed Class	4	High School Diploma or GED	BOP Employee BOP Certificate Only electrical and electronics installer and repairer	0 / 0

Institution: COLEMAN MED FCI   **(Cont'd)**

Electrician
Location: Camp
	Installation, Maintenance, and Repair
	  - Electrical and Electronics Installers and Repairers
	  - Apprenticeship
		48	No Pre-Requisites Required	BOP Employee
				Department of Labor Certificate
				Electrician
					0 / 0

Electrician
Location: Main
	Installation, Maintenance, and Repair
	  - Electrical and Electronics Installers and Repairers
	  - Apprenticeship
		48	No Pre-Requisites Required	BOP Employee
				Department of Labor Certificate
				electrician
					0 / 0

Horticulture
Location: Camp
	Building and Grounds Cleaning
	  - Grounds Maintenance Workers
	  - Occ Ed Class
		4	High School Diploma or GED	Accredited Post Secondary Institution
				Industry-Recognized Certificate
				Horticulturist
					0 / 0

HVAC
Location: Main
	Installation, Maintenance, and Repair
	  - Heating, Air Conditioning, and Refrigeration Mechanics and Installers
	  - Occ Ed Class
		4	High School Diploma or GED	BOP Employee
				BOP Certificate Only
				HVAC technician
					0 / 0

Institution: COLEMAN MED FCI (Cont'd)

Program / Location	Occupation	Months	Pre-Requisites	Certifications	
HVAC Location: Main	Installation, Maintenance, and Repair - Heating, Air Conditioning, and Refrigeration Mechanics and Installers - Apprenticeship	36	No Pre-Requisites Required	BOP Employee Department of Labor Certificate HVAC mechanic and installer	0 / 0
HVAC Location: Camp	Installation, Maintenance, and Repair - Heating, Air Conditioning, and Refrigeration Mechanics and Installers - Apprenticeship	36	No Pre-Requisites Required	BOP Employee Department of Labor Certificate HVAC Mechanic and Installer	0 / 0
Landscape Management Technician Location: Camp	Building and Grounds Cleaning - Grounds Maintenance Workers - Apprenticeship	12	No Pre-Requisites Required	BOP Employee Department of Labor Certificate Landscape Management Technician	0 / 0
Landscape Tech Location: Main	Building and Grounds Cleaning - Grounds Maintenance Workers - Apprenticeship	12	High School Diploma or GED	BOP Employee Department of Labor Certificate Landscape Technician	0 / 0
Plumber Location: Camp	Construction and Extraction - Plumbers, Pipefitters, and Steamfitters - Apprenticeship	48	No Pre-Requisites Required	BOP Employee Department of Labor Certificate Plumber	0 / 0

Plumber	Construction and Extraction	48	No Pre-Requisites Required	BOP Employee	0 / 0
Location: Main	- Plumbers, Pipefitters, and Steamfitters			Department of Labor Certificate	
	- Apprenticeship			Plumber	

Institution: CUMBERLAND FCI

Program	Occupation	Months	Prerequisite	Credential	Ratio
Automobile Mechanic Location: Camp	Installation, Maintenance, and Repair - Automotive Service Technicians and Mechanics - Apprenticeship	48	High School Diploma or GED	BOP Employee Department of Labor Certificate Automobile Mechanic	0 / 0
Baker Location: Main	Food Preparation and Serving - Food Preparation Workers - Apprenticeship	36	High School Diploma or GED	BOP Employee Department of Labor Certificate Baker	0 / 0
Baker Location: Main	Food Preparation and Serving - Food Preparation Workers - Apprenticeship	36	High School Diploma or GED	BOP Employee Department of Labor Certificate Baker	0 / 0
Carpentry Location: Main	Construction and Extraction - Carpenters - Occ Ed Class	9	High School Diploma or GED	BOP Employee Post-Secondary (College) Certificate Only Carpenter	0 / 0
Carpentry Maintenance Location: Main	Construction and Extraction - Carpenters - Apprenticeship	48	High School Diploma or GED	BOP Employee Department of Labor Certificate Carpentry Maintenance	0 / 0
Computer Peripheral Equipment Operator Location: Camp	Office and Administrative Support - Secretaries and Administrative Assistants - Apprenticeship	12	High School Diploma or GED	BOP Employee Department of Labor Certificate Computer Peripheral Equipment Operator	0 / 0

Institution: CUMBERLAND FCI   **(Cont'd)**

Computer Peripheral Equipment Operator	Office and Administrative Support	12	High School Diploma or GED	BOP Employee
	- Secretaries and Administrative Assistants			Department of Labor Certificate
Location: Main				Computer Peripheral Equipment Operator
	- Apprenticeship			
Cook	Food Preparation and Serving	36	High School Diploma or GED	BOP Employee
	- Cooks			Department of Labor Certificate
Location: Camp	- Apprenticeship			Cook
Cook	Food Preparation and Serving	36	High School Diploma or GED	BOP Employee
	- Cooks			Department of Labor Certificate
Location: Main	- Apprenticeship			Cook
Dog Trainer	Personal Care and Service	12	High School Diploma or GED	Accredited Vocational/Technical School
	- Animal Care and Service Workers			Post-Secondary (College) Certificate Only
Location: Camp	- Occ Ed Class			Dog Trainer
Drywall	Construction and Extraction	4	High School Diploma or GED	BOP Employee
	- Carpenters			Post-Secondary (College) Certificate Only
Location: Main	- Occ Ed Class			Drywall Installation and Finishing

The "0 / 0" values appear in the rightmost column for the Computer Peripheral Equipment Operator, Cook (Camp), Cook (Main), Dog Trainer, and Drywall entries.

196

Institution: CUMBERLAND FCI (Cont'd)

Electrical Maintenance Location: Camp	Installation, Maintenance, and Repair - Electrical and Electronics Installers and Repairers - Apprenticeship	48	High School Diploma or GED	BOP Employee Department of Labor Certificate Electrical Installer	0 / 0
Electrical Maintenance Location: Main	Installation, Maintenance, and Repair - Electrical and Electronics Installers and Repairers - Apprenticeship	48	High School Diploma or GED	BOP Employee Department of Labor Certificate Electrical Maintenance	0 / 0
Heating, Ventilation and Air Conditioning Location: Camp	Installation, Maintenance, and Repair - Heating, Air Conditioning, and Refrigeration Mechanics and Installers - Apprenticeship	48	High School Diploma or GED	BOP Employee Department of Labor Certificate Heating, Ventilation and Air Conditioning	0 / 0
Heating, Ventilation and Air Conditioning Location: Main	Installation, Maintenance, and Repair - Heating, Air Conditioning, and Refrigeration Mechanics and Installers - Apprenticeship	48	High School Diploma or GED	BOP Employee Department of Labor Certificate Heating, Ventilation and Air Conditioning	0 / 0

Institution: CUMBERLAND FCI   (Cont'd)

Landscape/Gardner Location: Camp	Building and Grounds Cleaning - Grounds Maintenance Workers - Apprenticeship	48	High School Diploma or GED	BOP Employee Department of Labor Certificate Landscape/Gardner	0 / 0
Landscape/Gardner Location: Main	Building and Grounds Cleaning - Grounds Maintenance Workers - Apprenticeship	48	High School Diploma or GED	BOP Employee Department of Labor Certificate Landscape/Gardner	0 / 0
Painter Location: Camp	Construction and Extraction - Painters, Construction and Maintenance - Apprenticeship	36	High School Diploma or GED	BOP Employee Department of Labor Certificate Painter	0 / 0
Painter Location: Main	Construction and Extraction - Painters, Construction and Maintenance - Apprenticeship	36	High School Diploma or GED	BOP Employee Department of Labor Certificate Painter	0 / 0
Pet Grooming Location: Camp	Personal Care and Service - Animal Care and Service Workers - Occ Ed Class	12	High School Diploma or GED	Accredited Vocational/Technical School Post-Secondary (College) Certificate Only Pet Groomer	0 / 0

Institution: CUMBERLAND FCI (Cont'd)

Powerhouse Mechanic Location: Camp	Installation, Maintenance, and Repair - Industrial Machinery Mechanics and Maintenance Workers - Apprenticeship	36	High School Diploma or GED	BOP Employee Department of Labor Certificate Powerhouse Mechanic	0 / 0
Veterinary Assistant Location: Camp	Personal Care and Service - Animal Care and Service Workers - Occ Ed Class	12	High School Diploma or GED	Accredited Vocational/Technical School Post-Secondary (College) Certificate Only Veterinary Assistant	0 / 0
Welder Fitter Location: Camp	Production - Welders, Cutters, Solderers, and Brazers - Apprenticeship	36	High School Diploma or GED	BOP Employee Department of Labor Certificate Welder Fitter	0 / 0
Welder Fitter Location: Main	Production - Welders, Cutters, Solderers, and Brazers - Apprenticeship	36	High School Diploma or GED	BOP Employee Department of Labor Certificate Welder Fitter	0 / 0

Institution: DANBURY FCI

Animal Trainer	Personal Care and Service	24	High School Diploma or GED	Independent Contractor	0 / 0
Location: Camp	– Animal Care and Service Workers		– Must be employed by specific work assignment.	BOP Certificate & Department of Labor Certificate	
	– Apprenticeship			Animal Trainer	
Baker	Food Preparation and Serving	36	High School Diploma or GED	BOP Employee	0 / 0
Location: Camp	– Chefs and Head Cooks		– Must be employed by specific work assignment.	BOP Certificate & Department of Labor Certificate	
	– Apprenticeship			Baker	
Baker	Food Preparation and Serving	36	High School Diploma or GED	BOP Employee	0 / 0
Location: Main	– Chefs and Head Cooks		– Must be employed by specific work assignment.	BOP Certificate & Department of Labor Certificate	
	– Apprenticeship			Baker	
Career Development Technician	Education, Training, and Library	27	High School Diploma or GED	BOP Employee	0 / 0
Location: Camp	– Career and Technical Education Teachers		– Must be employed by specific work assignment.	BOP Certificate & Department of Labor Certificate	
	– Apprenticeship			Human Resources and Training, and Labor Relations Specialist	
Career Development Technician	Education, Training, and Library	27	High School Diploma or GED	BOP Employee	0 / 0
Location: Camp	– Career and Technical Education Teachers		– Must be employed in specific work assignment	BOP Certificate & Department of Labor Certificate	
	– Apprenticeship			Human Resources and Training, and Labor Relations Specialist	

Institution: DANBURY FCI (Cont'd)

Carpenter Location: Main	Construction and Extraction - Carpenters - Apprenticeship	48	High School Diploma or GED - Must be employed in specific work assignment.	BOP Employee BOP Certificate & Department of Labor Certificate Carpenter	0 / 0
Carpenter Location: Camp	Construction and Extraction - Carpenters - Apprenticeship	48	High School Diploma or GED - Must be employed in specific work assignment.	BOP Employee BOP Certificate & Department of Labor Certificate Carpenter	0 / 0
Chaplain Service Support Location: Camp	Community and Social Service - Social and Human Service Assistants - Apprenticeship	12	High School Diploma or GED - Must be employed by specific work assignment.	BOP Employee BOP Certificate & Department of Labor Certificate Chaplain Assistant	0 / 0
Chaplain Service Support Location: Main	Community and Social Service - Social and Human Service Assistants - Apprenticeship	12	High School Diploma or GED - Must be employed by specific work assignment.	BOP Employee BOP Certificate & Department of Labor Certificate Chaplain Assistant	0 / 0
Cook Location: Camp	Food Preparation and Serving - Chefs and Head Cooks - Apprenticeship	36	High School Diploma or GED - Must be employed by specific work assignment.	BOP Employee BOP Certificate & Department of Labor Certificate Cook	0 / 0

Institution: DANBURY FCI   **(Cont'd)**

Program / Location	Occupation		Requirements	Certifications	
Cook Location: Main	Food Preparation and Serving - Chefs and Head Cooks - Apprenticeship	36	High School Diploma or GED - Must be employed by specific work assignment.	BOP Employee BOP Certificate & Department of Labor Certificate Cook	0 / 0
Culinary Arts - VT Location: Main	Food Preparation and Serving - Food and Beverage Serving and Related Workers - Occ Ed Class	4	High School Diploma or GED - English Proficient	BOP Employee BOP Certificate Only Food and Beverage Worker	0 / 0
Dental Assistant Location: Camp	Production - Dental Laboratory Technicians - Apprenticeship	12	High School Diploma or GED - Must be employed by specific work assignment.	BOP Employee BOP Certificate & Department of Labor Certificate Dental Assistant	0 / 0
Dental Assistant Location: Main	Production - Dental Laboratory Technicians - Apprenticeship	12	High School Diploma or GED - Must be employed by specific work assignment.	BOP Employee BOP Certificate & Department of Labor Certificate Dental Assistant	0 / 0
Education and Training Location: Main	Education, Training, and Library - Teacher Assistants - Apprenticeship	15	High School Diploma or GED - Must be employed by specific work assignment and must have completed the Teacher's Aide or Career Development Technician, or other qualified training equivalent	BOP Employee BOP Certificate & Department of Labor Certificate Training and Development Specialist	0 / 0

Institution: DANBURY FCI   (Cont'd)

Education and Training	Education, Training, and Library	15	High School Diploma or GED	BOP Employee	0 / 0
Location: Camp	- Teacher Assistants		- Must be employed by specific work assignment.	BOP Certificate & Department of Labor Certificate	
	- Apprenticeship			Training and Development Specialist	
Electrician	Construction and Extraction	48	High School Diploma or GED	BOP Employee	0 / 0
Location: Camp	- Electricians		- Must be employed by specific work assignment.	BOP Certificate & Department of Labor Certificate	
	- Apprenticeship			Electrician	
Electrician	Construction and Extraction	48	High School Diploma or GED	BOP Employee	0 / 0
Location: Main	- Electricians		- Must be employed by specific work assignment.	BOP Certificate & Department of Labor Certificate	
	- Apprenticeship			Electrician	
Horticulture-VT	Farming, Fishing, and Forestry	4	High School Diploma or GED	BOP Employee	0 / 0
Location: Main	- Agricultural Workers		- English Proficient	BOP Certificate Only	
	- Occ Ed Class			Horticulturist	
Horticulturist	Farming, Fishing, and Forestry	36	High School Diploma or GED	BOP Employee	0 / 0
Location: Main	- Agricultural Workers		- Must be employed by specific work assignment.	BOP Certificate & Department of Labor Certificate	
	- Apprenticeship			Horticulturist	

Institution: DANBURY FCI (Cont'd)

Program / Location	Occupation Area	Months	Requirements	Certification	
Horticulturist Location: Camp	Farming, Fishing, and Forestry - Agricultural Workers - Apprenticeship	36	High School Diploma or GED - Must be employed by specific work assignment.	BOP Employee BOP Certificate & Department of Labor Certificate Horticulturist	0 / 0
Housekeeper, Commercial, Residential, or Industrial Location: Camp	Building and Grounds Cleaning - Janitors and Building Cleaners - Apprenticeship	12	High School Diploma or GED - Must be employed by specific work assignment.	BOP Employee BOP Certificate & Department of Labor Certificate Building Cleaning Worker	0 / 0
Housekeeper, Commercial, Residential, or Industrial Location: Main	Building and Grounds Cleaning - Janitors and Building Cleaners - Apprenticeship	12	High School Diploma or GED - Must be employed by specific work assignment.	BOP Employee BOP Certificate & Department of Labor Certificate Building Cleaning Worker	0 / 0
HVAC Location: Main	Installation, Maintenance, and Repair - Heating, Air Conditioning, and Refrigeration Mechanics and Installers - Apprenticeship	48	High School Diploma or GED - Must be employed by specific work assignment.	BOP Employee BOP Certificate & Department of Labor Certificate HVAC Installer-Servicer	0 / 0
Landscape Management Technician Location: Camp	Building and Grounds Cleaning - Grounds Maintenance Workers - Apprenticeship	12	High School Diploma or GED - Must be employed in specific work assignment.	BOP Employee BOP Certificate & Department of Labor Certificate Grounds Maintenance Worker	0 / 0

Institution: DANBURY FCI (Cont'd)

Landscape Management Technician Location: Main	Building and Grounds Cleaning - Grounds Maintenance Workers - Apprenticeship	12	High School Diploma or GED - Must be employed in specific work assignment.	BOP Employee BOP Certificate & Department of Labor Certificate Grounds Maintenance Worker	0 / 0
Legal Secretary Location: Main	Office and Administrative Support - Secretaries and Administrative Assistants - Apprenticeship	12	High School Diploma or GED - Must be employed in specific work assignment.	BOP Employee BOP Certificate & Department of Labor Certificate Legal Secretary	0 / 0
Legal Secretary Location: Camp	Office and Administrative Support - Secretaries and Administrative Assistants - Apprenticeship	12	High School Diploma or GED - Must be employed by specific work assignment.	BOP Employee BOP Certificate & Department of Labor Certificate Legal Secretary	0 / 0
Material Coordinator Location: Camp	Office and Administrative Support - Material Recording Clerks - Apprenticeship	24	High School Diploma or GED - Must be employed in specific work assignment.	BOP Employee BOP Certificate & Department of Labor Certificate Production Planning and Expediting Clerk	0 / 0
Material Coordinator Location: Main	Office and Administrative Support - Material Recording Clerks - Apprenticeship	24	High School Diploma or GED - Must be employed in specific work assignment.	BOP Employee BOP Certificate & Department of Labor Certificate Production Planning and Expediting Clerk	0 / 0

Institution: DANBURY FCI (Cont'd)

Meat Cutter	Production - Food Processing Occupations - Apprenticeship	24	High School Diploma or GED - Must be employed in specific work assignment.	BOP Employee BOP Certificate & Department of Labor Certificate Meat Cutter	0 / 0
Location: Main					
Office Manager/Administrative Services	Office and Administrative Support - General Office Clerks - Apprenticeship	24	High School Diploma or GED - Must be employed by specific work assignment.	BOP Employee BOP Certificate & Department of Labor Certificate Office Manager	0 / 0
Location: Main					
Office Manager/Administrative Services	Office and Administrative Support - General Office Clerks - Apprenticeship	24	High School Diploma or GED - Must be employed by specific work assignment.	BOP Employee BOP Certificate & Department of Labor Certificate Office Manager	0 / 0
Location: Camp					
Painter	Construction and Extraction - Painters, Construction and Maintenance - Apprenticeship	36	High School Diploma or GED - Must be employed in specific work assignment.	BOP Employee BOP Certificate & Department of Labor Certificate Painter	0 / 0
Location: Main					
Painter	Construction and Extraction - Painters, Construction and Maintenance - Apprenticeship	36	High School Diploma or GED - Must be employed by specific work assignment.	BOP Employee BOP Certificate & Department of Labor Certificate Painter	0 / 0
Location: Camp					

Institution: DANBURY FCI   (Cont'd)

Peer Specialist	Community and Social Service	12	High School Diploma or GED	BOP Employee
Location: Main	- Rehabilitation Counselors		- Must be employed by specific work assignment.	BOP Certificate & Department of Labor Certificate
	- Apprenticeship			Peer Specialist
				0 / 0
Plumber	Construction and Extraction	48	High School Diploma or GED	BOP Employee
Location: Camp	- Plumbers, Pipefitters, and Steamfitters		- Must be employed by specific work assignment.	BOP Certificate & Department of Labor Certificate
	- Apprenticeship			Plumber
				0 / 0
Plumber	Construction and Extraction	48	High School Diploma or GED	BOP Employee
Location: Main	- Plumbers, Pipefitters, and Steamfitters		- Must be employed in specific work assignment.	BOP Certificate & Department of Labor Certificate
	- Apprenticeship			Plumber
				0 / 0
Puppies Behind Bars - VT	Personal Care and Service	18	High School Diploma or GED	Independent Contractor
Location: Camp	- Animal Care and Service Workers		- English Proficient	BOP Certificate & Industry Recognized Certificate
	- Occ Ed Class			Dog Trainer
				0 / 0
Quality Control Inspector	Production	24	High School Diploma or GED	BOP Employee
Location: Camp	- Quality Control Inspectors		- Must be employed in specific work assignment.	BOP Certificate & Department of Labor Certificate
	- Apprenticeship			Quality Control Inspector

Institution: DANBURY FCI   (Cont'd)

Quality Control Inspector Location: Main	Production - Quality Control Inspectors - Apprenticeship	24	High School Diploma or GED - Must be employed in specific work assignment.	BOP Employee BOP Certificate & Department of Labor Certificate Quality Control Inspector	0 / 0
Recreation Assistant Location: Main	Personal Care and Service - Recreation Workers - Apprenticeship	27	High School Diploma or GED - Must be employed in specific work assignment.	BOP Employee BOP Certificate & Department of Labor Certificate Recreation Assistant	0 / 0
Recreation Assistant Location: Camp	Personal Care and Service - Recreation Workers - Apprenticeship	27	High School Diploma or GED - Must be employed by specific work assignment.	BOP Employee BOP Certificate & Department of Labor Certificate Recreation Assistant	0 / 0
Stationary Engineer Location: Main	Production - Power Plant Operators, Distributors, and Dispatchers - Apprenticeship	48	High School Diploma or GED - Must be employed in specific work assignment.	BOP Employee BOP Certificate & Department of Labor Certificate Stationary Engineer	0 / 0
Teacher Aide Location: Camp	Education, Training, and Library - Teacher Assistants - Apprenticeship	24	High School Diploma or GED - Must be employed in specific work assignment.	BOP Employee BOP Certificate & Department of Labor Certificate Teacher Aide	0 / 0

Institution: DANBURY FCI (Cont'd)

Teacher Aide	Education, Training, and Library	24	High School Diploma or GED	BOP Employee
Location: Main	- Teacher Assistants		- Must be employed in specific work assignment.	BOP Certificate & Department of Labor Certificate
	- Apprenticeship			Teacher Aide
				0 / 0
Tool Machine Set-Up Operator	Production	36	High School Diploma or GED	BOP Employee
Location: Main	- Machinists and Tool and Die Makers		- Must be employed in specific work assignment.	BOP Certificate & Department of Labor Certificate
	- Apprenticeship			Tool Machine Set-Up Operator
				0 / 0
Undercar Specialist	Installation, Maintenance, and Repair	24	High School Diploma or GED	BOP Employee
Location: Camp	- Automotive Service Technicians and Mechanics		- Must be employed in specific work assignment.	BOP Certificate & Department of Labor Certificate
	- Apprenticeship			Undercar Specialist
				0 / 0
WELDER	Construction and Extraction	36	High School Diploma or GED	BOP Employee
Location: Main	- Reinforcing Iron and Rebar Workers			BOP Certificate & Department of Labor Certificate
	- Apprenticeship			WELDER
				0 / 0

Institution: DEVENS FMC

Program	Occupation	Months	Prerequisites	Outcome / Certificate	
Animal Trainer Apprenticeship Program Location: Camp	Personal Care and Service - Animal Care and Service Workers - Apprenticeship	24	Concurrent GED Enrollment	Independent Contractor Department of Labor Certificate Animal Trainer	0 / 0
Cook Apprenticeship Location: Camp	Food Preparation and Serving - Cooks - Apprenticeship	24	High School Diploma or GED - Must work in Food Service & maintain E or O evaluations	BOP Employee Department of Labor Certificate Cook	0 / 0
Education & Training Apprenticeship Program Location: Main	Education, Training, and Library - Teacher Assistants - Apprenticeship	24	High School Diploma or GED - College Degree	BOP Employee Department of Labor Certificate Teacher Assistant / Career Center Employee	0 / 0
HVAC Apprenticeship Location: Main	Installation, Maintenance, and Repair - Heating, Air Conditioning, and Refrigeration Mechanics and Installers - Apprenticeship	36	High School Diploma or GED	BOP Employee Department of Labor Certificate Heating & Air Conditioning Installer	0 / 0
VT Computer Applications/MS Office Location: Main	Office and Administrative Support - Secretaries and Administrative Assistants - Occ Ed Class	4	Concurrent GED Enrollment	BOP Employee BOP Certificate & Industry Recognized Certificate Administrative Assistant	0 / 0

Institution: DEVENS FMC   **(Cont'd)**

| VT Culinary Arts
Location: Main | Food Preparation and Serving

- Cooks
- Apprenticeship | 8 | High School Diploma or GED | BOP Employee

BOP Certificate & Industry
Recognized Certificate

Line Cook/Prep Cook/Sous
Chef/Chef | 0 / 0 |

Institution: DUBLIN FCI

Program / Location	Occupation		Hours	Prerequisites	Certifications	0/0
Carpenter Location: Camp	Construction and Extraction	- Carpenters - Apprenticeship	48	No Pre-Requisites Required	BOP Employee BOP Certificate & Department of Labor Certificate Carpenter	0 / 0
Carpenter Location: Main	Construction and Extraction	- Carpenters - Apprenticeship	48	No Pre-Requisites Required	BOP Employee Department of Labor Certificate Carpenter	0 / 0
Custodial Maintenance Location: Main	Building and Grounds Cleaning	- Janitors and Building Cleaners - Occ Ed Class	4	High School Diploma or GED	BOP Employee BOP Certificate & Industry Recognized Certificate Custodial Maintenance	0 / 0
Customer Service Representative Location: Main	Office and Administrative Support	- Customer Service Representatives - Apprenticeship	30	No Pre-Requisites Required	BOP Employee Department of Labor Certificate Customer Service Representative	0 / 0
Dental Assistant Location: Main	Personal Care and Service	- Animal Care and Service Workers - Apprenticeship	12	High School Diploma or GED	BOP Employee Department of Labor Certificate Dental Assistant	0 / 0

Institution: DUBLIN FCI (Cont'd)

Electrician Location: Camp	Installation, Maintenance, and Repair - Electrical and Electronics Installers and Repairers - Apprenticeship	48	No Pre-Requisites Required	BOP Employee BOP Certificate & Department of Labor Certificate Electrician	0 / 0
Electrician Location: Main	Installation, Maintenance, and Repair - Electrical and Electronics Installers and Repairers - Apprenticeship	48	High School Diploma or GED	BOP Employee Department of Labor Certificate Electrician	0 / 0
HVAC Location: Main	Installation, Maintenance, and Repair - Heating, Air Conditioning, and Refrigeration Mechanics and Installers - Apprenticeship	36	No Pre-Requisites Required	BOP Employee Department of Labor Certificate HVAC	0 / 0
HVAC Location: Camp	Installation, Maintenance, and Repair - Heating, Air Conditioning, and Refrigeration Mechanics and Installers - Apprenticeship	36	No Pre-Requisites Required	BOP Employee BOP Certificate & Department of Labor Certificate HVAC Technician	0 / 0

Institution: DUBLIN FCI (Cont'd)

Landscape Technician Location: Main	Building and Grounds Cleaning - Grounds Maintenance Workers - Apprenticeship	24	High School Diploma or GED	Accredited Post Secondary Institution Department of Labor Certificate Landscape	0 / 0
Landscape Technician Location: Camp	Building and Grounds Cleaning - Grounds Maintenance Workers - Apprenticeship	24	No Pre-Requisites Required	BOP Employee BOP Certificate & Department of Labor Certificate Landscape	0 / 0
Office Technology Location: Camp	Office and Administrative Support - General Office Clerks - Occ Ed Class	4	High School Diploma or GED	BOP Employee BOP Certificate Only Administrative Assistant	0 / 0
Office Technology Location: Main	Office and Administrative Support - General Office Clerks - Occ Ed Class	4	High School Diploma or GED	BOP Employee BOP Certificate Only Administrative Assistant	0 / 0
Plumber Location: Camp	Construction and Extraction - Plumbers, Pipefitters, and Steamfitters - Apprenticeship	48	No Pre-Requisites Required	BOP Employee BOP Certificate & Department of Labor Certificate Plumber	0 / 0

Institution: DUBLIN FCI (Cont'd)

Plumber	Construction and Extraction	48	No Pre-Requisites Required	BOP Employee	0 / 0
Location: Main	- Plumbers, Pipefitters, and Steamfitters			Department of Labor Certificate	
	- Apprenticeship			Plumber	
ServSafe Food Handler	Food Preparation and Serving	3	Concurrent GED Enrollment	BOP Employee	0 / 0
Location: Main	- Food Preparation Workers			Industry-Recognized Certificate	
	- Occ Ed Class			Food Preparer/Handler	
Welder	Production	36	No Pre-Requisites Required	BOP Employee	0 / 0
Location: Camp	- Welders, Cutters, Solderers, and Brazers			Department of Labor Certificate	
	- Apprenticeship			Welder	

215

Institution: DULUTH FPC

Program / Location	Occupation	Hours	Education Requirement	Certification	Ratio
Construction Tech/Carpentry Location: Camp	Construction and Extraction - Carpenters - Occ Ed Class	10	High School Diploma or GED	Accredited Vocational/Technical School Vocational/Technical School Certificate Only General Carpenter	0 / 15
Dentistry Apprenticeship Location: Camp	Community and Social Service - Health Educators - Apprenticeship	24	High School Diploma or GED	BOP Employee Department of Labor Certificate Dental Assistant	0 / 39
Electrical Apprenticeship Location: Camp	Construction and Extraction - Electricians - Apprenticeship	48	High School Diploma or GED	BOP Employee Department of Labor Certificate Electrician	0 / 0
HVAC Location: Camp	Installation, Maintenance, and Repair - Heating, Air Conditioning, and Refrigeration Mechanics and Installers - Apprenticeship	24	High School Diploma or GED	BOP Employee BOP Certificate & Department of Labor Certificate HVAC Technician	0 / 0

Institution: EDGEFIELD FCI

Course	Location	Enrolled	Education Requirement	Certification	Completed / Passed
Culinary Arts 1 Spanish	Main	2	Concurrent GED Enrollment	BOP Employee Industry-Recognized Certificate Food Handler	0 / 0
Food Preparation and Serving - Food Preparation Workers - Occ Ed Class					
Culinary Arts 3 English	Main	2	Concurrent GED Enrollment	BOP Employee Industry-Recognized Certificate Food Handler	0 / 0
Food Preparation and Serving - Food Preparation Workers - Occ Ed Class					
Culinary Arts 4 English	Main	2	Concurrent GED Enrollment	BOP Employee Industry-Recognized Certificate Food Handler	0 / 0
Food Preparation and Serving - Food Preparation Workers - Occ Ed Class					
Culinary Arts English	Camp	2	Concurrent GED Enrollment	BOP Employee Industry-Recognized Certificate Food Handler	0 / 0
Food Preparation and Serving - Cooks - Occ Ed Class					
Culinary Arts English	Main	2	Concurrent GED Enrollment	BOP Employee Industry-Recognized Certificate Food Handler	0 / 0
Food Preparation and Serving - Cooks - Occ Ed Class					
Culinary Arts Spanish	Camp	2	Concurrent GED Enrollment	BOP Employee Industry-Recognized Certificate Food Handler	0 / 0
Food Preparation and Serving - Cooks - Occ Ed Class					
Culinary Arts VT Apprenticeship	Main	36	High School Diploma or GED	BOP Employee Department of Labor Certificate Cook	0 / 0
Food Preparation and Serving - Chefs and Head Cooks - Apprenticeship					

Institution: EDGEFIELD FCI (Cont'd)

Forklift Operator	Construction and Extraction	3	High School Diploma or GED	BOP Employee	0 / 0
Location: Camp	- Construction Equipment Operators			BOP Certificate Only	
				Certified Forklift Operator	
	- Occ Ed Class				
General Services Automotive Technician	Installation, Maintenance, and Repair	3	High School Diploma or GED	BOP Employee	0 / 0
Location: Camp	- Automotive Service Technicians and Mechanics			Industry-Recognized Certificate	
				General Services Automotive Technician	
	- Occ Ed Class				

Institution: EL RENO FCI

Dental Assistant Location: Camp	Installation, Maintenance, and Repair - General Maintenance and Repair Workers - Apprenticeship	24	High School Diploma or GED - Medical Clearance	BOP Employee BOP Certificate & Department of Labor Certificate Dental Assistant	0 / 0
Dental Assistant Location: Main	Production - Dental Laboratory Technicians - Apprenticeship	24	High School Diploma or GED	BOP Employee BOP Certificate & Department of Labor Certificate Dental Assistant	0 / 0
Diesel Repair Location: Camp	Installation, Maintenance, and Repair - Diesel Service Technicians and Mechanics - Occ Ed Class	9	Concurrent GED Enrollment	Accredited Vocational/Technical School Vocational/Technical School Certificate Only Diesel Service Technician, Mechanic	0 / 0
Drafting Location: Main	Production - Semiconductor Processors - Apprenticeship	60	High School Diploma or GED	BOP Employee BOP Certificate & Department of Labor Certificate Drafter	0 / 0
Electric Location: Main	Installation, Maintenance, and Repair - Electrical and Electronics Installers and Repairers - Occ Ed Class	9	High School Diploma or GED	Accredited Vocational/Technical School Post-Secondary (College) Certificate Only Basic Residential or Commercial Electrician	0 / 0

Institution: EL RENO FCI   **(Cont'd)**

Program / Location	Occupational Cluster	Capacity	Entry Requirement	Provider / Certificate / Occupation	Enrollment
Horticulture Location: Camp	Farming, Fishing, and Forestry - Agricultural Workers - Occ Ed Class	12	Concurrent GED Enrollment	BOP Employee BOP Certificate Only Farmer, Landscaper	0 / 0
Machinist Location: Main	Production - Machinists and Tool and Die Makers - Apprenticeship	60	High School Diploma or GED	BOP Employee BOP Certificate & Department of Labor Certificate Machinist	0 / 0
Millwright Location: Main	Installation, Maintenance, and Repair - Millwrights - Apprenticeship	60	High School Diploma or GED	BOP Employee BOP Certificate & Department of Labor Certificate Millwrights	0 / 0
Painter Location: Main	Production - Painting and Coating Workers - Apprenticeship	60	High School Diploma or GED	BOP Employee BOP Certificate & Department of Labor Certificate Painter	0 / 0
Plumbing Location: Main	Construction and Extraction - Plumbers, Pipefitters, and Steamfitters - Occ Ed Class	9	High School Diploma or GED	Accredited Vocational/Technical School Vocational/Technical School Certificate Only Plumber	0 / 0

Institution: EL RENO FCI   (Cont'd)

Purchasing Agent	Business and Financial	60	High School Diploma or GED	BOP Employee	0 / 0
Location: Main	- Purchasing Managers, Buyers, and Purchasing Agents			BOP Certificate & Department of Labor Certificate
	- Apprenticeship			Purchasing Agent
Quality Control	Production	60	High School Diploma or GED	BOP Employee	0 / 0
Location: Main	- Quality Control Inspectors			BOP Certificate & Department of Labor Certificate
	- Apprenticeship			Quality Control
Tool and Die Maker	Production	60	High School Diploma or GED	BOP Employee	0 / 0
Location: Main	- Machinists and Tool and Die Makers			BOP Certificate & Department of Labor Certificate
	- Apprenticeship			Tool & Die Maker
Welding	Production	60	High School Diploma or GED	BOP Employee	0 / 0
Location: Main	- Welders, Cutters, Solderers, and Brazers			BOP Certificate & Department of Labor Certificate
	- Apprenticeship			Welder
Welding Apprenticeship	Production	6	High School Diploma or GED	BOP Employee	0 / 0
Location: Main	- Welders, Cutters, Solderers, and Brazers			BOP Certificate Only
	- Occ Ed Class			Welder

Institution: ELKTON FCI

Program / Location	Occupational Area	Months	Entry Requirements	Certification / Outcome	
Vocational Training--Culinary Arts I Location: Main	Food Preparation and Serving - Cooks - Occ Ed Class	6	High School Diploma or GED	BOP Employee BOP Certificate Only Cook	0 / 0
AOE Hospitality Management Location: Main	Food Preparation and Serving - Food and Beverage Serving and Related Workers - Occ Ed Class	18	High School Diploma or GED - completion of VT Culinary Arts Program or Cook Apprenticeship	Accredited Post Secondary Institution A.A, A.S., or A.A.S. Diploma Hospitality Manager	0 / 22
Apprenticeship-Computer Operator Location: Main	Office and Administrative Support - General Office Clerks - Apprenticeship	24	High School Diploma or GED - approval by UNICOR staff	BOP Employee BOP Certificate & Department of Labor Certificate Proofreader	0 / 0
Apprenticeship--Cook Location: Main	Food Preparation and Serving - Cooks - Apprenticeship	24	High School Diploma or GED - Approval of Food Service Administrator	BOP Employee BOP Certificate & Department of Labor Certificate Cook, Food Manager	0 / 0
Apprenticeship--Electrician Location: Main	Installation, Maintenance, and Repair - Electrical and Electronics Installers and Repairers - Apprenticeship	48	High School Diploma or GED - Approval of Facilities Staff	BOP Employee BOP Certificate & Department of Labor Certificate Electrician	0 / 0

Institution: ELKTON FCI   (Cont'd)

Apprenticeship--HVAC Location: Main	Installation, Maintenance, and Repair - Heating, Air Conditioning, and Refrigeration Mechanics and Installers - Apprenticeship	36	High School Diploma or GED - Approval of Facilities Staff	BOP Employee BOP Certificate & Department of Labor Certificate HVAC Mechanic	0 / 0
Vocational Training--Building Trades Location: Main	Construction and Extraction - Construction Laborers and Helpers - Occ Ed Class	9	High School Diploma or GED	BOP Employee BOP Certificate Only Laborer, Construction Worker	0 / 0
Vocational Training--Culinary Arts II Location: Main	Food Preparation and Serving - Cooks - Occ Ed Class	6	High School Diploma or GED	BOP Employee BOP Certificate Only Cook, Food Manager	0 / 0

Institution: ENGLEWOOD FCI

Culinary Arts	Food Preparation and Serving	No Pre-Requisites Required	BOP Employee	0 / 0
Location: Main	- Chefs and Head Cooks		BOP Certificate & Industry Recognized Certificate	
	- Occ Ed Class	6		
			Cook	
Customer Service	Office and Administrative Support	High School Diploma or GED	Accredited Post Secondary Institution	0 / 12
Location: Main	- Customer Service Representatives	- Pass College Placement Exam	Post-Secondary (College) Certificate Only	
	- Occ Ed Class	12	Customer Service Representative	
General Business	Business and Financial	High School Diploma or GED	Accredited Post Secondary Institution	0 / 12
Location: Main	- Market Research Analysts	- College Placement Exam	Post-Secondary (College) Certificate Only	
	- Occ Ed Class	12	Analyst	

Institution: ESTILL FCI

Baker - Apprenticeship Location: Camp	Food Preparation and Serving - Cooks - Apprenticeship	48	No Pre-Requisites Required	BOP Employee Department of Labor Certificate Baker	0 / 0
Baker - Apprenticeship Location: Main	Food Preparation and Serving - Cooks - Apprenticeship	48	No Pre-Requisites Required	BOP Employee Department of Labor Certificate Baker	0 / 0
Cook - Apprenticeship Location: Camp	Food Preparation and Serving - Chefs and Head Cooks - Apprenticeship	48	No Pre-Requisites Required	BOP Employee Department of Labor Certificate Cook/Chef	0 / 0
Cook - Apprenticeship Location: Main	Food Preparation and Serving - Chefs and Head Cooks - Apprenticeship	48	No Pre-Requisites Required	BOP Employee Department of Labor Certificate Cook/Chef	0 / 0
Electrical - Apprenticeship Location: Camp	Construction and Extraction - Electricians - Apprenticeship	48	No Pre-Requisites Required	BOP Employee Department of Labor Certificate Electrician	0 / 0
Electrical - Apprenticeship Location: Main	Construction and Extraction - Electricians - Apprenticeship	48	No Pre-Requisites Required	BOP Employee Department of Labor Certificate Electrician	0 / 0
Housekeeping - Apprenticeship Location: Camp	Building and Grounds Cleaning - Janitors and Building Cleaners - Apprenticeship	48	No Pre-Requisites Required	BOP Employee Department of Labor Certificate Janitor	0 / 0

Program	Course	Hours	Pre-Requisites	Outcome	
Housekeeping - Apprenticeship Location: Main	Building and Grounds Cleaning - Janitors and Building Cleaners - Apprenticeship	48	No Pre-Requisites Required	BOP Employee Department of Labor Certificate Janitor	0 / 0
HVAC - Apprenticeship Location: Camp	Installation, Maintenance, and Repair - Heating, Air Conditioning, and Refrigeration Mechanics and Installers - Apprenticeship	48	No Pre-Requisites Required	BOP Employee Department of Labor Certificate HVAC Technician	0 / 0
HVAC - Apprenticeship Location: Main	Installation, Maintenance, and Repair - Heating, Air Conditioning, and Refrigeration Mechanics and Installers - Apprenticeship	48	No Pre-Requisites Required	BOP Employee Department of Labor Certificate HVAC Technician	0 / 0
NCCER Carpentry Location: Main	Construction and Extraction - Structural Iron and Steel Workers - Occ Ed Class	24	High School Diploma or GED - Clear 6-month conduct/Time remaining for successful completion	BOP Employee Industry-Recognized Certificate Carpenter	0 / 0
NCCER HVAC Location: Main	Installation, Maintenance, and Repair - Heating, Air Conditioning, and Refrigeration Mechanics and Installers - Apprenticeship	24	High School Diploma or GED - Clear 6-month conduct/Time remaining for successful completion	BOP Employee BOP Certificate & Industry Recognized Certificate HVAC Technician	0 / 0

Institution: ESTILL FCI   (Cont'd)

NCCER HVAC Location: Camp	Installation, Maintenance, and Repair - Heating, Air Conditioning, and Refrigeration Mechanics and Installers - Apprenticeship	24	High School Diploma or GED - Clear 6-month conduct/Time remaining for successful completion	BOP Employee BOP Certificate & Industry Recognized Certificate HVAC Technician	0 / 0
NCCER Welding Location: Main	Construction and Extraction - Structural Iron and Steel Workers - Occ Ed Class	24	High School Diploma or GED - Clear 6-month Conduct/Time remaining for successful completion	BOP Employee BOP Certificate & Industry Recognized Certificate Welder	0 / 0
Plumber - Apprenticeship Location: Camp	Construction and Extraction - Plumbers, Pipefitters, and Steamfitters - Apprenticeship	48	No Pre-Requisites Required	BOP Employee Department of Labor Certificate Plumber	0 / 0
Plumber - Apprenticeship Location: Main	Construction and Extraction - Plumbers, Pipefitters, and Steamfitters - Apprenticeship	48	No Pre-Requisites Required	BOP Employee Department of Labor Certificate Plumber	0 / 0
ServSafe Location: Main	Food Preparation and Serving - Food Preparation Workers - Apprenticeship	4	Concurrent GED Enrollment - Clear 6-month conduct/Time remaining for successful completion	BOP Employee BOP Certificate & Industry Recognized Certificate Food Preparation Worker	0 / 0

Institution: ESTILL FCI   **(Cont'd)**

ServSafe
Location: Camp
	Food Preparation and Serving
	- Food Preparation Workers
	  - Apprenticeship
		4	Concurrent GED Enrollment
			
			  - Clear 6-month
			conduct/Time remaining for
			successful completion
				BOP Employee
				BOP Certificate & Industry
				Recognized Certificate
				Food Preparation Worker
					0 / 0

Welding - Apprenticeship Location: Camp	Construction and Extraction - Structural Iron and Steel Workers - Apprenticeship	48	No Pre-Requisites Required	BOP Employee Department of Labor Certificate Welder	0 / 0

228

Institution: FAIRTON FCI

Administrative Office Management Location: Main Office and Administrative Support - General Office Clerks - Apprenticeship	24	High School Diploma or GED - Employed by UNICOR	BOP Employee BOP Certificate & Department of Labor Certificate OFFICE MANAGER/ADMINISTRATIVE SERVICES	0 / 0
Building Maintenance Apprenticeship Location: Main Installation, Maintenance, and Repair - General Maintenance and Repair Workers - Apprenticeship	24	High School Diploma or GED	BOP Employee Department of Labor Certificate Maintenance Repairer, Building	0 / 0
Dog Trainer for Hearing Impaired Location: Camp Personal Care and Service - Animal Care and Service Workers - Apprenticeship	48	High School Diploma or GED	Independent Contractor Department of Labor Certificate Animal Trainer	0 / 0
Electrician Apprenticeship Location: Main Installation, Maintenance, and Repair - Electrical and Electronics Installers and Repairers - Apprenticeship	48	High School Diploma or GED	BOP Employee Department of Labor Certificate Electrician	0 / 0
Electrician, Maintenance Location: Main Construction and Extraction - Electricians - Apprenticeship	48	High School Diploma or GED	BOP Employee BOP Certificate & Department of Labor Certificate Maintenance Electrician	0 / 0

Institution: FAIRTON FCI   (Cont'd)

Program	Occupation Area		Slots	Requirements	Certifications	
Horticulture Location: Main	Farming, Fishing, and Forestry - Agricultural Workers - Occ Ed Class		9	Concurrent GED Enrollment - Prefer GED graduates	BOP Employee BOP Certificate Only Horticulturalist	0 / 0
HVAC Apprenticeship Location: Main	Installation, Maintenance, and Repair - Heating, Air Conditioning, and Refrigeration Mechanics and Installers - Apprenticeship		36	High School Diploma or GED	BOP Employee Department of Labor Certificate HVAC Technician	0 / 0
Landscape Management Technician Location: Main	Farming, Fishing, and Forestry - Agricultural Workers - Apprenticeship		12	High School Diploma or GED	BOP Employee Department of Labor Certificate Landscape Management Technician	0 / 0
Landscape Technician Location: Main	Farming, Fishing, and Forestry - Agricultural Workers - Apprenticeship		24	High School Diploma or GED	BOP Employee Department of Labor Certificate Landscape Technician	0 / 0
NCCER Carpentry Level One Location: Main	Construction and Extraction - Carpenters - Occ Ed Class		6	High School Diploma or GED - NCCER CORE Curriculum	BOP Employee Industry-Recognized Certificate Carpenter Helper	0 / 0
NCCER CORE Curriculum Location: Main	Construction and Extraction - Construction Laborers and Helpers - Occ Ed Class		3	High School Diploma or GED	BOP Employee Industry-Recognized Certificate Construction Helper	0 / 0

Institution: FAIRTON FCI (Cont'd)

Program / Location	Occupational Area		Prerequisite	Credential	
NCCER CORE Curriculum Location: PCU	Construction and Extraction - Construction Laborers and Helpers - Occ Ed Class	3	High School Diploma or GED	BOP Employee Industry-Recognized Certificate Construction Helper	0 / 0
NCCER Electrical Level One Location: Main	Construction and Extraction - Electricians - Occ Ed Class	6	High School Diploma or GED - NCCER CORE Curriculum	BOP Employee Industry-Recognized Certificate Electrician Helper	0 / 0
NCCER Plumbing Level One Location: Main	Construction and Extraction - Plumbers, Pipefitters, and Steamfitters - Occ Ed Class	6	High School Diploma or GED - NCCER CORE Curriculum	BOP Employee Industry-Recognized Certificate Plumber Helper	0 / 0
NCCER Project Management Location: Main	Construction and Extraction - Construction and Building Inspectors - Occ Ed Class	6	High School Diploma or GED - NCCER CORE, One Specialty, and Project Supervision	BOP Employee Industry-Recognized Certificate Project Manager Trainee	0 / 0
NCCER Project Management Location: Camp	Construction and Extraction - Construction and Building Inspectors - Occ Ed Class	6	High School Diploma or GED - NCCER Project Supervision	BOP Employee Industry-Recognized Certificate Project Manager Trainee	0 / 0
NCCER Project Supervision Location: Camp	Construction and Extraction - Construction and Building Inspectors - Occ Ed Class	6	High School Diploma or GED	BOP Employee Industry-Recognized Certificate Project Supervisor Trainee	0 / 0

Institution: FAIRTON FCI   **(Cont'd)**

NCCER Project Supervision Location: Main	Construction and Extraction - Construction and Building Inspectors - Occ Ed Class	6	High School Diploma or GED - NCCER CORE Curriculum and One Specialty Class	BOP Employee Industry-Recognized Certificate Project Supervisor	0 / 0
Plumber Apprenticeship Location: Main	Construction and Extraction - Plumbers, Pipefitters, and Steamfitters - Apprenticeship	48	High School Diploma or GED	BOP Employee Department of Labor Certificate Plumber	0 / 0
Quality Assurer Apprenticeship Location: Main	Production - Quality Control Inspectors - Apprenticeship	24	High School Diploma or GED	BOP Employee Department of Labor Certificate Quality Control Inspector	0 / 0

Institution: FLORENCE ADMAX USP

Restaurant Management/Culinary Arts	Food Preparation and Serving	10	High School Diploma or GED	BOP Employee	0 / 0
Location: Camp	- Cooks			BOP Certificate & Industry Recognized Certificate	
	- Occ Ed Class			Manager/Cook	

Institution: FLORENCE FCI

Building Trades Location: Main Construction and Extraction - Construction Laborers and Helpers - Occ Ed Class	10	High School Diploma or GED	BOP Employee BOP Certificate & Industry Recognized Certificate Construction Worker	0 / 0
Cabinet/Furniture Maker Location: Main Production - Woodworkers - Occ Ed Class	10	High School Diploma or GED	BOP Employee BOP Certificate & Industry Recognized Certificate Cabinet and Furniture Maker	0 / 0
Computer Assisted Drafting Location: Main Office and Administrative Support - Desktop Publishers - Occ Ed Class	10	High School Diploma or GED	BOP Employee BOP Certificate & Industry Recognized Certificate Computer Aided Draftsman	0 / 0
Green Energy Location: Main Installation, Maintenance, and Repair - Electrical and Electronics Installers and Repairers - Occ Ed Class	6	High School Diploma or GED	Accredited Post Secondary Institution Industry-Recognized Certificate Electrical Installer	0 / 0
Green Energy Location: Camp Installation, Maintenance, and Repair - Electrical and Electronics Installers and Repairers - Occ Ed Class	6	High School Diploma or GED	Accredited Post Secondary Institution Industry-Recognized Certificate Electrical Installer	

234

Institution: FLORENCE FCI   **(Cont'd)**

Restaurant Management/Culinary Arts	Food Preparation and Serving	10	High School Diploma or GED	BOP Employee
Location: Main	- Cooks			BOP Certificate & Industry Recognized Certificate
	- Occ Ed Class			Manager/Cook
				0 / 0

Institution: FLORENCE HIGH USP

Restaurant Management/Culinary Arts Location: Main	Food Preparation and Serving - Cooks - Occ Ed Class	10	High School Diploma or GED	BOP Employee BOP Certificate & Industry Recognized Certificate Manager/Cook	0 / 0

Institution: FORREST CITY FCI

Program	Occupation	Months	Requirements	Credential	
Building Trades Location: Main	Construction and Extraction - Carpenters - Occ Ed Class	12	High School Diploma or GED - Job Interview & Application	BOP Employee Industry-Recognized Certificate Carpenter	0 / 0
Diesel Technology Location: Main	Installation, Maintenance, and Repair - Diesel Service Technicians and Mechanics - Occ Ed Class	12	High School Diploma or GED - Pass the ASSET Test	Accredited Post Secondary Institution Post-Secondary (College) Certificate Only Diesel Service Technician	0 / 30
Drafting Technology Location: Main	Construction and Extraction - Painters, Construction and Maintenance - Occ Ed Class	12	High School Diploma or GED	Accredited Post Secondary Institution Post-Secondary (College) Certificate Only Drafting Specialist	0 / 30
Drafting Technology Location: Camp	Construction and Extraction - Painters, Construction and Maintenance - Occ Ed Class	12	High School Diploma or GED	Accredited Post Secondary Institution Post-Secondary (College) Certificate Only Drafting Specialist	0 / 30
Office Technology Location: Main	Office and Administrative Support - General Office Clerks - Occ Ed Class	12	High School Diploma or GED - Pass the ASSET Test	Accredited Post Secondary Institution Post-Secondary (College) Certificate Only Office Technology	0 / 30

Institution: FORREST CITY FCI   (Cont'd)

Office Technology Location: Camp	Office and Administrative Support - General Office Clerks - Occ Ed Class	12	High School Diploma or GED - Pass the ASSET Test	Accredited Post Secondary Institution Post-Secondary (College) Certificate Only Office Technology	0 / 30

Institution: FORREST CITY MED FCI

Building Trades	Construction and Extraction	6	High School Diploma or GED	BOP Employee	0 / 0
Location: Main	- Carpenters		- Job Interview & Application	Industry-Recognized Certificate	
	- Occ Ed Class			Carpenter	
Diesel Technology	Installation, Maintenance, and Repair	12	High School Diploma or GED	Accredited Post Secondary Institution	0 / 30
Location: Main			- Pass the ASSET Test	Post-Secondary (College) Certificate Only	
	- Diesel Service Technicians and Mechanics			Diesel Service Technician	
	- Occ Ed Class				
Office Technology	Office and Administrative Support	12	High School Diploma or GED	Accredited Post Secondary Institution	0 / 30
Location: Main			- Pass the ASSET Test	Post-Secondary (College) Certificate Only	
	- General Office Clerks			Office Technology	
	- Occ Ed Class				

Institution: FORT DIX FCI

Program / Location	Occupation Category	Duration (months)	Requirements	Certification	
Alteration Tailor Apprenticeship Location: Main	Production - Sewers and Tailors - Apprenticeship	24	High School Diploma or GED - US Citizen or Permanent Legal Resident	BOP Employee Department of Labor Certificate Tailor	0 / 0
Building Maintenance Repairer Apprenticeship Location: Main	Construction and Extraction - Construction and Building Inspectors - Apprenticeship	24	High School Diploma or GED - US Citizenship	BOP Employee Department of Labor Certificate Building Maintenance Repairer	0 / 0
Commercial Driver's License (AOE) Location: Camp	Business and Financial - Logisticians - Occ Ed Class	3	High School Diploma or GED - Class D driver's license, birth certificate, furlough eligible, US Citizenship or permanent legal resident	Independent Contractor State Certificate Class A Commercial Driver	0 / 0
Cook Apprenticeship Location: Main	Food Preparation and Serving - Chefs and Head Cooks - Apprenticeship	24	High School Diploma or GED - Apprenticeship enrolled	BOP Employee Department of Labor Certificate Food Service Specialist	0 / 0
Horticulturist Apprenticeship Location: Camp	Farming, Fishing, and Forestry - Agricultural Workers - Apprenticeship	36	High School Diploma or GED - US Citizenship or permanent legal resident	BOP Employee Department of Labor Certificate Horticulturist	0 / 0
HVAC (Heating, Ventilation, Air-conditioning) AOE Location: Main	Installation, Maintenance, and Repair - Heating, Air Conditioning, and Refrigeration Mechanics and Installers - Occ Ed Class	12	High School Diploma or GED - US Citizenship or permanent legal resident, 24+ months PRD, pass Wonderlic placement test 12+	Accredited Vocational/Technical School Both Vo-Tech School and Industry-Recognized Certificates HVAC Technician	0 / 57

Institution: FORT DIX FCI   (Cont'd)

Industrial Housekeeping Apprenticeship Location: Main	Building and Grounds Cleaning - Janitors and Building Cleaners - Apprenticeship	12	High School Diploma or GED - US Citizenship or permanent legal resident	BOP Employee Department of Labor Certificate Janitor	0 / 0
Landscaping Apprenticeship Location: Camp	Building and Grounds Cleaning - Grounds Maintenance Workers - Apprenticeship	24	High School Diploma or GED -	BOP Employee Department of Labor Certificate Building and Grounds Worker	0 / 0
Office Manager Apprenticeship Location: Main	Office and Administrative Support - General Office Clerks - Apprenticeship	24	High School Diploma or GED - US Citizenship or permanent legal resident	BOP Employee Department of Labor Certificate Office Clerk	0 / 0
Quality Control Apprenticeship Location: Main	Production - Quality Control Inspectors - Apprenticeship	24	High School Diploma or GED - US Citizenship or permanent legal resident	BOP Employee Department of Labor Certificate Quality Control Inspector	0 / 0
Teacher's Aide Apprenticeship Location: Main	Education, Training, and Library - Teacher Assistants - Apprenticeship	24	High School Diploma or GED - US Citizenship or permanent legal resident	BOP Employee Department of Labor Certificate Teacher's Aide	0 / 0
Vocational Training Floor Covering and Installation Location: Main	Installation, Maintenance, and Repair - General Maintenance and Repair Workers - Apprenticeship	3	High School Diploma or GED -	BOP Employee BOP Certificate & Industry Recognized Certificate Hardwood, Flooring, Carpet, Tile and Maintenance Worker	0 / 0

Institution: FORT DIX FCI   (Cont'd)

Vocational Training Computers Location: Main	Office and Administrative Support - General Office Clerks - Occ Ed Class	3	High School Diploma or GED -	BOP Employee BOP Certificate & Industry Recognized Certificate Office Automation	0 / 0
Vocational Training Electrical (Advanced) Location: Main	Installation, Maintenance, and Repair - Electrical and Electronics Installers and Repairers - Apprenticeship	4	High School Diploma or GED -	BOP Employee BOP Certificate Only Journeyman Electrical Worker/after national examination	0 / 0
Vocational Training Electrical (Basic Level) Location: Main	Installation, Maintenance, and Repair - Electrical and Electronics Installers and Repairers - Apprenticeship	4	Concurrent GED Enrollment -	BOP Employee BOP Certificate Only Basic Electrical Worker	0 / 0
Vocational Training Horticulture Location: Camp	Building and Grounds Cleaning - Grounds Maintenance Workers - Apprenticeship	3	Concurrent GED Enrollment -	BOP Employee BOP Certificate & Industry Recognized Certificate Grounds Maintenance Worker	0 / 0
Vocational Training Hydroponic Location: Camp	Farming, Fishing, and Forestry - Agricultural Workers - Apprenticeship	3	High School Diploma or GED -	BOP Employee BOP Certificate & Industry Recognized Certificate Green House Worker/Produce Specialist	0 / 0

Institution: FORT DIX FCI   **(Cont'd)**

Vocational Training Turf science	Building and Grounds Cleaning	3	Concurrent GED Enrollment	BOP Employee	0 / 0
Location: Camp	- Grounds Maintenance Workers		-	BOP Certificate & Industry Recognized Certificate	
	- Apprenticeship			Grounds Worker/Landscaping	
Vocational Training Woodworking and House Framing	Construction and Extraction	3	Concurrent GED Enrollment	BOP Employee	0 / 0
	- Carpenters		-	BOP Certificate Only	
Location: Main	- Apprenticeship			Carpenter and Woodworker	

Institution: FORT WORTH FCI

Program / Location	Occupation	#	Requirements	Certificate	
Cook Location: Main	Food Preparation and Serving - Cooks - Apprenticeship	36	High School Diploma or GED - minimum 60 days on Food Service Work Detail	BOP Employee BOP Certificate & Department of Labor Certificate Cook	0 / 0
Dental Assistant Location: Main	Production - Dental Laboratory Technicians - Apprenticeship	18	High School Diploma or GED - minimum 60 days on Dental Work Detail	BOP Employee BOP Certificate & Department of Labor Certificate Dental Assistant	0 / 0
HVAC - Vocational Training - Tarrant Community College Location: Main	Installation, Maintenance, and Repair - Heating, Air Conditioning, and Refrigeration Mechanics and Installers - Apprenticeship	6	High School Diploma or GED	Accredited Post Secondary Institution Industry-Recognized Certificate HVAC Technician/Installer	10 / 0
HVAC Apprenticeship Location: Main	Installation, Maintenance, and Repair - Heating, Air Conditioning, and Refrigeration Mechanics and Installers - Apprenticeship	60	High School Diploma or GED - minimum 60 days on HVAC Work Detail	BOP Employee BOP Certificate & Department of Labor Certificate HVAC Technician/Installer	0 / 0
Nurse Assistant Location: Main	Community and Social Service - Social and Human Service Assistants - Apprenticeship	18	High School Diploma or GED - minimum 60 days on Med Surge Work Detail	BOP Employee BOP Certificate & Department of Labor Certificate Nurse Assistant	0 / 0

Institution: FORT WORTH FCI (Cont'd)

Program	Details		Requirements	Certification	
Plumbing Apprenticeship Location: Main	Installation, Maintenance, and Repair - General Maintenance and Repair Workers - Apprenticeship	60	High School Diploma or GED - employed by Plumbing Work Detail for minimum 60 days	BOP Employee Department of Labor Certificate Plumber	0 / 0
Turf Grass Management Location: Main	Building and Grounds Cleaning - Grounds Maintenance Workers - Occ Ed Class	6	High School Diploma or GED	BOP Employee BOP Certificate & Industry Recognized Certificate Grounds Keeper	12 / 0

Institution: GILMER FCI

Associate's Degree in Science of Business Location: Main	Business and Financial - Accountants and Auditors - Occ Ed Class	42	High School Diploma or GED	Accredited Post Secondary Institution A.A, A.S., or A.A.S. Diploma Accounting Clerk, Bookkeeper, Office Manager, Supervisor	0 / 64
Cook Apprenticeship Location: Camp	Food Preparation and Serving - Cooks - Apprenticeship	36	High School Diploma or GED	BOP Employee Department of Labor Certificate Cook	0 / 0
Cook Apprenticeship Location: Main	Food Preparation and Serving - Cooks - Apprenticeship	36	No Pre-Requisites Required	BOP Employee Department of Labor Certificate Cook	0 / 0
Heating and Air Conditioning Installation Service Apprenticeship Location: Camp	Installation, Maintenance, and Repair - Heating, Air Conditioning, and Refrigeration Mechanics and Installers - Apprenticeship	48	High School Diploma or GED	BOP Employee Department of Labor Certificate HVAC Technician	0 / 0
Heating and Air Conditioning Installation Service Apprenticeship Location: Main	Installation, Maintenance, and Repair - Heating, Air Conditioning, and Refrigeration Mechanics and Installers - Apprenticeship	48	High School Diploma or GED	BOP Employee Department of Labor Certificate HVAC Technician	0 / 0

Institution: GILMER FCI   **(Cont'd)**

Heating Ventilation Air Conditioning Location: Main	Installation, Maintenance, and Repair - Heating, Air Conditioning, and Refrigeration Mechanics and Installers - Occ Ed Class	6	High School Diploma or GED	BOP Employee Both Vo-Tech School and Industry-Recognized Certificates HVAC Technician Entry Level	0 / 0
Housekeeper Commercial, Residential, Industrial Apprenticeship Location: Main	Building and Grounds Cleaning - Janitors and Building Cleaners - Apprenticeship	12	High School Diploma or GED	BOP Employee Department of Labor Certificate Housekeeper Commercial, Residential, Industrial	0 / 0
Painter Apprenticeship Location: Main	Production - Painting and Coating Workers - Apprenticeship	36	High School Diploma or GED	BOP Employee Department of Labor Certificate Automotive Painter	0 / 0
Plumber Apprenticeship Location: Main	Construction and Extraction - Plumbers, Pipefitters, and Steamfitters - Apprenticeship	48	High School Diploma or GED	BOP Employee Department of Labor Certificate Plumber	0 / 0
Polished Concrete and Floor Coverings Location: Main	Construction and Extraction - Cement Masons and Terrazzo Workers - Apprenticeship	6	Concurrent GED Enrollment	BOP Employee Vocational/Technical School Certificate Only Floor Coverings Installer & Polished Concrete Worker	0 / 0

Institution: GILMER FCI (Cont'd)

Program / Location	Occupational Area		Education Requirement	Credential	
Polished Concrete Apprenticeship Location: Main	Construction and Extraction - Cement Masons and Terrazzo Workers - Apprenticeship	48	High School Diploma or GED	BOP Employee Department of Labor Certificate Polished Concrete Worker	0 / 0
Residential Wiring Location: Main	Construction and Extraction - Electricians - Occ Ed Class	6	High School Diploma or GED	BOP Employee Both Vo-Tech School and Industry-Recognized Certificates Apprentice Electrician	0 / 0
Teacher Aide Apprenticeship Location: Main	Education, Training, and Library - Teacher Assistants - Apprenticeship	24	High School Diploma or GED	BOP Employee Department of Labor Certificate Teacher Aide	0 / 0
Teacher Aide Apprenticeship Location: Camp	Education, Training, and Library - Teacher Assistants - Apprenticeship	24	High School Diploma or GED	BOP Employee Department of Labor Certificate Teacher Aide	0 / 0
Welder/Fitter Apprenticeship Location: Camp	Production - Welders, Cutters, Solderers, and Brazers - Apprenticeship	48	High School Diploma or GED	BOP Employee Department of Labor Certificate Welder	0 / 0
Welder/Fitter Apprenticeship Location: Main	Production - Welders, Cutters, Solderers, and Brazers - Apprenticeship	48	High School Diploma or GED	BOP Employee Department of Labor Certificate Welder	0 / 0

Institution: GREENVILLE FCI

Apprenticeship Animal Trainer Location: Camp	Personal Care and Service - Animal Care and Service Workers - Apprenticeship	24	High School Diploma or GED	BOP Employee BOP Certificate & Department of Labor Certificate Journeyman Animal Trainer	0 / 0
Apprenticeship Electrician Location: Main	Construction and Extraction - Electricians - Apprenticeship	48	High School Diploma or GED	BOP Employee BOP Certificate & Department of Labor Certificate Journeyman Electrician	0 / 0
Apprenticeship HVAC Location: Camp	Installation, Maintenance, and Repair - Heating, Air Conditioning, and Refrigeration Mechanics and Installers - Apprenticeship	36	High School Diploma or GED	BOP Employee BOP Certificate & Department of Labor Certificate Journeyman HVAC	0 / 0
Apprenticeship Landscape Management Location: Camp	Building and Grounds Cleaning - Grounds Maintenance Workers - Apprenticeship	12	High School Diploma or GED	BOP Employee BOP Certificate & Department of Labor Certificate Journeyman Landscape Management	0 / 0
Apprenticeship Landscape Management Location: Main	Building and Grounds Cleaning - Grounds Maintenance Workers - Apprenticeship	12	High School Diploma or GED	BOP Employee BOP Certificate & Department of Labor Certificate Journeyman Landscape Manager	0 / 0

Institution: GREENVILLE FCI (Cont'd)

Program / Location	Occupation		Prerequisite	Outcome	
Apprenticeship Machinist Wood Location: Main	Production - Woodworkers - Apprenticeship	48	High School Diploma or GED	BOP Employee BOP Certificate & Department of Labor Certificate Journeyman Machinist Wood	0 / 0
Apprenticeship Sewing Location: Main	Production - Sewers and Tailors - Apprenticeship	48	High School Diploma or GED	BOP Employee BOP Certificate & Department of Labor Certificate Journeyman Sewer	0 / 0
Apprenticeship Teacher's Aide Location: Camp	Education, Training, and Library - Teacher Assistants - Apprenticeship	24	High School Diploma or GED	BOP Employee BOP Certificate & Department of Labor Certificate Journeyman Teacher's Aide	0 / 0
Apprenticeship Teacher's Aide Location: Main	Education, Training, and Library - Teacher Assistants - Apprenticeship	24	High School Diploma or GED	BOP Employee BOP Certificate & Department of Labor Certificate Journeyman Teacher's Aide	0 / 0
Apprenticeship Welding Location: Camp	Production - Welders, Cutters, Solderers, and Brazers - Apprenticeship	36	High School Diploma or GED	BOP Employee BOP Certificate & Department of Labor Certificate Journeyman Welder	0 / 0
Horticulture Location: Camp	Farming, Fishing, and Forestry - Agricultural Workers - Occ Ed Class	4	No Pre-Requisites Required	BOP Employee Industry-Recognized Certificate Master Gardner	0 / 0

Institution: GREENVILLE FCI   **(Cont'd)**

HVAC	36	High School Diploma or GED	BOP Employee	0 / 0
Location: Main			BOP Certificate & Department of Labor Certificate	
Construction and Extraction			Journeyman HVAC	
- Construction Laborers and Helpers				
- Apprenticeship				
Microsoft Office	4	High School Diploma or GED	Accredited Post Secondary Institution	0 / 27
Location: Main			Post-Secondary (College) Certificate Only	
Office and Administrative Support			Administrative Assistant	
- Secretaries and Administrative Assistants				
- Occ Ed Class				
Microsoft Office	4	High School Diploma or GED	Accredited Post Secondary Institution	0 / 27
Location: Camp			Post-Secondary (College) Certificate Only	
Office and Administrative Support			Administrative Assistant	
- Secretaries and Administrative Assistants				
- Occ Ed Class				
Prisoners Assisting with Support Dogs (PAWS)	12	High School Diploma or GED	Independent Contractor	0 / 0
Location: Camp			Industry-Recognized Certificate	
Personal Care and Service			Animal Trainer	
- Animal Care and Service Workers				
- Apprenticeship				
Quality & Assurance Apprenticeship	36	High School Diploma or GED	BOP Employee	0 / 0
Location: Main			BOP Certificate & Department of Labor Certificate	
Production			Journeyman Quality & Assurance	
- Quality Control Inspectors				
- Apprenticeship				

Institution: GREENVILLE FCI (Cont'd)

Program			Seats Filled / Available
Sewing	Production	3	0 / 0
Location: Camp	- Sewers and Tailors	No Pre-Requisites Required	BOP Employee
	- Occ Ed Class		Industry-Recognized Certificate
			Sewer
V.T. Cabinet Making 1	Construction and Extraction	6	0 / 15
Location: Main	- Carpenters	High School Diploma or GED	BOP Employee
	- Occ Ed Class		BOP Certificate Only
			Cabinet Maker
V.T. Cabinet Making 2	Construction and Extraction	4	0 / 3
Location: Main	- Carpenters	High School Diploma or GED	BOP Employee
	- Occ Ed Class		BOP Certificate Only
			Cabinet design

Institution: HAZELTON FCI

Building Trades Location: Main	Construction and Extraction - Carpenters - Occ Ed Class	12	High School Diploma or GED	BOP Employee BOP Certificate & Industry Recognized Certificate Carpenter	0 / 0
Carpenter Apprenticeship Location: Main	Construction and Extraction - Construction Laborers and Helpers - Apprenticeship	48	High School Diploma or GED	BOP Employee Department of Labor Certificate Carpenter	0 / 0
Cook Apprenticeship Location: SFF	Food Preparation and Serving - Food Preparation Workers - Apprenticeship	36	High School Diploma or GED	BOP Employee Department of Labor Certificate Cook	0 / 0
Cook Apprenticeship Location: Main	Food Preparation and Serving - Cooks - Apprenticeship	36	No Pre-Requisites Required	BOP Employee Department of Labor Certificate Cook	0 / 0
Dental Assistant Apprenticeship Location: Main	Production - Dental Laboratory Technicians - Apprenticeship	12	High School Diploma or GED	BOP Employee Department of Labor Certificate Dental Assistant	0 / 0
Dental Assistant Apprenticeship Location: SFF	Production - Dental Laboratory Technicians - Apprenticeship	12	High School Diploma or GED	BOP Employee Department of Labor Certificate Dental Assistant	0 / 0

Institution: **HAZELTON FCI** (Cont'd)

Health Care Sanitary Technician Location: Main	Building and Grounds Cleaning - Janitors and Building Cleaners - Apprenticeship	12	No Pre-Requisites Required	BOP Employee Department of Labor Certificate Health Care Sanitary Technician	0 / 0
Health Care Sanitary Technician Location: SFF	Building and Grounds Cleaning - Janitors and Building Cleaners - Apprenticeship	12	No Pre-Requisites Required	BOP Employee Department of Labor Certificate Health Care Sanitary Technician	0 / 0
Housekeeper, Commercial, Residential or Industrial Location: Main	Building and Grounds Cleaning - Janitors and Building Cleaners - Apprenticeship	12	No Pre-Requisites Required	BOP Employee Department of Labor Certificate Housekeeper, Commercial, Residential Industrial	0 / 0
Housekeeper, Commercial, Residential or Industrial Location: SFF	Building and Grounds Cleaning - Janitors and Building Cleaners - Apprenticeship	12	No Pre-Requisites Required	BOP Employee Department of Labor Certificate Housekeep, Commercial, Residential, Industrial	0 / 0
Microsoft Office 2010 Location: SFF	Office and Administrative Support - General Office Clerks - Occ Ed Class	3	High School Diploma or GED	BOP Employee BOP Certificate Only Microsoft Office Specialist	0 / 0
Microsoft Office 2010 Location: Main	Office and Administrative Support - General Office Clerks - Occ Ed Class	3	High School Diploma or GED	BOP Employee BOP Certificate Only Microsoft Office Specialist	0 / 0

Institution: HAZELTON FCI (Cont'd)

Teacher's Aide Apprenticeship	Education, Training, and Library	24	High School Diploma or GED	BOP Employee
Location: Main	- Teacher Assistants			Department of Labor Certificate
	- Apprenticeship			Teacher's Aide
				0 / 0
Teacher's Aide Apprenticeship	Education, Training, and Library	24	High School Diploma or GED	BOP Employee
Location: SFF	- Teacher Assistants			Department of Labor Certificate
	- Apprenticeship			Teacher's Aide
				0 / 0
VT Culinary Arts	Food Preparation and Serving	9	High School Diploma or GED	BOP Employee
Location: SFF	- Chefs and Head Cooks			BOP Certificate Only
	- Occ Ed Class			Chef
				0 / 0

Institution: HAZELTON USP

Cook Apprenticeship Location: Main	Food Preparation and Serving - Food Preparation Workers - Apprenticeship	36	No Pre-Requisites Required	BOP Employee Department of Labor Certificate Cook	0 / 0
Cook Apprenticeship Location: Camp	Food Preparation and Serving - Food Preparation Workers - Apprenticeship	36	No Pre-Requisites Required	BOP Employee Department of Labor Certificate Cook	0 / 0
Health Care Sanitary Technician Location: Main	Building and Grounds Cleaning - Janitors and Building Cleaners - Apprenticeship	12	No Pre-Requisites Required	BOP Employee Department of Labor Certificate Health Care Sanitary Technician	0 / 0
Housekeeper, Commercial, Residential, or Industrial Location: Main	Building and Grounds Cleaning - Janitors and Building Cleaners - Apprenticeship	12	No Pre-Requisites Required	BOP Employee Department of Labor Certificate Housekeeper, Commercial, Residential, Industrial	0 / 0
Housekeeper, Residential, Commercial, or Residential Location: Camp	Production - Quality Control Inspectors - Apprenticeship	12	High School Diploma or GED	BOP Employee Department of Labor Certificate Housekeeper, Residential, Commercial, Residential	0 / 0
Microsoft Office 2010 Location: Main	Office and Administrative Support - General Office Clerks - Occ Ed Class	3	High School Diploma or GED	BOP Employee BOP Certificate Only Microsoft Office Specialist	0 / 0

Institution: HAZELTON USP   **(Cont'd)**

Microsoft Office 2010 Location: Camp	Office and Administrative Support - General Office Clerks - Occ Ed Class	3	High School Diploma or GED	BOP Employee BOP Certificate Only Microsoft Office Specialist	0 / 0
Teacher's Aide Apprenticeship Location: Main	Education, Training, and Library - Teacher Assistants - Apprenticeship	24	High School Diploma or GED	BOP Employee Department of Labor Certificate Teacher's Aide	0 / 0
Teacher's Aide Apprenticeship Location: Camp	Education, Training, and Library - Teacher Assistants - Apprenticeship	24	High School Diploma or GED	BOP Employee Department of Labor Certificate Teacher's Aide	0 / 0

Institution: HERLONG FCI

Baker Location: Main	Food Preparation and Serving - Cooks - Apprenticeship	12	High School Diploma or GED - Supervisor's Approval	BOP Employee Department of Labor Certificate Baker	0 / 0
Baker Location: Camp	Food Preparation and Serving - Cooks - Apprenticeship	12	High School Diploma or GED	BOP Employee Department of Labor Certificate Baker	0 / 0
Carpentry Location: Main	Construction and Extraction - Carpenters - Apprenticeship	12	High School Diploma or GED	BOP Employee Department of Labor Certificate Carpenter	0 / 0
Computer Operator Location: Main	Office and Administrative Support - Desktop Publishers - Apprenticeship	36	High School Diploma or GED	BOP Employee Department of Labor Certificate Computer Operator, Desktop Publisher	0 / 0
Cook Location: Camp	Food Preparation and Serving - Cooks - Apprenticeship	12	High School Diploma or GED	BOP Employee Department of Labor Certificate Cook	0 / 0
Cook Location: Main	Food Preparation and Serving - Cooks - Apprenticeship	12	High School Diploma or GED - Supervisor's Approval	BOP Employee Department of Labor Certificate Cook	0 / 0
Dental Assistant Location: Main	Production - Dental Laboratory Technicians - Apprenticeship	12	High School Diploma or GED	BOP Employee Department of Labor Certificate Dental Assistant	0 / 0

Institution: HERLONG FCI (Cont'd)

Dental Assistant	Production	12	High School Diploma or GED	BOP Employee	0 / 0
Location: Camp	- Dental Laboratory Technicians			Department of Labor Certificate	
	- Apprenticeship			Dental Assistant	
Electrical Tech	Construction and Extraction	48	High School Diploma or GED	BOP Employee	0 / 0
Location: Main	- Electricians			Department of Labor Certificate	
	- Apprenticeship			Electrical Technician	
Engraver	Production	12	High School Diploma or GED	BOP Employee	0 / 0
Location: Camp	- Assemblers and Fabricators			Department of Labor Certificate	
	- Apprenticeship			Engraver Machine	
Engraver	Production	12	High School Diploma or GED	BOP Employee	0 / 0
Location: Main	- Assemblers and Fabricators			Department of Labor Certificate	
	- Apprenticeship			Engraver, Machine	
HVAC	Installation, Maintenance, and Repair	36	High School Diploma or GED	BOP Employee	0 / 0
Location: Camp	- Heating, Air Conditioning, and Refrigeration Mechanics and Installers			Department of Labor Certificate	
	- Apprenticeship			HVAC	

Institution: HERLONG FCI   **(Cont'd)**

HVAC Location: Main	Installation, Maintenance, and Repair - Heating, Air Conditioning, and Refrigeration Mechanics and Installers - Apprenticeship	36	High School Diploma or GED	BOP Employee Department of Labor Certificate Heating & Air Conditioner Installation and Service	0 / 0
Landscape Management Tech Location: Main	Building and Grounds Cleaning - Grounds Maintenance Workers - Apprenticeship	12	High School Diploma or GED	BOP Employee Department of Labor Certificate Landscape Management Technician	0 / 0
Landscape Tech Location: Camp	Building and Grounds Cleaning - Grounds Maintenance Workers - Apprenticeship	12	High School Diploma or GED	BOP Employee Department of Labor Certificate Landscape Management Tech	0 / 0
Plumber Location: Main	Construction and Extraction - Plumbers, Pipefitters, and Steamfitters - Apprenticeship	48	High School Diploma or GED	BOP Employee Department of Labor Certificate Plumber	0 / 0
Solar PV Installer Location: Camp	Production - Assemblers and Fabricators - Apprenticeship	12	High School Diploma or GED	BOP Employee Department of Labor Certificate Solar PV Installer	0 / 0

Institution: HERLONG FCI   (Cont'd)

Solar PV Installer Location: Main	Installation, Maintenance, and Repair - Electrical and Electronics Installers and Repairers - Apprenticeship	12	High School Diploma or GED	BOP Employee Department of Labor Certificate Solar PV Installer	0 / 0
Tutor/Instructor Location: Main	Education, Training, and Library - Teacher Assistants - Apprenticeship	18	High School Diploma or GED	BOP Employee Department of Labor Certificate Education and Training Instructor	0 / 0
Welder Location: Main	Production - Welders, Cutters, Solderers, and Brazers - Apprenticeship	36	High School Diploma or GED	BOP Employee Department of Labor Certificate Welder, Combination	0 / 0

Institution: JESUP FCI

Air Conditioning Technology Location: Main	Installation, Maintenance, and Repair - Heating, Air Conditioning, and Refrigeration Mechanics and Installers - Occ Ed Class	24	High School Diploma or GED - ASSET Test	Accredited Post Secondary Institution Post-Secondary (College) Certificate & Industry Recognized Certificate HVAC Technician	0 / 51
Electrical Construction Maintenance Location: Main	Installation, Maintenance, and Repair - Electrical and Electronics Installers and Repairers - Occ Ed Class	24	High School Diploma or GED - ASSET Test	Accredited Post Secondary Institution Post-Secondary (College) Certificate & Industry Recognized Certificate Electrical Journeyman's Helper	0 / 55
Microsoft Office Applications Professional Location: Main	Office and Administrative Support - General Office Clerks - Occ Ed Class	6	High School Diploma or GED	BOP Employee Post-Secondary (College) Certificate & Industry Recognized Certificate Office Clerk	0 / 22

Institution: LA TUNA FCI

HVAC Location: Main	Installation, Maintenance, and Repair - Electrical and Electronics Installers and Repairers - Occ Ed Class	12	High School Diploma or GED	Accredited Post Secondary Institution Vocational/Technical School Certificate Only HVAC Installation Technician/ HVAC Service Technician	0 / 0
HVAC Location: Main	Education, Training, and Library - Instructional Coordinators - Occ Ed Class	11	High School Diploma or GED	Accredited Vocational/Technical School Vocational/Technical School Certificate Only HVAC Technician	0 / 0
HVAC Location: Main	Education, Training, and Library - Instructional Coordinators - Occ Ed Class	11	High School Diploma or GED	Accredited Vocational/Technical School Post-Secondary (College) Certificate Only HVAC technician	0 / 0
HVAC Location: Main	Installation, Maintenance, and Repair - General Maintenance and Repair Workers - Occ Ed Class	12	High School Diploma or GED	Accredited Post Secondary Institution Post-Secondary (College) Certificate Only Installation Technician/Service Technician	0 / 0

Institution: LA TUNA FCI (Cont'd)

Microsoft Office Location: Main	Education, Training, and Library - Career and Technical Education Teachers - Occ Ed Class	6	High School Diploma or GED	Accredited Post Secondary Institution Post-Secondary (College) Certificate & Industry Recognized Certificate Information Systems Technician/Data Entry	0 / 0
Microsoft Office Location: Main	Education, Training, and Library - Instructional Coordinators - Occ Ed Class	6	High School Diploma or GED	Accredited Vocational/Technical School Post-Secondary (College) Certificate Only Office technician	0 / 0
Microsoft Office Location: SFF	Education, Training, and Library - Instructional Coordinators - Occ Ed Class	6	High School Diploma or GED	Accredited Vocational/Technical School Post-Secondary (College) Certificate Only Office Technician	0 / 0
Microsoft Office Location: SFF	Education, Training, and Library - Career and Technical Education Teachers - Occ Ed Class	6	High School Diploma or GED	Accredited Post Secondary Institution Post-Secondary (College) Certificate Only Information Systems Technician/Data Entry	0 / 0

264

Institution: LA TUNA FCI   (Cont'd)

Office Technology Location: Main	Education, Training, and Library - Career and Technical Education Teachers - Occ Ed Class	6	High School Diploma or GED	Accredited Post Secondary Institution Post-Secondary (College) Certificate Only Information Systems Technician/Data Entry	0 / 0
Office Technology Location: Main	Education, Training, and Library - Instructional Coordinators - Occ Ed Class	6	High School Diploma or GED	Accredited Vocational/Technical School Vocational/Technical School Certificate Only Microsoft Office Technician	0 / 0
Office Technology Location: SFF	Education, Training, and Library - Instructional Coordinators - Occ Ed Class	6	High School Diploma or GED	Accredited Post Secondary Institution Vocational/Technical School Certificate Only Microsoft Office Technician	0 / 0
VT Auto Location: Main	Installation, Maintenance, and Repair - Automotive Service Technicians and Mechanics - Occ Ed Class	12	High School Diploma or GED	Accredited Post Secondary Institution Industry-Recognized Certificate Service Technician/ Engine Repair Technician	0 / 0

Institution: LA TUNA FCI   (Cont'd)

Program / Location	Occupation		Education	Credential	Ratio
VT Auto Location: Main	Education, Training, and Library - Instructional Coordinators - Occ Ed Class	11	High School Diploma or GED	Accredited Vocational/Technical School Post-Secondary (College) Certificate Only Auto Technician	0 / 0
VT Auto Location: Main	Installation, Maintenance, and Repair - Automotive Service Technicians and Mechanics - Occ Ed Class	12	High School Diploma or GED	Accredited Post Secondary Institution Post-Secondary (College) Certificate & Industry Recognized Certificate Service Technician/Engine Repair Technician	0 / 0
VT Auto Location: Main	Education, Training, and Library - Instructional Coordinators - Occ Ed Class	11	High School Diploma or GED	Accredited Vocational/Technical School Post-Secondary (College) Certificate Only Auto Technician	0 / 0
VT Office Technology Location: SFF	Education, Training, and Library - Career and Technical Education Teachers - Occ Ed Class	6	High School Diploma or GED	Accredited Post Secondary Institution Post-Secondary (College) Certificate Only Information Systems Technician/Data Entry	0 / 0

Institution: LA TUNA FCI (Cont'd)

VT Welding	Education, Training, and Library	12	High School Diploma or GED	Independent Contractor	0 / 0
Location: Camp	- Instructional Coordinators			BOP Certificate Only
	- Occ Ed Class			Welder
VT Welding	Education, Training, and Library	12	High School Diploma or GED	Independent Contractor	0 / 0
Location: Camp	- Instructional Coordinators			BOP Certificate Only
	- Occ Ed Class			Welder
Welding	Construction and Extraction	12	High School Diploma or GED	Accredited Post Secondary Institution	0 / 0
Location: Camp	- Carpenters			Industry-Recognized Certificate
	- Occ Ed Class			Certified Pipe Welder
Welding	Construction and Extraction	12	High School Diploma or GED	Accredited Post Secondary Institution	0 / 0
Location: Camp	- Carpenters			Industry-Recognized Certificate
	- Occ Ed Class			Certified Pipe Welder

Institution: LEAVENWORTH USP

Program	Occupation		Pre-Requisites	Certifications	
Hospitality Employment and Retail Therapy (HEART) Location: Main	Food Preparation and Serving - Food and Beverage Serving and Related Workers - Occ Ed Class	4	No Pre-Requisites Required	BOP Employee BOP Certificate & Industry Recognized Certificate Hotel/Restaurant Employee	0 / 0
Janitorial Location: Main	Building and Grounds Cleaning - Janitors and Building Cleaners - Occ Ed Class	3	No Pre-Requisites Required	BOP Employee BOP Certificate & Industry Recognized Certificate Janitorial/Professional Cleaning	0 / 0
Servsafe Location: Main	Food Preparation and Serving - Food Preparation Workers - Occ Ed Class	3	Concurrent GED Enrollment	BOP Employee Industry-Recognized Certificate Servsafe Certified	0 / 0

268

Institution: LEE USP

Basic Home Construction (Building Trades) Location: Main	Construction and Extraction - Carpenters - Occ Ed Class	5	High School Diploma or GED - Clear Conduct	BOP Employee BOP Certificate Only Home Construction Worker	0 / 0
Horticulture/Gardening Location: Camp	Farming, Fishing, and Forestry - Agricultural Workers - Occ Ed Class	8	Concurrent GED Enrollment - Clear Conduct	BOP Employee BOP Certificate Only Master Gardener	0 / 0
Residential HVAC Location: Main	Installation, Maintenance, and Repair - Heating, Air Conditioning, and Refrigeration Mechanics and Installers - Occ Ed Class	6	High School Diploma or GED - Clear Conduct	BOP Employee BOP Certificate & Industry Recognized Certificate Residential HVAC Technician	0 / 0

Institution: LEWISBURG USP

Business English/Information Location: Main	Office and Administrative Support - Information Clerks - Occ Ed Class	6	High School Diploma or GED	BOP Employee BOP Certificate Only Information Clerk	0 / 0
Business English/Reading Location: Main	Office and Administrative Support - General Office Clerks - Occ Ed Class	6	High School Diploma or GED	BOP Employee BOP Certificate Only General Office Clerk	0 / 0
Business Math Location: Main	Office and Administrative Support - Financial Clerks - Occ Ed Class	6	High School Diploma or GED	BOP Employee BOP Certificate Only Financial Clerk	0 / 0
Commercial Housekeeping Location: Main	Building and Grounds Cleaning - Janitors and Building Cleaners - Apprenticeship	12	High School Diploma or GED	BOP Employee Department of Labor Certificate Janitor	0 / 0
Computer Fundamentals Location: Main	Office and Administrative Support - General Office Clerks - Occ Ed Class	6	High School Diploma or GED	BOP Employee BOP Certificate Only General Office Clerk	0 / 0
Desktop Publishing Location: Camp	Office and Administrative Support - Desktop Publishers - Occ Ed Class	12	High School Diploma or GED	BOP Employee BOP Certificate Only Desktop Publisher	0 / 0

Institution: LEWISBURG USP   **(Cont'd)**

Electrical Location: Main	Installation, Maintenance, and Repair - Electrical and Electronics Installers and Repairers - Apprenticeship	48	High School Diploma or GED	BOP Employee Department of Labor Certificate Electrician
Graphic Arts Location: Camp	Production - Printing Workers - Occ Ed Class	12	High School Diploma or GED	BOP Employee BOP Certificate Only Printer
HVAC Location: Main	Installation, Maintenance, and Repair - Heating, Air Conditioning, and Refrigeration Mechanics and Installers - Apprenticeship	48	High School Diploma or GED	BOP Employee Department of Labor Certificate Journeyman HVAC Worker
Plumbing Location: Main	Construction and Extraction - Plumbers, Pipefitters, and Steamfitters - Apprenticeship	48	High School Diploma or GED	BOP Employee Department of Labor Certificate Journeyman Plumber

Institution: LEXINGTON FMC

Automobile Mechanic Location: Camp	Installation, Maintenance, and Repair - Automotive Service Technicians and Mechanics - Apprenticeship	48	High School Diploma or GED	BOP Employee Department of Labor Certificate Automobile Mechanic	0 / 0
Building Maintenance Service - Repair Location: Main	Construction and Extraction - Painters, Construction and Maintenance - Apprenticeship	24	High School Diploma or GED	BOP Employee Department of Labor Certificate Building Maintenance Worker	0 / 0
Building Maintenance Service - Repair Location: Camp	Construction and Extraction - Painters, Construction and Maintenance - Apprenticeship	24	High School Diploma or GED	BOP Employee Department of Labor Certificate Building Maintenance Worker	0 / 0
Carpentry Location: Main	Construction and Extraction - Carpenters - Apprenticeship	48	High School Diploma or GED	BOP Employee Department of Labor Certificate Carpenter	0 / 0
Carpentry VT Location: Main	Construction and Extraction - Construction Laborers and Helpers - Occ Ed Class	6	High School Diploma or GED	BOP Employee BOP Certificate Only Construction Laborer	0 / 0

Institution: LEXINGTON FMC (Cont'd)

Program / Location	Occupation	Months	Requirements	Credentials	
Construction Craft Laborer Location: Main	Construction and Extraction - Construction Laborers and Helpers - Apprenticeship	24	High School Diploma or GED	BOP Employee Department of Labor Certificate Construction Laborer	0 / 0
Cook Location: Main	Food Preparation and Serving - Cooks - Apprenticeship	36	High School Diploma or GED	BOP Employee Department of Labor Certificate Cook	0 / 0
Cook Location: Camp	Food Preparation and Serving - Cooks - Apprenticeship	36	High School Diploma or GED	BOP Employee Department of Labor Certificate Cook	0 / 0
Culinary Arts VT Location: Main	Food Preparation and Serving - Cooks - Occ Ed Class	12	High School Diploma or GED - 1 yr. clear conduct, Food Service cleared	BOP Employee Industry-Recognized Certificate Cook/Restaurant Worker	0 / 0
Customer Service Representative Location: Main	Office and Administrative Support - Customer Service Representatives - Apprenticeship	24	High School Diploma or GED	BOP Employee Department of Labor Certificate Customer Service Representative	0 / 0
Electrician Location: Main	Construction and Extraction - Electricians - Apprenticeship	48	High School Diploma or GED	BOP Employee Department of Labor Certificate Electrician	0 / 0

Institution: LEXINGTON FMC   (Cont'd)

Greenhouse VT Location: Main	Farming, Fishing, and Forestry - Agricultural Workers - Apprenticeship	3	High School Diploma or GED	BOP Employee BOP Certificate Only Greenhouse Mechanic	0 / 0
Healthcare Sanitation Location: Main	Building and Grounds Cleaning - Janitors and Building Cleaners - Apprenticeship	12	High School Diploma or GED	BOP Employee Department of Labor Certificate Healthcare Sanitation Worker	0 / 0
Heating & Air Conditioning Installer/Servicer Location: Main	Installation, Maintenance, and Repair - Heating, Air Conditioning, and Refrigeration Mechanics and Installers - Apprenticeship	36	High School Diploma or GED	BOP Employee Department of Labor Certificate Heating & Air Conditioning Installer/Servicer	0 / 0
Horticulture VT Location: Main	Farming, Fishing, and Forestry - Agricultural Workers - Occ Ed Class	4	High School Diploma or GED	BOP Employee BOP Certificate Only Greenhouse/Landscape/Nursery Worker	0 / 0
Horticulture VT SCP Location: Camp	Farming, Fishing, and Forestry - Agricultural Workers - Occ Ed Class	8	Concurrent GED Enrollment	BOP Employee BOP Certificate Only Greenhouse/Landscape/Nursery Worker	0 / 0

Institution: LEXINGTON FMC   (Cont'd)

Program / Location	Occupation	Months	Education	Credential	
Horticulturist Location: Main	Farming, Fishing, and Forestry - Agricultural Workers - Apprenticeship	36	High School Diploma or GED	BOP Employee Department of Labor Certificate Greenhouse/Landscape/Nursery Worker	0 / 0
Machinist Location: Main	Production - Machinists and Tool and Die Makers - Apprenticeship	48	High School Diploma or GED	BOP Employee Department of Labor Certificate Machinist	0 / 0
Maintenance Mechanic (Any Industry) Location: Main	Installation, Maintenance, and Repair - Industrial Machinery Mechanics and Maintenance Workers - Apprenticeship	48	High School Diploma or GED	BOP Employee Department of Labor Certificate Maintenance Mechanic	0 / 0
Masonry VT Location: Main	Construction and Extraction - Brickmasons, Blockmasons, and Stonemasons - Occ Ed Class	6	Concurrent GED Enrollment	BOP Employee BOP Certificate Only Brick mason	0 / 0
Material Coordinator Location: Main	Office and Administrative Support - Material Recording Clerks - Apprenticeship	24	High School Diploma or GED	BOP Employee Department of Labor Certificate Warehouse Worker	0 / 0

Institution: LEXINGTON FMC (Cont'd)

Material Coordinator Location: Camp	Office and Administrative Support - Material Recording Clerks - Apprenticeship	24	High School Diploma or GED	BOP Employee Department of Labor Certificate Warehouse Worker	0 / 0
Office Manager/Administrative Services Location: Main	Office and Administrative Support - Secretaries and Administrative Assistants - Apprenticeship	24	High School Diploma or GED	BOP Employee Department of Labor Certificate Office Manager/Administrative Assistant	0 / 0
Painter Location: Main	Construction and Extraction - Painters, Construction and Maintenance - Apprenticeship	36	High School Diploma or GED	BOP Employee Department of Labor Certificate Painter	0 / 0
Pipefitter-Steamfitter Location: Main	Construction and Extraction - Plumbers, Pipefitters, and Steamfitters - Apprenticeship	48	High School Diploma or GED	BOP Employee Department of Labor Certificate Pipefitter-Steamfitter	0 / 0
Plumber Location: Main	Construction and Extraction - Plumbers, Pipefitters, and Steamfitters - Apprenticeship	48	High School Diploma or GED	BOP Employee Department of Labor Certificate Plumber	0 / 0

Institution: LEXINGTON FMC (Cont'd)

Power Plant Operator Location: Main	Production - Power Plant Operators, Distributors, and Dispatchers - Apprenticeship	48	High School Diploma or GED	BOP Employee Department of Labor Certificate Power Plant Operator	0 / 0
Quality Assurance Inspector Location: Main	Production - Quality Control Inspectors - Apprenticeship	36	High School Diploma or GED	BOP Employee Department of Labor Certificate Quality Assurance Inspector	0 / 0
Residential Electrical VT Location: Main	Construction and Extraction - Electricians - Occ Ed Class	10	High School Diploma or GED	BOP Employee BOP Certificate Only Residential Electrician	0 / 0
Small Business Management Location: Main	Business and Financial - Meeting, Convention, and Event Planners - Occ Ed Class	3	High School Diploma or GED	BOP Employee BOP Certificate Only Small Business Manager	0 / 0
Small Business Management Location: Camp	Business and Financial - Meeting, Convention, and Event Planners - Occ Ed Class	3	High School Diploma or GED	BOP Employee BOP Certificate Only Small Business Manager	0 / 0
Small-Engine Mechanic Location: Camp	Installation, Maintenance, and Repair - Small Engine Mechanics - Apprenticeship	24	High School Diploma or GED	BOP Employee Department of Labor Certificate Small-Engine Mechanic	0 / 0

Institution: LEXINGTON FMC (Cont'd)

Welder		36	High School Diploma or GED	BOP Employee
Location: Main	Production			Department of Labor Certificate
	- Welders, Cutters, Solderers, and Brazers			Welder
	- Apprenticeship			
Welding VT		6	Concurrent GED Enrollment	BOP Employee
Location: Main	Production			BOP Certificate Only
	- Welders, Cutters, Solderers, and Brazers			Welder
	- Occ Ed Class			

0 / 0

0 / 0

Institution: LOMPOC FCI

VT LNDSCP	Building and Grounds Cleaning	6	Concurrent GED Enrollment	BOP Employee	0 / 0
Location: Main	- Grounds Maintenance Workers			BOP Certificate Only	
	- Occ Ed Class			Landscaper designer/maintenance	

Institution: LOMPOC USP

Program / Location	Occupational Class	Count	Entry Requirement	Credential	Ratio
AOE WELDING Location: Main	Construction and Extraction - Structural Iron and Steel Workers - Occ Ed Class	12	Concurrent GED Enrollment	Accredited Post Secondary Institution Industry-Recognized Certificate WELDER	0 / 19
Barber 1 Location: Main	Personal Care and Service - Barbers, Hairdressers, and Cosmetologists - Occ Ed Class	6	High School Diploma or GED - Completion of Barber Services	BOP Employee BOP Certificate Only Barber Tradesman	0 / 0
Barber 2 Location: Main	Personal Care and Service - Barbers, Hairdressers, and Cosmetologists - Occ Ed Class	6	High School Diploma or GED - Completion of Barber 1	BOP Employee BOP Certificate Only Barber Apprentice	0 / 0
Barber Services Location: Main	Personal Care and Service - Barbers, Hairdressers, and Cosmetologists - Occ Ed Class	6	High School Diploma or GED	BOP Employee BOP Certificate Only Barber Technician	0 / 0
MTL FABWELD Location: Main	Construction and Extraction - Structural Iron and Steel Workers - Occ Ed Class	4	Concurrent GED Enrollment	BOP Employee BOP Certificate & Industry Recognized Certificate Metal Fabricator	0 / 0
VT Hydroponics Location: Camp	Farming, Fishing, and Forestry - Agricultural Workers - Occ Ed Class	6	Concurrent GED Enrollment	BOP Employee BOP Certificate Only Greenhouse Manager	0 / 0

Institution: LOMPOC USP   **(Cont'd)**

Location: Main

			Concurrent GED Enrollment		
VT Wood	Construction and Extraction	4		BOP Employee	0 / 0
	- Construction Laborers and Helpers			BOP Certificate Only	
	- Occ Ed Class			Construction Laborer	

Institution: LORETTO FCI

Program / Location		Prerequisites	Certification Awarded	
ASE Automotive Repair Location: Camp	6	High School Diploma or GED	Accredited Vocational/Technical School Both Vo-Tech School and Industry-Recognized Certificates Automotive Service Technician/Mechanic	0 / 0
- Automotive Service Technicians and Mechanics - Occ Ed Class				
CDL Location: Camp	2	High School Diploma or GED - Valid Driver License	Independent Contractor Both Vo-Tech School and Industry-Recognized Certificates CDL Class A Driver	0 / 0
- Power Plant Operators, Distributors, and Dispatchers - Occ Ed Class				
Cook Apprenticeship Location: Camp	24	High School Diploma or GED - Must be employed in specific trade	BOP Employee Department of Labor Certificate General Cook	0 / 0
- Cooks - Apprenticeship				
Cook Apprenticeship Location: Main	24	High School Diploma or GED - Must be employed in specific trade	BOP Employee Department of Labor Certificate General Cook	0 / 0
- Cooks - Apprenticeship				
Personal Trainer Location: Main	3	High School Diploma or GED	BOP Employee Industry-Recognized Certificate Personal Fitness Trainer	0 / 0
- Fitness Trainers and Instructors - Occ Ed Class				

Institution: LORETTO FCI (Cont'd)

Personal Trainer Location: Camp	Personal Care and Service - Fitness Trainers and Instructors - Occ Ed Class	3	High School Diploma or GED	BOP Employee Industry-Recognized Certificate Personal Fitness Trainer	0 / 0
Teacher Aide Apprenticeship Location: Main	Education, Training, and Library - Teacher Assistants - Apprenticeship	24	High School Diploma or GED - Must be employed in specific trade	BOP Employee Department of Labor Certificate Teacher Aide	0 / 0
Teacher Aide Apprenticeship Location: Camp	Education, Training, and Library - Teacher Assistants - Apprenticeship	24	High School Diploma or GED - Must be employed in specific trade	BOP Employee Department of Labor Certificate Teacher Aide	0 / 0

Institution: MANCHESTER FCI

Program / Location	Program Area	Hours	Requirement	Certification	
Baker Location: Main	Production - Bakers - Apprenticeship	36	High School Diploma or GED - Must be employed in specific trade	BOP Employee Department of Labor Certificate Baker Assistant	0 / 0
Baker Location: Camp	Production - Bakers - Apprenticeship	36	High School Diploma or GED - Must be employed in specific trade	BOP Employee Department of Labor Certificate Baker Assistant	0 / 0
Boiler Room Operator Location: Camp	Construction and Extraction - Boilermakers - Apprenticeship	48	High School Diploma or GED - Must be employed in specific trade	BOP Employee Department of Labor Certificate Boiler Room Operator Assistant	0 / 0
Cabinetmaker Location: Main	Construction and Extraction - Carpenters - Apprenticeship	48	High School Diploma or GED - Must be employed in specific trade	BOP Employee Department of Labor Certificate Cabinetmaker Assistant	0 / 0
Carpentry Location: Main	Construction and Extraction - Carpenters - Apprenticeship	48	High School Diploma or GED - Must be employed in specific trade	BOP Employee Department of Labor Certificate Carpentry Assistant	0 / 0
Carpentry Location: Main	Construction and Extraction - Carpenters - Occ Ed Class	6	Concurrent GED Enrollment	BOP Employee Vocational/Technical School Certificate Only Carpentry Assistant	0 / 0

Institution: MANCHESTER FCI   **(Cont'd)**

Program / Location		Months	Prerequisites	Certifications	
Combination Welder Location: Camp	Production - Welders, Cutters, Solderers, and Brazers - Apprenticeship	36	High School Diploma or GED - Must be employed in specific trade	BOP Employee Department of Labor Certificate Combination Welder Assistant	0 / 0
Cook Location: Main	Food Preparation and Serving - Cooks - Apprenticeship	24	High School Diploma or GED - Must be employed in specific trade	BOP Employee Department of Labor Certificate Cook Assistant	0 / 0
Cook Location: Camp	Food Preparation and Serving - Cooks - Apprenticeship	24	High School Diploma or GED - Must be employed in specific trade	BOP Employee Department of Labor Certificate Cook Assistant	0 / 0
Culinary Arts Location: Camp	Food Preparation and Serving - Chefs and Head Cooks - Occ Ed Class	12	High School Diploma or GED - Pass TABE Test	Accredited Post Secondary Institution Post-Secondary (College) Certificate Only Chef/Cook	0 / 2
Culinary Arts Location: Main	Food Preparation and Serving - Chefs and Head Cooks - Occ Ed Class	12	High School Diploma or GED - Pass TABE Test	Accredited Post Secondary Institution Post-Secondary (College) Certificate Only Chef/Cook	0 / 2

Institution: MANCHESTER FCI (Cont'd)

Program / Location	Occupation	Months	Requirements	Certification	
Drafting Location: Main	Installation, Maintenance, and Repair - Computer, ATM, and Office Machine Repairers - Apprenticeship	48	High School Diploma or GED - Must be employed in specific trade	BOP Employee Department of Labor Certificate Drafting Assistant	0 / 0
Electrical Location: Main	Construction and Extraction - Electricians - Occ Ed Class	6	Concurrent GED Enrollment	BOP Employee Vocational/Technical School Certificate Only Electrical Assistant	0 / 0
Electrician Location: Main	Construction and Extraction - Electricians - Apprenticeship	48	High School Diploma or GED - Must be employed in specific trade	BOP Employee Department of Labor Certificate Electrician Assistant	0 / 0
Electrician Location: Camp	Construction and Extraction - Electricians - Apprenticeship	48	High School Diploma or GED - Must be employed in specific trade	BOP Employee Department of Labor Certificate Electrician Assistant	0 / 0
Horticulture Location: Camp	Farming, Fishing, and Forestry - Agricultural Workers - Occ Ed Class	6	Concurrent GED Enrollment	BOP Employee BOP Certificate Only Horticulturalist Assistant	0 / 0

Institution: MANCHESTER FCI   **(Cont'd)**

HVAC Location: Main	Installation, Maintenance, and Repair - Heating, Air Conditioning, and Refrigeration Mechanics and Installers - Apprenticeship	36	High School Diploma or GED - Must be employed in specific trade	BOP Employee Department of Labor Certificate HVAC Assistant	0 / 0
HVAC Location: Camp	Installation, Maintenance, and Repair - Heating, Air Conditioning, and Refrigeration Mechanics and Installers - Apprenticeship	36	High School Diploma or GED - Must be employed in specific trade	BOP Employee Department of Labor Certificate HVAC Assistant	0 / 0
Hydroponics Location: Camp	Farming, Fishing, and Forestry - Agricultural Workers - Occ Ed Class	6	Concurrent GED Enrollment	BOP Employee BOP Certificate Only Hydroponic Assistant	0 / 0
Landscape Management Technician Location: Main	Building and Grounds Cleaning - Grounds Maintenance Workers - Apprenticeship	12	High School Diploma or GED - Must be employed in specific trade	BOP Employee Department of Labor Certificate Landscape Assistant	0 / 0
Landscape Management Technician Location: Camp	Building and Grounds Cleaning - Grounds Maintenance Workers - Apprenticeship	12	High School Diploma or GED - Must be employed in specific trade	BOP Employee Department of Labor Certificate Landscape Assistant	0 / 0

287

Institution: MANCHESTER FCI   (Cont'd)

Machine Operator I (Sewing)	Production	24	High School Diploma or GED	BOP Employee	0 / 0
Location: Main	- Sewers and Tailors		- Must be employed in specific trade	Department of Labor Certificate	
	- Apprenticeship			Sewing Machine Operator	
Masonry Bricklayer	Construction and Extraction	12	High School Diploma or GED	Accredited Post Secondary Institution	0 / 3
Location: Main	- Brickmasons, Blockmasons, and Stonemasons		- Pass TABE test	Post-Secondary (College) Certificate Only	
	- Occ Ed Class			Masonry Position	
Painter	Construction and Extraction	36	High School Diploma or GED	BOP Employee	0 / 0
Location: Main	- Painters, Construction and Maintenance		- Must be employed in specific trade	Department of Labor Certificate	
	- Apprenticeship			Painter Assistant	
Plumber	Construction and Extraction	48	High School Diploma or GED	BOP Employee	0 / 0
Location: Main	- Plumbers, Pipefitters, and Steamfitters		- Must be employed in specific trade	Department of Labor Certificate	
	- Apprenticeship			Plumber Assistant	

Institution: MARIANNA FCI

Program	Occupation		Education	Credentials	
2nd Chance K-9 Program Location: Camp	Personal Care and Service - Animal Care and Service Workers - Occ Ed Class	4	High School Diploma or GED	BOP Employee BOP Certificate Only Animal Care Provider	0 / 0
2nd Chance K-9 Program Location: PCU	Personal Care and Service - Animal Care and Service Workers - Occ Ed Class	4	High School Diploma or GED	BOP Employee BOP Certificate Only Animal Care Provider	0 / 0
Adult Diversified Career Training - Building Maintenance Location: Camp	Installation, Maintenance, and Repair - General Maintenance and Repair Workers - Occ Ed Class	5	High School Diploma or GED	BOP Employee BOP Certificate Only Basic Building Maintenance Employee	0 / 0
Adult Diversified Career Training - Cosmetologist Location: Camp	Personal Care and Service - Barbers, Hairdressers, and Cosmetologists - Occ Ed Class	5	High School Diploma or GED	BOP Employee BOP Certificate Only Basic Cosmetologist	0 / 0
Adult Diversified Career Training - Culinary Arts Location: Camp	Food Preparation and Serving - Food Preparation Workers - Occ Ed Class	5	High School Diploma or GED	BOP Employee BOP Certificate Only Basic Culinary Skilled Employee	0 / 0

289

Institution: MARIANNA FCI   (Cont'd)

Program / Location	Courses		Requirement	Credentials
Adult Diversified Career Training - Lube Technician Location: Camp	Installation, Maintenance, and Repair - Automotive Service Technicians and Mechanics - Occ Ed Class	5	High School Diploma or GED	BOP Employee BOP Certificate Only Lube Technician	0 / 0
Adult Diversified Career Training - Mechanic Technician Location: Camp	Installation, Maintenance, and Repair - Automotive Service Technicians and Mechanics - Occ Ed Class	5	High School Diploma or GED	BOP Employee BOP Certificate Only Basic Mechanic Technician	0 / 0
Adult Diversified Career Training - Safety Technician Location: Camp	Installation, Maintenance, and Repair - General Maintenance and Repair Workers - Occ Ed Class	5	High School Diploma or GED	BOP Employee BOP Certificate Only Basic Safety Technician	0 / 0
Continental Canine Training Program Location: Camp	Personal Care and Service - Animal Care and Service Workers - Occ Ed Class	5	High School Diploma or GED	BOP Employee BOP Certificate & Industry Recognized Certificate Canine Trainer	0 / 0
Electrical Helper Location: Main	Installation, Maintenance, and Repair - Electrical and Electronics Installers and Repairers - Occ Ed Class	18	High School Diploma or GED	BOP Employee BOP Certificate Only Electrical Helper Technician	0 / 0

290

Institution: MARIANNA FCI (Cont'd)

Program / Location	Occupation		Requirement	Outcomes	0 / 0
Electrician Apprenticeship Location: Main	Installation, Maintenance, and Repair - Electrical and Electronics Installers and Repairers - Apprenticeship	48	High School Diploma or GED	BOP Employee BOP Certificate & Department of Labor Certificate Electrician Technician	0 / 0
EPA 608 (Refrigerant Certification) Location: Main	Installation, Maintenance, and Repair - Home Appliance Repairers - Occ Ed Class	6	High School Diploma or GED	BOP Employee BOP Certificate & Industry Recognized Certificate Refrigerant Certified Employee	0 / 0
Foundations of Business Location: Main	Business and Financial - Purchasing Managers, Buyers, and Purchasing Agents - Occ Ed Class	2	High School Diploma or GED	BOP Employee BOP Certificate Only Business Owner	0 / 0
Horticulture Location: Camp	Building and Grounds Cleaning - Grounds Maintenance Workers - Occ Ed Class	5	High School Diploma or GED	BOP Employee BOP Certificate & Industry Recognized Certificate Horticulture Employee	0 / 0
Horticulture - Professional Location: Camp	Building and Grounds Cleaning - Grounds Maintenance Workers - Occ Ed Class	6	High School Diploma or GED - Completion of Horticulture - Worker	BOP Employee Industry-Recognized Certificate Greenhouse/Landscape/Nursery Worker/Agricultural Worker/Horticulture Worker	0 / 0

Institution: MARIANNA FCI   **(Cont'd)**

Horticulture - Professional Location: Main	Building and Grounds Cleaning - Grounds Maintenance Workers - Occ Ed Class	6	High School Diploma or GED - Completion of Horticulture - Worker	BOP Employee Industry-Recognized Certificate Greenhouse/Landscape/Nursery Worker/Agricultural Worker/Horticulture Worker	0 / 0
Horticulture - Professional Location: PCU	Building and Grounds Cleaning - Grounds Maintenance Workers - Occ Ed Class	6	High School Diploma or GED - Horticulture - Worker	BOP Employee Industry-Recognized Certificate Greenhouse/Landscape/Nursery Worker/Agriculture Worker/Horticulture Worker	0 / 0
Horticulture - Worker Location: Camp	Building and Grounds Cleaning - Grounds Maintenance Workers - Occ Ed Class	2	High School Diploma or GED	BOP Employee BOP Certificate Only Greenhouse/Landscape/Nursery/ Worker/Agriculture Workers/ Horticulture Workers	0 / 0
Horticulture - Worker Location: Main	Building and Grounds Cleaning - Grounds Maintenance Workers - Occ Ed Class	2	High School Diploma or GED	BOP Employee BOP Certificate Only Greenhouse/Landscape/Nursery Worker/Agricultural Worker/Horticulture Worker	0 / 0

Institution: MARIANNA FCI   (Cont'd)

Program / Location	Months	Education Requirement	Certifications / Job Titles	Enrolled/Completed
HVAC Apprenticeship Location: Main Installation, Maintenance, and Repair - Heating, Air Conditioning, and Refrigeration Mechanics and Installers - Apprenticeship	36	High School Diploma or GED	BOP Employee BOP Certificate & Department of Labor Certificate HVAC Technician	0 / 0
HVAC Helper Location: Main Installation, Maintenance, and Repair - Heating, Air Conditioning, and Refrigeration Mechanics and Installers - Occ Ed Class	12	High School Diploma or GED	BOP Employee BOP Certificate Only HVAC Helper Technician	0 / 0
Landscaping and Grounds keeping Workers Location: Camp Building and Grounds Cleaning - Grounds Maintenance Workers - Apprenticeship	24	High School Diploma or GED - Completion of Horticulture - Worker and Horticulture - Professional	BOP Employee Department of Labor Certificate Gardener, Grounds maintenance Worker, Grounds Person, Grounds Worker, Grounds/Maintenance Specialist, Groundskeeper, Landscape Specialist, Landscape Technician, Outside Maintenance Worker	0 / 0
NCCER Building & Trades Core Location: Main Construction and Extraction - Construction Laborers and Helpers - Occ Ed Class	5	High School Diploma or GED	BOP Employee BOP Certificate & Industry Recognized Certificate Building & Trades Technician	0 / 0

Institution: MARIANNA FCI (Cont'd)

Plumbing Apprenticeship Location: Main	Construction and Extraction - Plumbers, Pipefitters, and Steamfitters - Apprenticeship	48	High School Diploma or GED	BOP Employee BOP Certificate & Department of Labor Certificate Plumbing Technician	0 / 0
Plumbing Helper Location: Main	Construction and Extraction - Plumbers, Pipefitters, and Steamfitters - Occ Ed Class	12	High School Diploma or GED	BOP Employee BOP Certificate Only Plumbing Helper Technician	0 / 0

Institution: MARION USP

Program / Location	Occupational Area		Requirement	Credential	0 / 0
Building Trades / Location: Main	Construction and Extraction	12	High School Diploma or GED	BOP Employee	0 / 0
	- Carpenters			Post-Secondary (College) Certificate Only	
	- Occ Ed Class			Construction Laborer	
Certified Production Technician / Location: Main	Production	6	High School Diploma or GED	BOP Employee	0 / 0
	- Metal and Plastic Machine Workers			Post-Secondary (College) Certificate Only	
	- Occ Ed Class			Certified Production Technician	
Electrical / Location: Camp	Construction and Extraction	48	High School Diploma or GED	BOP Employee	0 / 0
	- Electricians			BOP Certificate & Department of Labor Certificate	
	- Apprenticeship			Electrician	
Electrician / Location: Main	Construction and Extraction	48	High School Diploma or GED	BOP Employee	0 / 0
	- Electricians			BOP Certificate & Department of Labor Certificate	
	- Apprenticeship			Electrician	
HVAC / Location: Main	Installation, Maintenance, and Repair	48	High School Diploma or GED	BOP Employee	0 / 0
	- Heating, Air Conditioning, and Refrigeration Mechanics and Installers			BOP Certificate & Department of Labor Certificate	
	- Apprenticeship			HVAC Technician	

Institution: MARION USP   **(Cont'd)**

Information Processing	Office and Administrative Support	12	High School Diploma or GED	BOP Employee
Location: Main	- General Office Clerks			Post-Secondary (College) Certificate Only
	- Occ Ed Class			General Office Worker
Painting	Construction and Extraction	36	High School Diploma or GED	BOP Employee
Location: Main	- Painters, Construction and Maintenance			BOP Certificate & Department of Labor Certificate
	- Apprenticeship			Painter
Residential and Commercial Plumbing	Installation, Maintenance, and Repair	48	High School Diploma or GED	BOP Employee
Location: Main	- General Maintenance and Repair Workers		- 1 year working in the plumbing shop	BOP Certificate & Department of Labor Certificate
	- Apprenticeship			Residential & Commercial Pluming
Waste Water Treatment	Production	48	High School Diploma or GED	BOP Employee
Location: Camp	- Water and Wastewater Treatment Plant and System Operators			Department of Labor Certificate
	- Apprenticeship			Wastewater Plant Operator
Water Treatment	Production	48	High School Diploma or GED	BOP Employee
Location: Camp	- Water and Wastewater Treatment Plant and System Operators			BOP Certificate & Department of Labor Certificate
	- Apprenticeship			Water Plant Operator

				0 / 0
				0 / 0
				0 / 0
				0 / 0
				0 / 0

296

Institution: MCCREARY USP

Program	Duration (months)	Requirement	Provider	Certificate	Ratio
A-HVAC Location: Main Installation, Maintenance, and Repair - Heating, Air Conditioning, and Refrigeration Mechanics and Installers - Apprenticeship	36	High School Diploma or GED	BOP Employee	Department of Labor Certificate HEATING&AIE CONDITIONING INSTALLER/SERVICER	0 / 0
A-PAINTER Location: Main Construction and Extraction - Painters, Construction and Maintenance - Apprenticeship	36	High School Diploma or GED	BOP Employee	Department of Labor Certificate PAINTER	0 / 0
Auto Mechanic Apprenticeship Location: Camp Installation, Maintenance, and Repair - Automotive Service Technicians and Mechanics - Apprenticeship	48	High School Diploma or GED	BOP Employee	Department of Labor Certificate Automobile Mechanic	0 / 0
Cook Apprenticeship Location: Camp Food Preparation and Serving - Cooks - Apprenticeship	24	High School Diploma or GED	BOP Employee	Department of Labor Certificate Cook	0 / 0
Cook Apprenticeship Location: Main Food Preparation and Serving - Cooks - Apprenticeship	24	High School Diploma or GED	BOP Employee	Department of Labor Certificate Cook	0 / 0

Institution: MCCREARY USP   **(Cont'd)**

Electrical Apprenticeship Location: Main	Construction and Extraction - Electricians - Apprenticeship	48	High School Diploma or GED	BOP Employee Department of Labor Certificate Electrician	0 / 0
Landscape Management Technician Apprenticeship Location: Camp	Building and Grounds Cleaning - Grounds Maintenance Workers - Apprenticeship	12	High School Diploma or GED	BOP Employee Department of Labor Certificate Landscape Management Technician	0 / 0
Landscape Technician Apprenticeship Location: Camp	Building and Grounds Cleaning - Grounds Maintenance Workers - Apprenticeship	24	High School Diploma or GED	BOP Employee Department of Labor Certificate Landscape Technician	0 / 0
Powerhouse Mechanic Location: Camp	Production - Power Plant Operators, Distributors, and Dispatchers - Apprenticeship	48	High School Diploma or GED	BOP Employee Department of Labor Certificate Powerhouse Mechanic	0 / 0
VT Master Gardener Location: Camp	Farming, Fishing, and Forestry - Agricultural Workers - Occ Ed Class	3	High School Diploma or GED	Accredited Post Secondary Institution BOP Certificate & Industry Recognized Certificate Master Gardener	0 / 0

Institution: MCCREARY USP   **(Cont'd)**

VT Office Clerk Location: Main	Office and Administrative Support - General Office Clerks - Occ Ed Class	6	High School Diploma or GED	BOP Employee BOP Certificate Only Microsoft Office Clerk	0 / 0
VT Residential Wiring Location: Main	Installation, Maintenance, and Repair - General Maintenance and Repair Workers - Occ Ed Class	5	High School Diploma or GED	BOP Employee BOP Certificate Only None	0 / 0
VT Web Page Designer Location: Main	Office and Administrative Support - Information Clerks - Occ Ed Class	6	High School Diploma or GED	BOP Employee BOP Certificate Only Web Designer	0 / 0
Welding Apprenticeship Location: Camp	Production - Welders, Cutters, Solderers, and Brazers - Apprenticeship	36	High School Diploma or GED	BOP Employee Department of Labor Certificate Welder	0 / 0

Institution: MCDOWELL FCI

Program	Occupation Area	Hours	Eligibility	Provider / Certificate	0/0
Cook Apprentice Location: Main	Food Preparation and Serving - Cooks - Apprenticeship	24	High School Diploma or GED - No incident reports within one year, 12 months left on sentence	BOP Employee Department of Labor Certificate Cook	0 / 0
Cook Apprentice Location: Camp	Food Preparation and Serving - Cooks - Apprenticeship	24	High School Diploma or GED - No incident reports within one year, 12 months left on sentence	BOP Employee Department of Labor Certificate Cook	0 / 0
Dental Assistant Apprenticeship Program Location: Main	Production - Dental Laboratory Technicians - Apprenticeship	18	High School Diploma or GED - No incident reports within one year, 12 months left on sentence	BOP Employee Department of Labor Certificate Dental Assistant	0 / 0
Electrical Apprentice Location: Main	Construction and Extraction - Electricians - Apprenticeship	24	High School Diploma or GED - No incident reports within one year, 12 months left on sentence	BOP Employee Department of Labor Certificate Electrician	0 / 0
Electrical Apprentice Location: Camp	Construction and Extraction - Electricians - Apprenticeship	24	High School Diploma or GED - No incident reports within one year, 12 months left on sentence	BOP Employee Department of Labor Certificate Electrician	0 / 0
HVAC Apprentice Location: Main	Installation, Maintenance, and Repair - Heating, Air Conditioning, and Refrigeration Mechanics and Installers - Apprenticeship	18	High School Diploma or GED - No incident reports within one year, 12 months left on sentence	BOP Employee Department of Labor Certificate HVAC Installer/Repairer	0 / 0

Institution: MCDOWELL FCI   **(Cont'd)**

HVAC Apprentice Location: Camp	Installation, Maintenance, and Repair - Heating, Air Conditioning, and Refrigeration Mechanics and Installers - Apprenticeship	18	High School Diploma or GED - No incident reports within one year, 12 months left on sentence	BOP Employee Department of Labor Certificate HVAC Installer/Repairer	0 / 0
Material Coordinator Location: Camp	Office and Administrative Support - Material Recording Clerks - Apprenticeship	24	High School Diploma or GED	BOP Employee Department of Labor Certificate warehouse worker	0 / 0
Material Coordinator Apprentice Location: Main	Office and Administrative Support - Material Recording Clerks - Apprenticeship	24	High School Diploma or GED	BOP Employee Department of Labor Certificate Warehouse worker	0 / 0
Plumber Apprentice Location: Main	Construction and Extraction - Plumbers, Pipefitters, and Steamfitters - Apprenticeship	24	High School Diploma or GED - No incident reports within one year, 12 months left on sentence	BOP Employee Department of Labor Certificate Plumber	0 / 0
Plumber Apprentice Location: Camp	Construction and Extraction - Plumbers, Pipefitters, and Steamfitters - Apprenticeship	24	High School Diploma or GED - No incident reports within one year, 12 months left on sentence	BOP Employee Department of Labor Certificate Plumber	0 / 0

Institution: MCDOWELL FCI   (Cont'd)

Program		Number	Requirements	Certifications	
Teacher Assistant Apprentice Location: Main	Education, Training, and Library - Teacher Assistants - Apprenticeship	12	High School Diploma or GED - No incident reports within one year, 12 months left on sentence	BOP Employee Department of Labor Certificate Teacher Assistant	0 / 0
Teacher Assistant Apprentice Location: Camp	Education, Training, and Library - Teacher Assistants - Apprenticeship	12	High School Diploma or GED - No incident reports within one year, 12 months left on sentence	BOP Employee Department of Labor Certificate Teacher Assistant	0 / 0
VT Carpentry Location: Main	Construction and Extraction - Carpenters - Occ Ed Class	5	High School Diploma or GED	BOP Employee Industry-Recognized Certificate Carpenter	0 / 0
VT Masonry Location: Main	Construction and Extraction - Brickmasons, Blockmasons, and Stonemasons - Occ Ed Class	5	High School Diploma or GED	BOP Employee Industry-Recognized Certificate Mason	0 / 0
VT Residential Wiring Location: Main	Construction and Extraction - Electricians - Occ Ed Class	5	High School Diploma or GED	BOP Employee Industry-Recognized Certificate Electrician	0 / 0
Welding Apprentice Location: Camp	Production - Welders, Cutters, Solderers, and Brazers - Apprenticeship	24	High School Diploma or GED - No incident reports within one year, 12 months left on sentence	BOP Employee Department of Labor Certificate Welder	0 / 0

Institution: MCKEAN FCI

Program	Work Assignment	Hours	Requirement	Outcomes	Slots
Cook Apprentice Location: Main	Food Preparation and Serving - Cooks - Apprenticeship	60	High School Diploma or GED	BOP Employee BOP Certificate & Department of Labor Certificate Cook	0 / 0
Culinary Arts Location: Camp	Food Preparation and Serving - Cooks - Occ Ed Class	60	High School Diploma or GED	BOP Employee Industry-Recognized Certificate Cook	0 / 0
Culinary Arts Location: Main	Food Preparation and Serving - Cooks - Occ Ed Class	24	Concurrent GED Enrollment	BOP Employee Industry-Recognized Certificate Cook	0 / 0
NCCER Carpentry Level 1 Location: Main	Construction and Extraction - Carpenters - Occ Ed Class	6	High School Diploma or GED	BOP Employee Industry-Recognized Certificate Basic Carpenter	0 / 0
NCCER Carpentry Level 2 Location: Main	Construction and Extraction - Carpenters - Occ Ed Class	6	High School Diploma or GED - NCCER Carpentry Level 1	BOP Employee Industry-Recognized Certificate Basic Carpenter	0 / 0
Teacher's Aide Location: Main	Education, Training, and Library - Teacher Assistants - Apprenticeship	60	High School Diploma or GED	BOP Employee BOP Certificate & Department of Labor Certificate Teacher's Assistant	0 / 0

Institution: MCKEAN FCI   (Cont'd)

Education, Training, and Library	60	High School Diploma or GED	BOP Employee	0 / 0
- Teacher Assistants			BOP Certificate & Department of Labor Certificate	
- Occ Ed Class			Teacher's Aide	

Teacher's Aide

Location: Camp

Institution: MEMPHIS FCI

Program / Location	Occupation		Requirements	Certification / Employer	Ratio
Career Development Technician Location: Main	Education, Training, and Library - Career and Technical Education Teachers - Apprenticeship	29	High School Diploma or GED - Secured institution employment in the education department, career resource center.	BOP Employee Department of Labor Certificate Career Development Technician	0 / 0
Career Development Technician Location: Camp	Education, Training, and Library - Career and Technical Education Teachers - Apprenticeship	29	High School Diploma or GED - Secured institution employment in the education department, career resource center.	BOP Employee Department of Labor Certificate Career Development Technician	0 / 0
Carpenter (Maintenance) Location: Main	Construction and Extraction - Carpenters - Apprenticeship	50	High School Diploma or GED - Secured institution employment in the facilities construction shop.	BOP Employee Department of Labor Certificate Carpenter (Maintenance)	0 / 0
Carpenter (Maintenance) Location: Camp	Construction and Extraction - Carpenters - Apprenticeship	50	High School Diploma or GED - Secured institution employment in the facilities construction shop.	BOP Employee Department of Labor Certificate Carpenter (Maintenance)	0 / 0
Cook (Hotel and Restaurant) Location: Camp	Food Preparation and Serving - Cooks - Apprenticeship	38	High School Diploma or GED - Secured institution employment as a cook in the food service department.	BOP Employee Department of Labor Certificate Hotel and Restaurant Cook	0 / 0
Cook (Hotel and Restaurant) Location: Main	Food Preparation and Serving - Cooks - Apprenticeship	38	High School Diploma or GED - Secured institution employment as a cook in the food service department.	BOP Employee Department of Labor Certificate Hotel and Restaurant Cook	0 / 0

Institution: MEMPHIS FCI   **(Cont'd)**

Dental Assistant Location: Main	Personal Care and Service - Animal Care and Service Workers - Apprenticeship	13	High School Diploma or GED - Secured institution employment in the dental office.	BOP Employee Department of Labor Certificate Dental Assistant	0 / 0
Dental Assistant Location: Camp	Personal Care and Service - Animal Care and Service Workers - Apprenticeship	13	High School Diploma or GED - Secured employment in the institution dental office.	BOP Employee Department of Labor Certificate Dental Assistant	0 / 0
Drafter (Architectural) Location: Main	Construction and Extraction - Construction and Building Inspectors - Apprenticeship	50	High School Diploma or GED - Secured institution employment in the facilities drafting department.	BOP Employee Department of Labor Certificate Drafter	0 / 0
Electrician Location: Main	Construction and Extraction - Electricians - Apprenticeship	50	High School Diploma or GED - Secured institution employment in the facilities department electric shop.	BOP Employee Department of Labor Certificate Electrician	0 / 0
Electrician Location: Camp	Construction and Extraction - Electricians - Apprenticeship	50	High School Diploma or GED - Secured employment in the institution facilities electric shop.	BOP Employee Department of Labor Certificate Electrician	0 / 0
Engraver Location: Camp	Office and Administrative Support - Desktop Publishers - Apprenticeship	38	High School Diploma or GED - Secured employment in the institution print shop.	BOP Employee Department of Labor Certificate Engraver	0 / 0

Program	Training Areas	#	Education	Employment	Certification / Job Title	
Golf Course Management Location: Camp	Building and Grounds Cleaning - Grounds Maintenance Workers - Apprenticeship	25	High School Diploma or GED	- Secured institution employment in the facilities landscape department.	Independent Contractor Department of Labor Certificate Golf Course Grounds Keeper	0 / 0
Heating and Air-conditioning Location: Main	Installation, Maintenance, and Repair - Heating, Air Conditioning, and Refrigeration Mechanics and Installers - Apprenticeship	38	High School Diploma or GED	- Secured institution employment in the facilities HVAC shop.	BOP Employee Department of Labor Certificate Heating and Air-conditioning Repairman	0 / 0
Heating and Air-conditioning Location: Camp	Installation, Maintenance, and Repair - Heating, Air Conditioning, and Refrigeration Mechanics and Installers - Apprenticeship	38	High School Diploma or GED	- Secured institution employment in the facilities HVAC shop.	BOP Employee Department of Labor Certificate Heating and Air-conditioning Repairman	0 / 0
Landscape Gardener Location: Main	Building and Grounds Cleaning - Grounds Maintenance Workers - Apprenticeship	50	High School Diploma or GED	- Secured institution employment in the facilities landscape shop.	BOP Employee Department of Labor Certificate Landscape Gardner	0 / 0
Landscape Gardner Location: Camp	Building and Grounds Cleaning - Grounds Maintenance Workers - Apprenticeship	50	High School Diploma or GED	- Secured institution employment in the facilities landscape department.	BOP Employee Department of Labor Certificate Landscape Gardner	0 / 0

Institution: MEMPHIS FCI   (Cont'd)

Program / Location	Occupation		Requirements	Credentials	
Logistics/Transportation Management Location: Main	Business and Financial - Logisticians - Occ Ed Class	9	High School Diploma or GED - A minimum of 18 months remaining on sentence to ensure program completion	Accredited Post Secondary Institution Post-Secondary (College) Certificate Only Entry Level Warehouse or Distribution Supervisor	0 / 18
Logistics/Transportation Management Location: Camp	Business and Financial - Logisticians - Occ Ed Class	9	High School Diploma or GED - A minimum of 18 months remaining on sentence to ensure program completion	Accredited Post Secondary Institution Post-Secondary (College) Certificate Only Entry Level Warehouse/Distribution Supervisor	0 / 18
NCCER-Building Trades Location: Main	Construction and Extraction - Construction Laborers and Helpers - Occ Ed Class	12	High School Diploma or GED - A minimum of 18 months remaining on sentence to ensure program completion.	BOP Employee Industry-Recognized Certificate Construction Laborers and Helpers	0 / 0
Painter (Construction) Location: Main	Construction and Extraction - Painters, Construction and Maintenance - Apprenticeship	38	High School Diploma or GED - Secured institution employment in the facilities department paint shop.	BOP Employee Department of Labor Certificate Painter (Construction)	0 / 0
Plumber Location: Main	Construction and Extraction - Plumbers, Pipefitters, and Steamfitters - Apprenticeship	50	High School Diploma or GED - Secured institution employment in the facilities department plumbing shop.	BOP Employee Department of Labor Certificate Plumber	0 / 0

Institution: MEMPHIS FCI   **(Cont'd)**

Printer-Slotter Operator Location: Camp	Office and Administrative Support - Desktop Publishers - Apprenticeship	50	High School Diploma or GED - Secured institution employment in the education department print shop.	BOP Employee Department of Labor Certificate Printer Operator	0 / 0
Purchasing Agent Location: Main	Business and Financial - Purchasing Managers, Buyers, and Purchasing Agents - Apprenticeship	50	High School Diploma or GED - Secured institution employment in UNICOR	BOP Employee Department of Labor Certificate Purchasing Agent	0 / 0
Quality Assurance and Supervision Location: Main	Business and Financial - Purchasing Managers, Buyers, and Purchasing Agents - Occ Ed Class	9	High School Diploma or GED - A minimum of 18 months remaining on sentence to ensure program completion.	Accredited Post Secondary Institution Post-Secondary (College) Certificate Only Entry Level Service Manager	0 / 18
Quality Assurance and Supervision Location: Camp	Business and Financial - Purchasing Managers, Buyers, and Purchasing Agents - Occ Ed Class	9	High School Diploma or GED - A minimum of 18 months remaining on sentence to ensure program completion.	Accredited Post Secondary Institution Post-Secondary (College) Certificate Only Entry Level Service Manager	0 / 18
Quality Control Technician Location: Main	Production - Quality Control Inspectors - Apprenticeship	25	High School Diploma or GED - Secured Institution employment in UNICOR	BOP Employee Department of Labor Certificate Quality Control Inspectors	0 / 0

Institution: MEMPHIS FCI   (Cont'd)

Program	Cluster		Requirements	Certifications	
Teacher Aide Location: Main	Education, Training, and Library - Teacher Assistants - Apprenticeship	25	High School Diploma or GED - Secured institution employment in the education department as a teacher assistant.	BOP Employee Department of Labor Certificate Teacher Assistant	0 / 0
Teacher Aide Location: Camp	Education, Training, and Library - Teacher Assistants - Apprenticeship	25	High School Diploma or GED - Secured institution employment in the education department as a teacher assistant.	BOP Employee Department of Labor Certificate Teacher Assistant	0 / 0
VT Administrative Assistant Location: Main	Office and Administrative Support - Secretaries and Administrative Assistants - Occ Ed Class	4	Concurrent GED Enrollment	BOP Employee BOP Certificate Only Secretaries and Administrative Assistants	0 / 0
Welder (Combination) Location: Camp	Construction and Extraction - Structural Iron and Steel Workers - Apprenticeship	50	High School Diploma or GED - Secured institution employment in the facilities welding department.	BOP Employee Department of Labor Certificate Welder	0 / 0

310

Institution: MENDOTA FCI

Vocational Building Trades Location: Main	Construction and Extraction - Construction Laborers and Helpers - Occ Ed Class	5	High School Diploma or GED	BOP Employee BOP Certificate Only Construction Laborers	0 / 0
Vocational Trades Automotive Location: Main	Installation, Maintenance, and Repair - Automotive Service Technicians and Mechanics - Occ Ed Class	2	High School Diploma or GED	BOP Employee BOP Certificate & Industry Recognized Certificate Automotive Air Conditioning Mechanic	0 / 0
Vocational Trades Warehouse Location: Main	Office and Administrative Support - Cargo and Freight Agents - Occ Ed Class	2	High School Diploma or GED	BOP Employee BOP Certificate Only Warehouse Technician	0 / 0
Vocational Trades Warehouse Location: Camp	Office and Administrative Support - Cargo and Freight Agents - Occ Ed Class	2	High School Diploma or GED	BOP Employee BOP Certificate Only Warehouse Technician	0 / 0

Institution: MIAMI FCI

Program / Location	Hours	Education	Details	Enrollment
Custodial Maintenance Location: Main Building and Grounds Cleaning - Janitors and Building Cleaners - Occ Ed Class	6	High School Diploma or GED	BOP Employee BOP Certificate Only Custodian	0 / 0
Electrical Apprenticeship Location: Main Installation, Maintenance, and Repair - Electrical and Electronics Installers and Repairers - Apprenticeship	48	High School Diploma or GED	BOP Employee BOP Certificate & Department of Labor Certificate Electrician Technician	0 / 0
Electrical Apprenticeship Location: Camp Installation, Maintenance, and Repair - Electrical and Electronics Installers and Repairers - Apprenticeship	48	High School Diploma or GED	BOP Employee BOP Certificate & Department of Labor Certificate Electrician Tech	0 / 0
HVAC Apprenticeship Location: Main Construction and Extraction - Insulation Workers - Apprenticeship	48	High School Diploma or GED	BOP Employee BOP Certificate & Department of Labor Certificate HVAC Technician	0 / 0
Plumbing Apprenticeship Location: Main Installation, Maintenance, and Repair - General Maintenance and Repair Workers - Apprenticeship	48	High School Diploma or GED	BOP Employee BOP Certificate & Department of Labor Certificate Plumber	0 / 0

Institution: MIAMI FDC

Computerized Engraving	Production	1 High School Diploma or GED	Independent Contractor	0 / 0
Location: Main	- Printing Workers		Industry-Recognized Certificate
	- Occ Ed Class		Engraving Operator
Custodial Technician	Building and Grounds Cleaning	1 No Pre-Requisites Required	BOP Employee	0 / 0
Location: Main	- Janitors and Building Cleaners		Industry-Recognized Certificate
	- Occ Ed Class		Custodial Technician
Food Handler	Food Preparation and Serving	1 No Pre-Requisites Required	BOP Employee	0 / 0
Location: Main	- Food Preparation Workers		BOP Certificate & Industry Recognized Certificate
	- Occ Ed Class		Food Handler

Institution: MILAN FCI

Bricklayer (O*NET - 47-2021.00) Location: Main	Construction and Extraction - Brickmasons, Blockmasons, and Stonemasons - Apprenticeship	36	High School Diploma or GED	BOP Employee BOP Certificate & Department of Labor Certificate Bricklayer	0 / 0
Carpenter (O*NET - 47-2031.01) Location: Main	Construction and Extraction - Carpenters - Apprenticeship	48	High School Diploma or GED	BOP Employee BOP Certificate & Department of Labor Certificate Carpenter	0 / 0
Combination Welder (O*NET - 51-4121.02) Location: Main	Production - Welders, Cutters, Solderers, and Brazers - Apprenticeship	36	High School Diploma or GED	BOP Employee BOP Certificate & Department of Labor Certificate Combination Welder	0 / 0
Electrician (O*NET - 47-2111.00) Location: Main	Construction and Extraction - Electricians - Apprenticeship	48	High School Diploma or GED	BOP Employee BOP Certificate & Department of Labor Certificate Electrician	0 / 0
Machinist (O*NET - 51-4041.00) Location: Main	Installation, Maintenance, and Repair - Industrial Machinery Mechanics and Maintenance Workers - Apprenticeship	48	High School Diploma or GED	BOP Employee BOP Certificate & Department of Labor Certificate Machinist	0 / 0

314

Program	Location	Occupation / Class		Education	Certification	
Millwright (O*NET - 49-9044.00)	Location: Main	Installation, Maintenance, and Repair - Millwrights - Apprenticeship	48	High School Diploma or GED	BOP Employee BOP Certificate & Department of Labor Certificate Millwright	0 / 0
National Federation of Professional Trainers (NFPT)	Location: Main	Personal Care and Service - Fitness Trainers and Instructors - Occ Ed Class	3	High School Diploma or GED	BOP Employee BOP Certificate & Industry Recognized Certificate Certified Personal Trainer	32 / 0
Parks & Recreation	Location: Main	Personal Care and Service - Recreation Workers - Occ Ed Class	9	High School Diploma or GED	BOP Employee BOP Certificate Only Recreation Worker	0 / 0
Pipefitter (O*NET - 47-2152.01)	Location: Main	Construction and Extraction - Plumbers, Pipefitters, and Steamfitters - Apprenticeship	48	High School Diploma or GED	BOP Employee BOP Certificate & Department of Labor Certificate Pipefitter	0 / 0
Plumber (O*NET - 47-2152.02)	Location: Main	Construction and Extraction - Plumbers, Pipefitters, and Steamfitters - Apprenticeship	48	High School Diploma or GED	BOP Employee BOP Certificate & Department of Labor Certificate Plumber	0 / 0
Quality Control (O*NET - 51-9061.01)	Location: Main	Production - Quality Control Inspectors - Apprenticeship	24	High School Diploma or GED	BOP Employee BOP Certificate & Department of Labor Certificate Quality Assurance Specialist	0 / 0

Institution: MILAN FCI   (Cont'd)

Refrigeration Mechanic (O*NET - 49-9021.02) Location: Main	Installation, Maintenance, and Repair - Heating, Air Conditioning, and Refrigeration Mechanics and Installers - Apprenticeship	36	High School Diploma or GED	BOP Employee BOP Certificate & Department of Labor Certificate Refrigeration Mechanic	0 / 0
Stationary Engineer (O*NET - 51-8021.02) Location: Main	Production - Stationary Engineers and Boiler Operators - Apprenticeship	48	High School Diploma or GED - Gate Pass Inmates Only	BOP Employee BOP Certificate & Department of Labor Certificate Stationary Engineer	0 / 0
Tool & Die (O*NET - 51-4111.00) Location: Main	Production - Machinists and Tool and Die Makers - Apprenticeship	48	High School Diploma or GED	BOP Employee BOP Certificate & Department of Labor Certificate Tool & Die Machinist	0 / 0

Institution: MONTGOMERY FPC

Animal Trainer Location: Camp	Personal Care and Service – Animal Care and Service Workers – Apprenticeship	24	High School Diploma or GED – Must be in the job prior to entering the apprenticeship.	BOP Employee Department of Labor Certificate Animal Trainer	0 / 0
Barber Location: Camp	Personal Care and Service – Barbers, Hairdressers, and Cosmetologists – Apprenticeship	24	High School Diploma or GED – Must be in the job prior to entering the apprenticeship.	BOP Employee Department of Labor Certificate Barber	0 / 0
Carpenter Location: Camp	Construction and Extraction – Carpenters – Apprenticeship	60	High School Diploma or GED – Must be in the job prior to entering the apprenticeship.	BOP Employee Department of Labor Certificate Carpenter	0 / 0
Cook Location: Camp	Food Preparation and Serving – Cooks – Apprenticeship	48	High School Diploma or GED – Must be in the job prior to entering the apprenticeship.	BOP Employee Department of Labor Certificate Cook	0 / 0
Dry Cleaning Location: Camp	Production – Laundry and Dry-cleaning Workers – Apprenticeship	36	High School Diploma or GED – Must be in the job prior to entering the apprenticeship.	BOP Employee Department of Labor Certificate Dry Cleaner	0 / 0
Electric Technician Location: Camp	Installation, Maintenance, and Repair – Electrical and Electronics Installers and Repairers – Apprenticeship	60	High School Diploma or GED – Must be in the job prior to entering the apprenticeship.	BOP Employee Department of Labor Certificate Electrician	0 / 0

317

Institution: MONTGOMERY FPC   (Cont'd)

Greens Keeper	Building and Grounds Cleaning	24	High School Diploma or GED	BOP Employee	0 / 0
Location: Camp	– Grounds Maintenance Workers		– Must be in the job prior to entering the apprenticeship.	Department of Labor Certificate	
	– Apprenticeship			Greens Keeper	
Horticulture	Farming, Fishing, and Forestry	24	High School Diploma or GED	BOP Employee	0 / 0
Location: Camp	– Agricultural Workers		– Must be in the job prior to entering the apprenticeship.	Department of Labor Certificate	
	– Apprenticeship			Horticulturist	
Housekeeper	Building and Grounds Cleaning	24	High School Diploma or GED	BOP Employee	0 / 0
Location: Camp	– Maids and Housekeeping Cleaners		– Must be in the job prior to entering the apprenticeship.	Department of Labor Certificate	
	– Apprenticeship			Housekeeper	
HVAC	Installation, Maintenance, and Repair	36	High School Diploma or GED	BOP Employee	0 / 0
Location: Camp	– Heating, Air Conditioning, and Refrigeration Mechanics and Installers		– Must be in the job prior to entering the apprenticeship.	Department of Labor Certificate	
	– Apprenticeship			HVAC	
Landscape Management Tech	Building and Grounds Cleaning	24	High School Diploma or GED	BOP Employee	0 / 0
Location: Camp	– Grounds Maintenance Workers		– Must be in the job prior to entering the apprenticeship.	Department of Labor Certificate	
	– Apprenticeship			Landscape Management Tech	

Institution: MONTGOMERY FPC (Cont'd)

Mechanic Location: Camp	Installation, Maintenance, and Repair - Automotive Service Technicians and Mechanics - Occ Ed Class	48	High School Diploma or GED - Must be in the job prior to entering the apprenticeship.	BOP Employee Department of Labor Certificate Auto Mechanic	0 / 0
Plumbing Location: Main	Construction and Extraction - Plumbers, Pipefitters, and Steamfitters - Apprenticeship	48	High School Diploma or GED - Must be in the job prior to entering the apprenticeship.	BOP Employee Department of Labor Certificate Plumber	0 / 0
Small Engine Repair Location: Camp	Installation, Maintenance, and Repair - Small Engine Mechanics - Apprenticeship	24	Concurrent GED Enrollment - Must be in the job prior to entering the apprenticeship.	BOP Employee Department of Labor Certificate Small Engine Mechanic	0 / 0

Institution: MORGANTOWN FCI

Microsoft Office Location: Main	Office and Administrative Support - General Office Clerks - Occ Ed Class	4	Concurrent GED Enrollment	BOP Employee BOP Certificate Only Data Entry Clerk/Office Assistant
Microsoft Office Location: Main	Office and Administrative Support - General Office Clerks - Occ Ed Class	4	Concurrent GED Enrollment	BOP Employee BOP Certificate Only Data Entry Clerk/Office Assistant
Welder Location: Main	Production - Welders, Cutters, Solderers, and Brazers - Apprenticeship	6	Concurrent GED Enrollment	BOP Employee Industry-Recognized Certificate Welder

0 / 0

0 / 0

0 / 0

Institution: OAKDALE FCI I

Building Trades Location: Main	Construction and Extraction - Carpenters - Apprenticeship	4	High School Diploma or GED	Accredited Vocational/Technical School Post-Secondary (College) Certificate Only Carpenter	0 / 5
Horticulture Location: Main	Building and Grounds Cleaning - Grounds Maintenance Workers - Apprenticeship	4	High School Diploma or GED	Accredited Vocational/Technical School Post-Secondary (College) Certificate Only Nursery and Grounds Technician	0 / 5

Institution: OAKDALE FCI II

Welding	Construction and Extraction	4	High School Diploma or GED	Accredited Vocational/Technical School	0 / 5
Location: Camp	- Construction Equipment Operators			Post-Secondary (College) Certificate Only	
	- Apprenticeship			Welder	

Institution: OKLAHOMA CITY FTC

Dental Apprenticeship	Production	24	High School Diploma or GED	BOP Employee	0 / 0
Location: Main	- Dental Laboratory Technicians		- Medical clearance	BOP Certificate & Department of Labor Certificate	
	- Apprenticeship			Dental Assistant	

Institution: OTTISVILLE FCI

		Concurrent GED Enrollment	
Computer Skills Location: Main	Office and Administrative Support - Desktop Publishers - Occ Ed Class	6	BOP Employee BOP Certificate Only Computer Clerical	0 / 0
Floor Care Maintenance Custodial Technician Location: Main	Building and Grounds Cleaning - Janitors and Building Cleaners - Occ Ed Class	12	High School Diploma or GED	BOP Employee BOP Certificate & Industry Recognized Certificate Maintenance Custodial Technician	0 / 0
Horticulture/Landscape Location: Main	Farming, Fishing, and Forestry - Agricultural Workers - Occ Ed Class	18	High School Diploma or GED	BOP Employee BOP Certificate Only Horticulturist / Landscaper	0 / 0
Textiles and Production Location: Main	Production - Upholsterers - Occ Ed Class	6	High School Diploma or GED	BOP Employee BOP Certificate Only Sewer/ Upholsterer	0 / 0

Institution: OXFORD FCI

Program	Occupation / Course		Requirement	Certification	
Animal Trainer Dept. of Labor Apprenticeship Location: Camp	Personal Care and Service - Animal Care and Service Workers - Apprenticeship	24	High School Diploma or GED	BOP Employee Department of Labor Certificate Animal Trainer	0 / 0
Bricklayer Dept. of Labor Apprenticeship Location: Camp	Construction and Extraction - Brickmasons, Blockmasons, and Stonemasons - Apprenticeship	60	High School Diploma or GED	BOP Employee Department of Labor Certificate Brick mason	0 / 0
Bricklayer Dept. of Labor Apprenticeship Location: Main	Construction and Extraction - Brickmasons, Blockmasons, and Stonemasons - Apprenticeship	60	High School Diploma or GED	BOP Employee Department of Labor Certificate Brick mason	0 / 0
Carpenter Dept. of Labor Apprenticeship Location: Camp	Construction and Extraction - Carpenters - Apprenticeship	60	High School Diploma or GED	BOP Employee Department of Labor Certificate Carpenter	0 / 0
Carpenter Dept. of Labor Apprenticeship Location: Main	Construction and Extraction - Carpenters - Apprenticeship	60	High School Diploma or GED	BOP Employee Department of Labor Certificate Carpenter	0 / 0
Certified Production Technician VT Location: Main	Production - Assemblers and Fabricators - Occ Ed Class	12	High School Diploma or GED	BOP Employee Industry-Recognized Certificate Certified Production Technician	0 / 0

Institution: OXFORD FCI   **(Cont'd)**

Culinary Arts Dept. of Labor Apprenticeship Location: Main	Food Preparation and Serving - Chefs and Head Cooks - Apprenticeship	18	High School Diploma or GED	BOP Employee Department of Labor Certificate Chef	0 / 22
Culinary Arts VT Location: Main	Food Preparation and Serving - Chefs and Head Cooks - Apprenticeship	18	High School Diploma or GED	BOP Employee Post-Secondary (College) Certificate & Industry Recognized Certificate Sous Chef	0 / 22
Dental Assistant Dept. of Labor Apprenticeship Location: Main	Production - Dental Laboratory Technicians - Apprenticeship	60	High School Diploma or GED	BOP Employee Department of Labor Certificate Dental Assistant	0 / 0
Electrician Dept. of Labor Apprenticeship Location: Camp	Construction and Extraction - Electricians - Apprenticeship	60	High School Diploma or GED	BOP Employee Department of Labor Certificate Electrician	0 / 0
Electrician Dept. of Labor Apprenticeship Location: Main	Construction and Extraction - Electricians - Apprenticeship	60	High School Diploma or GED	BOP Employee Department of Labor Certificate Electrician	0 / 0
Housekeeper Dept. of Labor Apprenticeship Location: Main	Building and Grounds Cleaning - Maids and Housekeeping Cleaners - Apprenticeship	24	High School Diploma or GED	BOP Employee Department of Labor Certificate Housekeeper	0 / 0

Institution: OXFORD FCI (Cont'd)

Housekeeper Dept. of Labor Apprenticeship Location: Camp	Building and Grounds Cleaning - Maids and Housekeeping Cleaners - Apprenticeship	24	High School Diploma or GED	BOP Employee Department of Labor Certificate Housekeeper	0 / 0
HVAC Dept. of Labor Apprenticeship Location: Camp	Installation, Maintenance, and Repair - Heating, Air Conditioning, and Refrigeration Mechanics and Installers - Apprenticeship	60	High School Diploma or GED	BOP Employee Department of Labor Certificate HVAC Technician	0 / 0
HVAC Dept. of Labor Apprenticeship Location: Main	Installation, Maintenance, and Repair - Heating, Air Conditioning, and Refrigeration Mechanics and Installers - Apprenticeship	60	High School Diploma or GED	BOP Employee Department of Labor Certificate HVAC Technician	0 / 0
Maintenance Repair Dept. of Labor Apprenticeship Location: Main	Installation, Maintenance, and Repair - General Maintenance and Repair Workers - Apprenticeship	60	High School Diploma or GED	BOP Employee Department of Labor Certificate Maintenance Repair Worker	0 / 0

Maintenance Repair Dept. of Labor Apprenticeship Location: Camp	Installation, Maintenance, and Repair - General Maintenance and Repair Workers - Apprenticeship	60	High School Diploma or GED	BOP Employee Department of Labor Certificate Maintenance Repair Worker	0 / 0
Painter Dept. of Labor Apprenticeship Location: Camp	Construction and Extraction - Painters, Construction and Maintenance - Apprenticeship	60	High School Diploma or GED	BOP Employee Department of Labor Certificate Painter	0 / 0
Painter Dept. of Labor Apprenticeship Location: Main	Construction and Extraction - Painters, Construction and Maintenance - Apprenticeship	60	High School Diploma or GED	BOP Employee Department of Labor Certificate Painter	0 / 0
Pipefitter Dept. of Labor Apprenticeship Location: Camp	Installation, Maintenance, and Repair - Line Installers and Repairers - Apprenticeship	60	High School Diploma or GED	BOP Employee Department of Labor Certificate Pipefitter	0 / 0
Pipefitter Dept. of Labor Apprenticeship Location: Main	Installation, Maintenance, and Repair - Line Installers and Repairers - Apprenticeship	60	High School Diploma or GED	BOP Employee Department of Labor Certificate Pipefitter	0 / 0

Institution: OXFORD FCI   **(Cont'd)**

Plumbing Dept. of Labor Apprenticeship Location: Camp	Construction and Extraction - Plumbers, Pipefitters, and Steamfitters - Apprenticeship	60	High School Diploma or GED	BOP Employee Department of Labor Certificate Plumber	0 / 0
Plumbing Dept. of Labor Apprenticeship Location: Main	Construction and Extraction - Plumbers, Pipefitters, and Steamfitters - Apprenticeship	60	High School Diploma or GED	BOP Employee Department of Labor Certificate Plumber	0 / 0
Stationary Engineer Dept. of Labor Apprenticeship Location: Camp	Installation, Maintenance, and Repair - Heating, Air Conditioning, and Refrigeration Mechanics and Installers - Apprenticeship	60	High School Diploma or GED	BOP Employee Department of Labor Certificate Boiler Operator	0 / 0
Waste Water Treatment Dept. of Labor Apprenticeship Location: Camp	Production - Water and Wastewater Treatment Plant and System Operators - Apprenticeship	36	High School Diploma or GED	BOP Employee Department of Labor Certificate Wastewater Treatment Plant Operator	0 / 0

Institution: PEKIN FCI

Certified Production Technician	Production	12	High School Diploma or GED	BOP Employee
Location: Main	- Assemblers and Fabricators		- One Year Clear Conduct	Industry-Recognized Certificate
	- Occ Ed Class			Certified Production Technician
				0 / 0
Computer Applications	Office and Administrative Support	10	High School Diploma or GED	BOP Employee
Location: Main	- Desktop Publishers		- One Year Clear Conduct	Post-Secondary (College) Certificate Only
	- Occ Ed Class			Computer Operator
				0 / 0
Computer Applications	Office and Administrative Support	10	High School Diploma or GED	BOP Employee
Location: Camp	- Desktop Publishers		- One Year Clear Conduct	Post-Secondary (College) Certificate Only
	- Occ Ed Class			Computer Operator
				0 / 0
Institutional Cook Apprenticeship	Food Preparation and Serving	36	High School Diploma or GED	BOP Employee
Location: Main	- Food Preparation Workers		- One Year Clear Conduct	Department of Labor Certificate
	- Apprenticeship			Institutional Cook
				0 / 0
Maintenance Electrician Apprenticeship	Construction and Extraction	48	High School Diploma or GED	BOP Employee
Location: Main	- Electricians		- One Year Clear Conduct	Department of Labor Certificate
	- Apprenticeship			Electrician
				0 / 0
Sheet Metal Worker Apprenticeship	Production	48	High School Diploma or GED	BOP Employee
Location: Main	- Assemblers and Fabricators		- One Year Clear Conduct	Department of Labor Certificate
	- Apprenticeship			Sheet Metal Worker

Institution: PENSACOLA FPC

Program	Location	Occupational Area	Months	Requirements	Certifications	
Baker	Location: Camp	Food Preparation and Serving - Cooks - Apprenticeship	36	Concurrent GED Enrollment	BOP Employee Department of Labor Certificate Baker	0 / 0
Carpenter	Location: Camp	Construction and Extraction - Carpenters - Apprenticeship	48	Concurrent GED Enrollment	BOP Employee Department of Labor Certificate Carpenter	0 / 0
CDL Class B	Location: Camp	Installation, Maintenance, and Repair - Automotive Service Technicians and Mechanics - Occ Ed Class	6	Concurrent GED Enrollment	Accredited Vocational/Technical School State Certificate CDL Class B Driver	0 / 0
Cook	Location: Camp	Food Preparation and Serving - Cooks - Apprenticeship	24	Concurrent GED Enrollment - 18 months remaining on sentence	BOP Employee Department of Labor Certificate Cook	0 / 0
Cook	Location: Camp	Food Preparation and Serving - Cooks - Apprenticeship	24	Concurrent GED Enrollment	BOP Employee Department of Labor Certificate Cook	0 / 0
Electrician	Location: Camp	Construction and Extraction - Electricians - Apprenticeship	48	Concurrent GED Enrollment	BOP Employee Department of Labor Certificate Electrician	0 / 0

Institution: PENSACOLA FPC   **(Cont'd)**

Greenskeeper II Location: Camp	Personal Care and Service - Recreation Workers - Apprenticeship	24	Concurrent GED Enrollment	BOP Employee Department of Labor Certificate Greenskeeper	0 / 0
Horticulturist Location: Camp	Building and Grounds Cleaning - Grounds Maintenance Workers - Apprenticeship	36	Concurrent GED Enrollment	BOP Employee Department of Labor Certificate Horticulturist	0 / 0
HVAC Technician Location: Camp	Installation, Maintenance, and Repair - Heating, Air Conditioning, and Refrigeration Mechanics and Installers - Apprenticeship	36	Concurrent GED Enrollment	BOP Employee Department of Labor Certificate HVAC Technician	0 / 0
Landscape Technician Location: Camp	Building and Grounds Cleaning - Grounds Maintenance Workers - Apprenticeship	24	Concurrent GED Enrollment	BOP Employee Department of Labor Certificate Landscape Technician	0 / 0
Marine Outboard Mechanic Location: Camp	Installation, Maintenance, and Repair - Small Engine Mechanics - Apprenticeship	48	Concurrent GED Enrollment	BOP Employee Department of Labor Certificate Marine Outboard Mechanic	0 / 0

Institution: PENSACOLA FPC   **(Cont'd)**

Plumber Location: Camp	Construction and Extraction - Plumbers, Pipefitters, and Steamfitters - Apprenticeship	48	Concurrent GED Enrollment	BOP Employee Department of Labor Certificate Plumber	0 / 0
Small Engine Mechanic Location: Camp	Installation, Maintenance, and Repair - Small Engine Mechanics - Apprenticeship	24	Concurrent GED Enrollment	BOP Employee Department of Labor Certificate Small Engine Mechanic	0 / 0

Institution: PETERSBURG FCI

Program	Occupation	Months	Education Requirement	Certificate	
Binder Apprenticeship Location: Main	Office and Administrative Support - Desktop Publishers - Apprenticeship	24	Concurrent GED Enrollment	Accredited Vocational/Technical School Department of Labor Certificate Binder	0 / 0
Carpentry VT Location: Main	Construction and Extraction - Carpenters - Occ Ed Class	12	High School Diploma or GED	Independent Contractor BOP Certificate & Industry Recognized Certificate Carpenter	0 / 0
Cook Apprenticeship Location: Main	Food Preparation and Serving - Cooks - Apprenticeship	36	High School Diploma or GED	Accredited Vocational/Technical School Department of Labor Certificate Cook	0 / 0
HVAC Apprenticeship Location: Main	Installation, Maintenance, and Repair - Heating, Air Conditioning, and Refrigeration Mechanics and Installers - Apprenticeship	48	High School Diploma or GED	Accredited Vocational/Technical School Department of Labor Certificate HVAC Technician	0 / 0
Landscape Apprenticeship Location: Main	Building and Grounds Cleaning - Grounds Maintenance Workers - Apprenticeship	48	High School Diploma or GED	Accredited Vocational/Technical School Department of Labor Certificate Landscape Technician	0 / 0

Institution: PETERSBURG FCI   (Cont'd)

Program / Location	Occupation		Requirement	Credential	
Machinist Apprenticeship Location: Main	Construction and Extraction - Construction Equipment Operators - Apprenticeship	48	High School Diploma or GED	BOP Employee BOP Certificate & Department of Labor Certificate Machinist	0 / 0
Machinist VT Location: Main	Construction and Extraction - Construction Equipment Operators - Occ Ed Class	12	High School Diploma or GED	BOP Employee BOP Certificate & Industry Recognized Certificate Machinist	0 / 0
Maintenance Electrician Apprenticeship Location: Main	Installation, Maintenance, and Repair - Electrical and Electronics Installers and Repairers - Apprenticeship	48	High School Diploma or GED	Accredited Post Secondary Institution Department of Labor Certificate Maintenance Electrician	0 / 0
Masonry VT Location: Main	Construction and Extraction - Brickmasons, Blockmasons, and Stonemasons - Occ Ed Class	12	High School Diploma or GED	BOP Employee BOP Certificate & Industry Recognized Certificate Brick mason	0 / 0
Plumbing Apprenticeship Location: Main	Installation, Maintenance, and Repair - Home Appliance Repairers - Apprenticeship	48	High School Diploma or GED	Accredited Vocational/Technical School Department of Labor Certificate Plumber	0 / 0

335

Institution: PETERSBURG MED FCI

AutoCAD VT Location: Main	Construction and Extraction - Construction Laborers and Helpers - Occ Ed Class	12	High School Diploma or GED	BOP Employee BOP Certificate & Industry Recognized Certificate AutoCAD Technician	0 / 0
Carpentry VT Location: Main	Construction and Extraction - Carpenters - Apprenticeship	48	High School Diploma or GED	BOP Employee BOP Certificate & Industry Recognized Certificate Carpenter	0 / 0
HVAC Apprenticeship Location: Main	Installation, Maintenance, and Repair - Heating, Air Conditioning, and Refrigeration Mechanics and Installers - Apprenticeship	36	High School Diploma or GED	Accredited Vocational/Technical School Department of Labor Certificate HVAC Technician	0 / 0
Landscape Apprenticeship Location: Main	Farming, Fishing, and Forestry - Agricultural Workers - Apprenticeship	48	High School Diploma or GED	Accredited Vocational/Technical School BOP Certificate & Department of Labor Certificate Landscape Worker	0 / 0
Plumbing Apprenticeship Location: Main	Installation, Maintenance, and Repair - General Maintenance and Repair Workers - Apprenticeship	48	High School Diploma or GED	Accredited Vocational/Technical School Department of Labor Certificate Plumber	0 / 0

336

Institution: PHOENIX FCI

Program	Occupation	Duration	Prerequisite	Certification	
Cook Apprenticeship Location: Camp	Food Preparation and Serving – Chefs and Head Cooks – Apprenticeship	30	High School Diploma or GED -	BOP Employee Department of Labor Certificate Cook	0 / 0
Cook Apprenticeship Location: Main	Food Preparation and Serving – Chefs and Head Cooks – Apprenticeship	30	High School Diploma or GED -	BOP Employee Department of Labor Certificate Cook	0 / 0
Electrical Apprenticeship Location: Camp	Installation, Maintenance, and Repair – Electrical and Electronics Installers and Repairers – Apprenticeship	60	High School Diploma or GED -	BOP Employee Department of Labor Certificate Electrician	0 / 0
Electrical Apprenticeship Location: Main	Installation, Maintenance, and Repair – Electrical and Electronics Installers and Repairers – Apprenticeship	60	High School Diploma or GED -	BOP Employee Department of Labor Certificate Electrician	0 / 0
Electronics Tester Apprenticeship Location: Camp	Production – Quality Control Inspectors – Apprenticeship	45	High School Diploma or GED -	BOP Employee Department of Labor Certificate Electronics Tester	0 / 0
Electronics Tester Apprenticeship Location: Main	Production – Quality Control Inspectors – Apprenticeship	45	High School Diploma or GED -	BOP Employee Department of Labor Certificate Electronics Tester	0 / 0

Institution: PHOENIX FCI   (Cont'd)

Electronics Utility Worker Apprenticeship Location: Main	Installation, Maintenance, and Repair - Electrical and Electronics Installers and Repairers - Apprenticeship	60	High School Diploma or GED -	BOP Employee Department of Labor Certificate Electronics Utility Worker	0 / 0
Electronics Utility Worker Apprenticeship Location: Camp	Installation, Maintenance, and Repair - Electrical and Electronics Installers and Repairers - Apprenticeship	60	High School Diploma or GED -	BOP Employee Department of Labor Certificate Electronics Utility Worker	0 / 0
Front-End Mechanic Apprenticeship Location: Camp	Installation, Maintenance, and Repair - General Maintenance and Repair Workers - Apprenticeship	20	High School Diploma or GED -	BOP Employee Department of Labor Certificate Front-End Mechanic	0 / 0
HVAC Apprenticeship Location: Camp	Installation, Maintenance, and Repair - Heating, Air Conditioning, and Refrigeration Mechanics and Installers - Apprenticeship	60	High School Diploma or GED -	BOP Employee Department of Labor Certificate HVAC Technician	0 / 0

Institution: PHOENIX FCI   (Cont'd)

HVAC Apprenticeship Location: Main	Installation, Maintenance, and Repair - Heating, Air Conditioning, and Refrigeration Mechanics and Installers - Apprenticeship	60	High School Diploma or GED -	BOP Employee Department of Labor Certificate HVAC Technician	0 / 0
Landscape Management Technician Apprenticeship Location: Camp	Installation, Maintenance, and Repair - General Maintenance and Repair Workers - Apprenticeship	30	High School Diploma or GED -	BOP Employee Department of Labor Certificate Landscape Management Technician	0 / 0
Landscape Management Technician Apprenticeship Location: Main	Installation, Maintenance, and Repair - General Maintenance and Repair Workers - Apprenticeship	30	High School Diploma or GED -	BOP Employee Department of Labor Certificate Landscape Management Technician	0 / 0
Plumbing Apprenticeship Location: Camp	Installation, Maintenance, and Repair - General Maintenance and Repair Workers - Apprenticeship	60	High School Diploma or GED -	BOP Employee Department of Labor Certificate Plumber	0 / 0

Institution: PHOENIX FCI   (Cont'd)

Program / Location	Occupation		Education	Credential	Completions
Plumbing Apprenticeship Location: Main	Installation, Maintenance, and Repair - General Maintenance and Repair Workers - Apprenticeship	60	High School Diploma or GED -	BOP Employee Department of Labor Certificate Plumber	0 / 0
Principles of Construction Location: Main	Construction and Extraction - Construction Laborers and Helpers - Occ Ed Class	3	High School Diploma or GED	BOP Employee BOP Certificate & Industry Recognized Certificate General Laborer	0 / 0
Quality Control Apprenticeship Location: Camp	Production - Quality Control Inspectors - Apprenticeship	30	High School Diploma or GED -	BOP Employee Department of Labor Certificate Quality Control Specialist	0 / 0
Quality Control Apprenticeship Location: Main	Production - Quality Control Inspectors - Apprenticeship	30	High School Diploma or GED -	BOP Employee Department of Labor Certificate Quality Control Specialist	0 / 0
VT Basic Principles of Construction Location: Camp	Construction and Extraction - Construction Laborers and Helpers - Occ Ed Class	3	High School Diploma or GED	BOP Employee BOP Certificate & Industry Recognized Certificate Construction	0 / 0
VT Basic Principles of Construction Location: PCU	Construction and Extraction - Construction Laborers and Helpers - Occ Ed Class	3	High School Diploma or GED	BOP Employee BOP Certificate & Industry Recognized Certificate Construction Worker	0 / 0

Institution: PHOENIX FCI   (Cont'd)

VT Carpentry Location: Camp	Construction and Extraction - Carpenters - Occ Ed Class	4	Concurrent GED Enrollment	BOP Employee BOP Certificate & Industry Recognized Certificate Carpenter	0 / 0
VT Carpentry Location: PCU	Construction and Extraction - Carpenters - Occ Ed Class	4	High School Diploma or GED	BOP Employee BOP Certificate & Industry Recognized Certificate Carpenter	0 / 0
VT Carpentry Location: Main	Construction and Extraction - Construction Laborers and Helpers - Occ Ed Class	3	Concurrent GED Enrollment -	BOP Employee BOP Certificate & Industry Recognized Certificate Apprentice Carpenter	0 / 0
VT Electrical Location: Main	Construction and Extraction - Construction Laborers and Helpers - Occ Ed Class	3	Concurrent GED Enrollment -	BOP Employee BOP Certificate & Industry Recognized Certificate Electrical Apprentice	0 / 0
VT Electrical Location: Camp	Construction and Extraction - Carpenters - Occ Ed Class	3	High School Diploma or GED	BOP Employee BOP Certificate & Industry Recognized Certificate Electrician	0 / 0

Institution: PHOENIX FCI   **(Cont'd)**

VT Plumbing	Construction and Extraction	3	Concurrent GED Enrollment	BOP Employee	0 / 0
Location: Main	- Construction Laborers and Helpers		-	BOP Certificate & Industry Recognized Certificate	
	- Occ Ed Class			Plumbing Apprentice	
VT ServSafe	Food Preparation and Serving	3	Concurrent GED Enrollment	BOP Employee	0 / 0
Location: Camp	- Food Preparation Workers			Industry-Recognized Certificate	
	- Occ Ed Class			ServSafe Certified Food Service Worker	

Institution: POLLOCK MED FCI

Program			Credential	Outcomes
Building Trades Location: Main	Construction and Extraction - Painters, Construction and Maintenance - Occ Ed Class	12	High School Diploma or GED	Accredited Vocational/Technical School Both Vo-Tech School and Industry-Recognized Certificates Painter, Construction Worker, or Maintenance Worker	0 / 0
Business Management Location: Main	Office and Administrative Support - Bookkeeping, Accounting, and Auditing Clerks - Occ Ed Class	12	High School Diploma or GED	BOP Employee Vocational/Technical School Certificate Only Bookkeeping, Accounting and/or Auditing Clerk	0 / 45
Culinary Arts Location: Main	Food Preparation and Serving - Food and Beverage Serving and Related Workers - Occ Ed Class	12	High School Diploma or GED	BOP Employee BOP Certificate & Industry Recognized Certificate Food Service Worker	0 / 0
Custodial Maintenance Location: Main	Building and Grounds Cleaning - Janitors and Building Cleaners - Occ Ed Class	3	Concurrent GED Enrollment	BOP Employee BOP Certificate & Industry Recognized Certificate Janitor and/or Floor Care Technician	0 / 0
Outdoor Motors Location: Main	Installation, Maintenance, and Repair - Small Engine Mechanics - Occ Ed Class	12	High School Diploma or GED	Accredited Vocational/Technical School Both Vo-Tech School and Industry-Recognized Certificates Small Engine Mechanic	0 / 0

Institution: POLLOCK MED FCI   (Cont'd)

Sewing	Production	6	Concurrent GED Enrollment	BOP Employee	0 / 0
Location: Main	- Sewers and Tailors - Occ Ed Class			Vocational/Technical School Certificate Only Sewer or Tailor	

Institution: POLLOCK USP

Program / Location		Credential		Certifications	
Building Trades Location: Main	Construction and Extraction - Painters, Construction and Maintenance - Occ Ed Class	12	High School Diploma or GED	BOP Employee Both Vo-Tech School and Industry-Recognized Certificates Painter, Construction Worker, or Maintenance Worker	0 / 0
Business Management Location: Main	Office and Administrative Support - Bookkeeping, Accounting, and Auditing Clerks - Occ Ed Class	12	High School Diploma or GED	Accredited Vocational/Technical School Vocational/Technical School Certificate Only Bookkeeping, Accounting, or Auditing Clerk	0 / 45
Business Management Location: Camp	Office and Administrative Support - Bookkeeping, Accounting, and Auditing Clerks - Occ Ed Class	12	High School Diploma or GED	Accredited Vocational/Technical School Vocational/Technical School Certificate Only Bookkeeping, Accounting, or Auditing Clerk	0 / 45
Culinary Arts Location: Main	Food Preparation and Serving - Food and Beverage Serving and Related Workers - Occ Ed Class	12	High School Diploma or GED	BOP Employee BOP Certificate & Industry Recognized Certificate Food Service Worker	0 / 0

Institution: POLLOCK USP   **(Cont'd)**

Custodial Maintenance Location: Main	Building and Grounds Cleaning - Janitors and Building Cleaners - Occ Ed Class	3	Concurrent GED Enrollment	BOP Employee BOP Certificate & Industry Recognized Certificate Janitor and/or Floor Care Technician	0 / 0
Custodial Maintenance Location: Camp	Building and Grounds Cleaning - Janitors and Building Cleaners - Occ Ed Class	3	Concurrent GED Enrollment	BOP Employee BOP Certificate & Industry Recognized Certificate Janitor and/or Floor Care Technician	0 / 0
Microcomputer Applications Location: Main	Office and Administrative Support - General Office Clerks - Occ Ed Class	6	High School Diploma or GED	BOP Employee Vocational/Technical School Certificate Only General Office Clerk	0 / 0
Microcomputer Applications Location: Camp	Office and Administrative Support - General Office Clerks - Occ Ed Class	6	High School Diploma or GED	BOP Employee Vocational/Technical School Certificate Only General Office Clerk	0 / 0

Institution: RAY BROOK FCI

Course		Enrollment	Prerequisites	Certifications	0 / 0
Associate Certified Electronics Technician Location: Main	Installation, Maintenance, and Repair - Electrical and Electronics Installers and Repairers - Occ Ed Class	10	High School Diploma or GED	BOP Employee Industry-Recognized Certificate Electronics Technician	0 / 0
Building Maintenance Repairer Location: Main	Installation, Maintenance, and Repair - General Maintenance and Repair Workers - Apprenticeship	24	High School Diploma or GED - Must be employed in specific work assignment	BOP Employee BOP Certificate & Department of Labor Certificate Building Maintenance and Repairer	0 / 0
Business Math 1 Location: Main	Office and Administrative Support - General Office Clerks - Occ Ed Class	5	Concurrent GED Enrollment	BOP Employee BOP Certificate Only Administrative Assistant	0 / 0
Business Math 2 Location: Main	Office and Administrative Support - General Office Clerks - Occ Ed Class	5	Concurrent GED Enrollment	BOP Employee BOP Certificate Only Administrative Assistant	0 / 0
Business Word 1 Location: Main	Office and Administrative Support - General Office Clerks - Occ Ed Class	5	Concurrent GED Enrollment	BOP Employee BOP Certificate Only Administrative Assistant	

Program / Location	Occupation	Number	Requirements	Credential	
Business Word 2 Location: Main	Office and Administrative Support - General Office Clerks - Occ Ed Class	4	Concurrent GED Enrollment	BOP Employee BOP Certificate Only Administrative Assistant	0 / 0
Career Development Technician Location: Main	Education, Training, and Library - Career and Technical Education Teachers - Apprenticeship	27	High School Diploma or GED - Must be employed in specific work assignment	BOP Employee BOP Certificate & Department of Labor Certificate Human Resources and Training, and Labor Relations Specialist	0 / 0
Credentialed Alcohol Substance Abuse Counselor Location: Main	Community and Social Service - Rehabilitation Counselors - Occ Ed Class	10	High School Diploma or GED	Independent Contractor Industry-Recognized Certificate Substance Abuse/Rehabilitation Counselor	0 / 0
Customer Service Specialist Location: Main	Office and Administrative Support - Customer Service Representatives - Occ Ed Class	4	Concurrent GED Enrollment	BOP Employee Industry-Recognized Certificate Customer Service Representative	0 / 0
Education and Training Location: Main	Education, Training, and Library - Teacher Assistants - Apprenticeship	24	High School Diploma or GED - Must be employed in specific work assignment	BOP Employee BOP Certificate & Department of Labor Certificate Teacher Assistant and Career Center Employee	0 / 0

Institution: RAY BROOK FCI   (Cont'd)

Course	Occupation	Count	Requirements	Certification	0 / 0
Housekeeping Location: Main	Building and Grounds Cleaning - Janitors and Building Cleaners - Apprenticeship	48	High School Diploma or GED - Must be employed in specific work assignment	BOP Employee BOP Certificate & Department of Labor Certificate Janitor	0 / 0
Introduction to Customer Service Specialist Location: Main	Office and Administrative Support - Customer Service Representatives - Occ Ed Class	4	Concurrent GED Enrollment	BOP Employee BOP Certificate Only Customer Service	0 / 0
Office Manager/Administrative Services Location: Main	Office and Administrative Support - Material Recording Clerks - Apprenticeship	24	High School Diploma or GED - Must be employed in specific work assignment	BOP Employee BOP Certificate & Department of Labor Certificate Office Manager	0 / 0
Recreation Assistant Location: Main	Personal Care and Service - Recreation Workers - Apprenticeship	27	High School Diploma or GED - Must be employed in specific work assignment	BOP Employee BOP Certificate & Department of Labor Certificate Recreation Assistant	0 / 0

Institution: ROCHESTER FMC

Program	Program Area	Hours	Education Requirement	Provider / Credential	Capacity
Biomedical Equipment Repair Apprenticeship Location: Main	Installation, Maintenance, and Repair - Medical Equipment Repairers - Apprenticeship	36	High School Diploma or GED	BOP Employee Department of Labor Certificate Medical Equipment Repairer	0 / 0
Electrical Apprenticeship Location: Main	Construction and Extraction - Electricians - Apprenticeship	48	High School Diploma or GED	BOP Employee Department of Labor Certificate Electrician	0 / 0
HVAC Apprenticeship Location: Main	Installation, Maintenance, and Repair - Heating, Air Conditioning, and Refrigeration Mechanics and Installers - Apprenticeship	48	High School Diploma or GED	BOP Employee Department of Labor Certificate Heating, Air Conditioning, and Refrigeration Mechanic	0 / 0
Landscape Management Technician VT Location: Main	Building and Grounds Cleaning - Grounds Maintenance Workers - Occ Ed Class	12	High School Diploma or GED	Independent Contractor Vocational/Technical School Certificate Only Landscaper	60 / 0
Painting Apprenticeship Location: Main	Construction and Extraction - Painters, Construction and Maintenance - Apprenticeship	36	High School Diploma or GED	BOP Employee Department of Labor Certificate Painter	0 / 0

Institution: ROCHESTER FMC   **(Cont'd)**

Plumbing Apprenticeship Location: Main	Construction and Extraction - Plumbers, Pipefitters, and Steamfitters - Apprenticeship	48	High School Diploma or GED	BOP Employee Department of Labor Certificate Plumber	0 / 0

Institution: SAFFORD FCI

Program	Occupation	Duration	Requirements	Credentials	Enrolled/Completed
Cabinetmaker Apprenticeship Location: Main	Production - Woodworkers - Apprenticeship	48	High School Diploma or GED - English Proficient	BOP Employee BOP Certificate & Department of Labor Certificate Journeyman Cabinetmaker	0 / 0
Culinary Apprenticeship Location: Main	Food Preparation and Serving - Cooks - Apprenticeship	24	High School Diploma or GED	BOP Employee BOP Certificate & Department of Labor Certificate Journeyman Cook	0 / 0
Dental Assistant Apprenticeship Location: Main	Production - Dental Laboratory Technicians - Apprenticeship	24	High School Diploma or GED - English Proficient	BOP Employee BOP Certificate & Department of Labor Certificate Journeyman Dental Assistant	0 / 0
Electrical Apprenticeship Location: Main	Construction and Extraction - Electricians - Apprenticeship	48	High School Diploma or GED	BOP Employee BOP Certificate & Department of Labor Certificate Journeyman Electrician Maintenance	0 / 0
HVAC Apprenticeship Location: Main	Construction and Extraction - Electricians - Apprenticeship	48	High School Diploma or GED	BOP Employee BOP Certificate & Department of Labor Certificate Journeyman HVAC Repairman	0 / 0

Institution: SAFFORD FCI   **(Cont'd)**

Program	Location	Count	Requirements		Credentials
Plumbing Apprenticeship	Location: Main	Construction and Extraction - Plumbers, Pipefitters, and Steamfitters - Apprenticeship	48	High School Diploma or GED	BOP Employee BOP Certificate & Department of Labor Certificate Journeyman Plumber	0 / 0
VT Business	Location: Main	Business and Financial - Accountants and Auditors - Occ Ed Class	3	High School Diploma or GED - English Proficient	Accredited Post Secondary Institution Post-Secondary (College) Certificate & Industry Recognized Certificate Small Business Manager	0 / 17
VT Carpentry	Location: Main	Construction and Extraction - Carpenters - Occ Ed Class	4	High School Diploma or GED - English Proficient	Accredited Post Secondary Institution Post-Secondary (College) Certificate & Industry Recognized Certificate Residential Framer	0 / 17
VT HVAC	Location: Main	Construction and Extraction - Electricians - Occ Ed Class	3	High School Diploma or GED - English Proficient	Accredited Post Secondary Institution Post-Secondary (College) Certificate & Industry Recognized Certificate HVAC Repairman	0 / 19

Institution: SAFFORD FCI (Cont'd)

VT Retail Management	3	High School Diploma or GED	Accredited Post Secondary Institution	0 / 18
Location: Main		- English Proficient		
Business and Financial			Post-Secondary (College) Certificate & Industry Recognized Certificate	
- Purchasing Managers, Buyers, and Purchasing Agents				
- Occ Ed Class			Retail Manager	

Institution: SANDSTONE FCI

Baker Location: Main	Food Preparation and Serving - Cooks - Apprenticeship	36	High School Diploma or GED	BOP Employee BOP Certificate & Department of Labor Certificate Baker	0 / 0
Bindery Worker Location: Main	Production - Printing Workers - Apprenticeship	48	High School Diploma or GED	BOP Employee BOP Certificate & Department of Labor Certificate Print Binding and Finishing Workers	0 / 0
Can Do Canines VT Program Location: PCU	Personal Care and Service - Animal Care and Service Workers - Occ Ed Class	12	High School Diploma or GED	Independent Contractor Post-Secondary (College) Certificate Only Dog Trainer	0 / 0
Career Development Technician Location: Main	Education, Training, and Library - Career and Technical Education Teachers - Apprenticeship	27	High School Diploma or GED	BOP Employee BOP Certificate & Department of Labor Certificate Human Resources and Training, and Labor Relations Specialist	0 / 0
Cook Location: Main	Food Preparation and Serving - Food Preparation Workers - Apprenticeship	24	High School Diploma or GED	BOP Employee BOP Certificate & Department of Labor Certificate Cook	0 / 0

Institution: SANDSTONE FCI   **(Cont'd)**

Program	Occupation	Months	Education	Certification	
Dental Assistant Location: Main	Production - Dental Laboratory Technicians - Apprenticeship	12	High School Diploma or GED	BOP Employee BOP Certificate & Department of Labor Certificate Dental Assistant	0 / 0
Heating & Air conditioning Installer-Servicer Location: Main	Installation, Maintenance, and Repair - Heating, Air Conditioning, and Refrigeration Mechanics and Installers - Apprenticeship	36	High School Diploma or GED	BOP Employee BOP Certificate & Department of Labor Certificate Heating & Air conditioning Installer-Servicer	0 / 0
Housekeeper, Commercial, Residential, or Industrial Location: Main	Building and Grounds Cleaning - Janitors and Building Cleaners - Apprenticeship	12	High School Diploma or GED	BOP Employee BOP Certificate & Department of Labor Certificate Janitors and Cleaners	0 / 0
Landscape Management Technician Location: Main	Building and Grounds Cleaning - Grounds Maintenance Workers - Apprenticeship	12	High School Diploma or GED	BOP Employee BOP Certificate & Department of Labor Certificate Grounds Maintenance Worker	0 / 0
Maintenance Mechanic Location: Main	Installation, Maintenance, and Repair - Automotive Service Technicians and Mechanics - Apprenticeship	48	High School Diploma or GED	BOP Employee BOP Certificate & Department of Labor Certificate Maintenance Mechanic	0 / 0

Institution: SANDSTONE FCI   **(Cont'd)**

Office Manager/Admin Services Location: Main	Office and Administrative Support - General Office Clerks - Apprenticeship	24	High School Diploma or GED	BOP Employee BOP Certificate & Department of Labor Certificate Administrative Services Manager	0 / 0
Offset-Press Operator 1 Location: Main	Production - Printing Workers - Apprenticeship	48	High School Diploma or GED	BOP Employee BOP Certificate & Department of Labor Certificate Press Operator	0 / 0
Photographer Location: Main	Production - Printing Workers - Apprenticeship	48	High School Diploma or GED	BOP Employee BOP Certificate & Department of Labor Certificate Graphic Design	0 / 0
Quality Control Inspector Location: Main	Production - Quality Control Inspectors - Apprenticeship	24	High School Diploma or GED	BOP Employee BOP Certificate & Department of Labor Certificate Quality Assurance Technician	0 / 0
ServSafe Food Handler Location: Main	Food Preparation and Serving - Food Preparation Workers - Occ Ed Class	3	High School Diploma or GED	BOP Employee Industry-Recognized Certificate Food Preparer/Handler	0 / 0

Institution: SANDSTONE FCI   (Cont'd)

Program / Location	Occupation		Education	Outcome	
Sewing Machine Repairer Location: Main	Installation, Maintenance, and Repair - Industrial Machinery Mechanics and Maintenance Workers - Apprenticeship	36	High School Diploma or GED	BOP Employee BOP Certificate & Department of Labor Certificate Sewing Machine Repairer	0 / 0
Vocational Auto Location: Main	Installation, Maintenance, and Repair - Automotive Service Technicians and Mechanics - Occ Ed Class	6	High School Diploma or GED -	BOP Employee Post-Secondary (College) Certificate & Industry Recognized Certificate Auto Mechanic/Technician	0 / 0
Vocational Building Trades Location: Main	Construction and Extraction - Carpenters - Occ Ed Class	6	High School Diploma or GED -	Independent Contractor Post-Secondary (College) Certificate Only Carpenter/ Masonry Worker	0 / 0
Vocational Culinary Location: Main	Food Preparation and Serving - Chefs and Head Cooks - Apprenticeship	12	High School Diploma or GED -	BOP Employee Post-Secondary (College) Certificate & Industry Recognized Certificate Chef/Cook	0 / 0
Vocational Welding Location: Main	Production - Welders, Cutters, Solderers, and Brazers - Apprenticeship	6	High School Diploma or GED -	BOP Employee Post-Secondary (College) Certificate Only Welder	0 / 0

Institution: SANDSTONE FCI   **(Cont'd)**

Welder, Combination	Production	36	High School Diploma or GED	BOP Employee	0 / 0
Location: Main	- Welders, Cutters, Solderers, and Brazers			BOP Certificate & Department of Labor Certificate	
	- Apprenticeship			Welder	

Institution: SCHUYLKILL FCI

Program / Location	Occupation		Education Requirement	Credentials	Completed
Basic Residential Wiring Location: Main	Construction and Extraction - Electricians - Occ Ed Class	4	High School Diploma or GED	BOP Employee BOP Certificate Only Residential Electrician Helper	0 / 0
Commercial Driver's License Class A Location: Camp	Office and Administrative Support - Cargo and Freight Agents - Occ Ed Class	2	High School Diploma or GED - Valid PA Driver's License	Accredited Vocational/Technical School State Certificate Class A Truck Driver	0 / 0
Cook Location: Main	Food Preparation and Serving - Cooks - Apprenticeship	24	High School Diploma or GED	BOP Employee Department of Labor Certificate Cook	0 / 0
Cook Location: Camp	Food Preparation and Serving - Cooks - Apprenticeship	24	High School Diploma or GED	BOP Employee Department of Labor Certificate Cook	0 / 0
Culinary Arts Location: Main	Food Preparation and Serving - Cooks - Occ Ed Class	5	High School Diploma or GED	BOP Employee Industry-Recognized Certificate Cook	0 / 0
Horticulture Location: Camp	Building and Grounds Cleaning - Grounds Maintenance Workers - Occ Ed Class	3	High School Diploma or GED	BOP Employee Industry-Recognized Certificate Lawn Care Worker	0 / 0

Institution: SCHUYLKILL FCI (Cont'd)

Landscaping	Building and Grounds Cleaning	3	High School Diploma or GED	BOP Employee	0 / 0
Location: Camp	- Grounds Maintenance Workers			Industry-Recognized Certificate	
	- Occ Ed Class			Landscape Worker	

Institution: SEAGOVILLE FCI

Program	Category	Count	Enrollment Requirement	Accreditation / Certificate	Ratio
Auto Mechanic Location: Main	Installation, Maintenance, and Repair - Automotive Service Technicians and Mechanics - Occ Ed Class	4	Concurrent GED Enrollment	Accredited Vocational/Technical School Vocational/Technical School Certificate Only Auto Mechanic	32 / 0
Automotive Technician Location: Main	Installation, Maintenance, and Repair - Automotive Service Technicians and Mechanics - Occ Ed Class	25	Concurrent GED Enrollment	Accredited Post Secondary Institution Vocational/Technical School Certificate Only Automotive Technician	42 / 0
Computer Graphics and Design Location: Main	Office and Administrative Support - Desktop Publishers - Occ Ed Class	2	High School Diploma or GED	Accredited Vocational/Technical School Vocational/Technical School Certificate Only Computer Graphics and Design	12 / 0
Construction Tech Location: Main	Construction and Extraction - Construction Laborers and Helpers - Occ Ed Class	3	Concurrent GED Enrollment	Accredited Post Secondary Institution Industry-Recognized Certificate Construction Technician	34 / 0
Core Construction Location: Main	Construction and Extraction - Construction Laborers and Helpers - Occ Ed Class	2	Concurrent GED Enrollment	Accredited Post Secondary Institution Industry-Recognized Certificate Construction Technician	34 / 0

Institution: SEAGOVILLE FCI   (Cont'd)

Heating and Air Conditioning (HVAC)	Construction and Extraction	3	Concurrent GED Enrollment	Accredited Post Secondary Institution
Location: Main	- Plumbers, Pipefitters, and Steamfitters			Industry-Recognized Certificate
	- Occ Ed Class			Heating and Air Conditioning Tech
				36 / 0
Landscape Design	Building and Grounds Cleaning	4	Concurrent GED Enrollment	Accredited Post Secondary Institution
Location: Main	- Grounds Maintenance Workers			Vocational/Technical School Certificate Only
	- Occ Ed Class			Landscape Design Technician
				26 / 0
Turfgrass	Building and Grounds Cleaning	4	Concurrent GED Enrollment	Accredited Post Secondary Institution
Location: Main	- Grounds Maintenance Workers			Vocational/Technical School Certificate Only
	- Occ Ed Class			Turfgrass Technician
				34 / 0

Institution: SHERIDAN FCI

Program / Location	Occupation	Count	Prerequisite	Certification	Ratio
AOE QuickBooks Location: Main	Business and Financial - Accountants and Auditors - Occ Ed Class	3	High School Diploma or GED	Accredited Post Secondary Institution Post-Secondary (College) Certificate Only Book Keeper	0 / 3
Baker Location: Main	Food Preparation and Serving - Chefs and Head Cooks - Apprenticeship	60	High School Diploma or GED	BOP Employee BOP Certificate & Department of Labor Certificate Baker/Cook	60 / 0
Barber Apprenticeship Location: Camp	Personal Care and Service - Barbers, Hairdressers, and Cosmetologists - Apprenticeship	24	High School Diploma or GED - Sanitation ACE Course	BOP Employee Department of Labor Certificate Barber	0 / 0
Basic Woodworking Location: Main	Production - Woodworkers - Occ Ed Class	4	High School Diploma or GED	BOP Employee BOP Certificate Only Woodworker	0 / 0
Building Maintenance Location: Main	Installation, Maintenance, and Repair - General Maintenance and Repair Workers - Apprenticeship	40	High School Diploma or GED	BOP Employee BOP Certificate & Department of Labor Certificate General Maintenance and Repair Workers	40 / 0

Institution: SHERIDAN FCI   (Cont'd)

Program	Occupation	Seats	Requirements	Certifications	Completions
Building Trades Location: Main	Construction and Extraction - Construction Laborers and Helpers - Occ Ed Class	4	High School Diploma or GED - Math Pre-Enrollment Exam	BOP Employee BOP Certificate Only Construction/Framer	0 / 0
Building Trades Location: Camp	Construction and Extraction - Construction Laborers and Helpers - Occ Ed Class	4	High School Diploma or GED - Math Pre-Enrollment Exam	BOP Employee BOP Certificate Only Construction/Framer	0 / 0
Cabinet Worker Location: Main	Production - Woodworkers - Apprenticeship	40	High School Diploma or GED	BOP Employee BOP Certificate & Department of Labor Certificate Cabinet Worker/Woodworker	40 / 0
Career Center Clerk Location: Main	Community and Social Service - School and Career Counselors - Apprenticeship	20	High School Diploma or GED	BOP Employee BOP Certificate & Department of Labor Certificate Career Counselor	20 / 0
Career Clerk Location: Camp	Community and Social Service - School and Career Counselors - Apprenticeship	20	High School Diploma or GED	BOP Employee BOP Certificate & Department of Labor Certificate Career Counselor	20 / 0

365

Institution: SHERIDAN FCI   **(Cont'd)**

Computer Aided Design (CAD) Location: Camp	Construction and Extraction - Construction and Building Inspectors - Occ Ed Class	3	High School Diploma or GED	BOP Employee BOP Certificate Only Drafting, home design assistant	0 / 0
Computer-Aided Design (CAD) Location: Main	Construction and Extraction - Construction and Building Inspectors - Occ Ed Class	3	High School Diploma or GED	BOP Employee BOP Certificate Only Architect/Contractor	0 / 0
Cook Location: Main	Food Preparation and Serving - Cooks - Apprenticeship	60	High School Diploma or GED	BOP Employee BOP Certificate & Department of Labor Certificate Cooks	60 / 0
Dental Assistant Location: Camp	Community and Social Service - Health Educators - Apprenticeship	12	High School Diploma or GED	BOP Employee BOP Certificate & Department of Labor Certificate Dental Assistant	20 / 0
Desktop Publisher Location: Main	Office and Administrative Support - General Office Clerks - Occ Ed Class	3	High School Diploma or GED - Typing 30 WPM	Accredited Post Secondary Institution Post-Secondary (College) Certificate Only Administrative Support	0 / 2

Institution: SHERIDAN FCI (Cont'd)

Desktop Publisher Location: Camp	Office and Administrative Support - General Office Clerks - Occ Ed Class	3	High School Diploma or GED - Typing 30 WPM	Accredited Post Secondary Institution Post-Secondary (College) Certificate Only Administrative Support	0 / 2
Electrical Location: Main	Construction and Extraction - Electricians - Apprenticeship	60	High School Diploma or GED	BOP Employee BOP Certificate & Department of Labor Certificate Electrician	60 / 0
Electrical Location: Camp	Construction and Extraction - Electricians - Apprenticeship	60	High School Diploma or GED	BOP Employee BOP Certificate & Department of Labor Certificate Electrician	60 / 0
Farmworker Location: Camp	Farming, Fishing, and Forestry - Agricultural Workers - Apprenticeship	20	High School Diploma or GED	BOP Employee BOP Certificate & Department of Labor Certificate Farmworker	20 / 0
HVAC Location: Main	Installation, Maintenance, and Repair - Heating, Air Conditioning, and Refrigeration Mechanics and Installers - Apprenticeship	60	High School Diploma or GED	BOP Employee BOP Certificate & Department of Labor Certificate HVAC	60 / 0

Program / Location	Occupation	Count	Prerequisites	Certification	Ratio
HVAC Location: Camp	Installation, Maintenance, and Repair - Heating, Air Conditioning, and Refrigeration Mechanics and Installers - Apprenticeship	60	High School Diploma or GED	BOP Employee BOP Certificate & Department of Labor Certificate HVAC	60 / 0
Landscape Design Location: Camp	Building and Grounds Cleaning - Grounds Maintenance Workers - Occ Ed Class	6	High School Diploma or GED - Exception to GED if 480+ hours achieved	BOP Employee BOP Certificate Only Landscaper	0 / 0
Landscape Management Technician Location: Main	Farming, Fishing, and Forestry - Agricultural Workers - Apprenticeship	24	No Pre-Requisites Required	BOP Employee Department of Labor Certificate Gardener, landscaper	0 / 0
Landscape Technician Location: Camp	Farming, Fishing, and Forestry - Agricultural Workers - Apprenticeship	40	High School Diploma or GED	BOP Employee BOP Certificate & Department of Labor Certificate Landscape Designer	40 / 0
Microsoft Excel Location: Main	Office and Administrative Support - General Office Clerks - Occ Ed Class	3	High School Diploma or GED - Typing 30 WPM	Accredited Post Secondary Institution Post-Secondary (College) Certificate Only Administrative Support	0 / 3

Institution: SHERIDAN FCI   (Cont'd)

Program / Location	Occupation		Requirements	Credential	
Microsoft Excel Location: Camp	Office and Administrative Support - General Office Clerks - Occ Ed Class	3	High School Diploma or GED - Typing 30 WPM	Accredited Post Secondary Institution Post-Secondary (College) Certificate Only Administrative Support	0 / 3
Microsoft PowerPoint Location: Main	Office and Administrative Support - General Office Clerks - Occ Ed Class	3	High School Diploma or GED - Typing 30 WPM	Accredited Post Secondary Institution Post-Secondary (College) Certificate Only Administrative Support	0 / 3
Microsoft PowerPoint Location: Camp	Office and Administrative Support - General Office Clerks - Occ Ed Class	3	High School Diploma or GED - Typing 30 WPM	Accredited Post Secondary Institution Post-Secondary (College) Certificate Only Administrative Support	0 / 3
Microsoft PowerPoint (AOE) Location: Camp	Office and Administrative Support - General Office Clerks - Occ Ed Class	1	High School Diploma or GED	Accredited Post Secondary Institution Post-Secondary (College) Certificate Only Office Support, Clerk	0 / 1
Microsoft PowerPoint Basic AOE Location: Main	Office and Administrative Support - General Office Clerks - Occ Ed Class	1	High School Diploma or GED	Accredited Post Secondary Institution Post-Secondary (College) Certificate Only Office Support, Clerk	0 / 1

Institution: SHERIDAN FCI (Cont'd)

Program / Location	Occupational Area			Required Education	Certification	Ratio
Microsoft Publisher Location: Main	Office and Administrative Support - General Office Clerks - Occ Ed Class	3	High School Diploma or GED - Typing 30 WPM	Accredited Post Secondary Institution Post-Secondary (College) Certificate Only Administrative Support	0 / 4
Microsoft Publisher Location: Camp	Office and Administrative Support - General Office Clerks - Occ Ed Class	3	High School Diploma or GED - Typing 30 WPM	Accredited Post Secondary Institution Post-Secondary (College) Certificate Only Administrative Support	0 / 4
Microsoft Windows, Basic (AOE) Location: Main	Office and Administrative Support - General Office Clerks - Occ Ed Class	1	High School Diploma or GED	Accredited Post Secondary Institution Post-Secondary (College) Certificate Only Office Support, Clerk	0 / 1
Microsoft Windows, Basic (AOE) Location: Camp	Office and Administrative Support - General Office Clerks - Occ Ed Class	1	High School Diploma or GED	Accredited Post Secondary Institution Post-Secondary (College) Certificate Only Office Support, Clerk	0 / 1
Microsoft Word Location: Main	Office and Administrative Support - General Office Clerks - Occ Ed Class	3	High School Diploma or GED - Typing 30 WPM	Accredited Post Secondary Institution Post-Secondary (College) Certificate Only Administrative Support	0 / 3

Program / Location	Occupation		Requirement	Certification / Outcome	
Microsoft Word Location: Camp	Office and Administrative Support - General Office Clerks - Occ Ed Class	3	High School Diploma or GED - Typing 30 WPM	Accredited Post Secondary Institution Post-Secondary (College) Certificate Only Administrative Support	0 / 3
Microsoft Word 2 (AOE) Location: Main	Office and Administrative Support - General Office Clerks - Occ Ed Class	3	High School Diploma or GED	Accredited Post Secondary Institution Post-Secondary (College) Certificate Only Office Support, Clerk	0 / 3
Microsoft Word 2 (AOE) Location: Camp	Office and Administrative Support - General Office Clerks - Occ Ed Class	3	High School Diploma or GED	Accredited Post Secondary Institution Post-Secondary (College) Certificate Only Office Support, clerk	0 / 3
Office Management Clerk Location: Main	Office and Administrative Support - General Office Clerks - Apprenticeship	40	High School Diploma or GED	BOP Employee BOP Certificate & Department of Labor Certificate Office Clerk, Receptionist, Secretary	40 / 0
Personal Fitness Trainer Location: Camp	Personal Care and Service - Fitness Trainers and Instructors - Apprenticeship	20	High School Diploma or GED	BOP Employee BOP Certificate & Department of Labor Certificate Personal Fitness Trainer	20 / 0

Institution: SHERIDAN FCI (Cont'd)

Program / Location	Details	Capacity	Requirements	Certifications	Ratio
Physical Fitness Trainer Location: Main	Personal Care and Service - Fitness Trainers and Instructors - Apprenticeship	20	High School Diploma or GED	BOP Employee BOP Certificate & Department of Labor Certificate Personal Fitness Trainer	20 / 0
Plumber Location: Main	Construction and Extraction - Plumbers, Pipefitters, and Steamfitters - Apprenticeship	60	High School Diploma or GED - Time on sentence left to complete the 8000 hour program	BOP Employee BOP Certificate & Department of Labor Certificate Plumbers, Pipefitters, and Steamfitters	60 / 0
QuickBooks AOE Location: Camp	Business and Financial - Accountants and Auditors - Occ Ed Class	3	High School Diploma or GED	Accredited Post Secondary Institution Post-Secondary (College) Certificate Only Book Keeper	0 / 3
Sanitation Technician Location: Main	Building and Grounds Cleaning - Janitors and Building Cleaners - Apprenticeship	20	High School Diploma or GED	BOP Employee BOP Certificate & Department of Labor Certificate Janitors and Building Cleaners	20 / 0
Solar Technician Location: Main	Production - Assemblers and Fabricators - Apprenticeship	40	High School Diploma or GED	BOP Employee BOP Certificate & Department of Labor Certificate Solar Technician	40 / 0

Program / Location	Occupational Category		Requirement	Credential / Type	
Teacher Aide I Location: Main	Education, Training, and Library - Teacher Assistants - Apprenticeship	40	High School Diploma or GED	BOP Employee BOP Certificate & Department of Labor Certificate Teacher Assistant	40 / 0
Teacher Aide I Location: Camp	Education, Training, and Library - Teacher Assistants - Apprenticeship	40	High School Diploma or GED	BOP Employee BOP Certificate & Department of Labor Certificate Teacher Assistants	40 / 0
VT Basic Horticulture Location: Camp	Building and Grounds Cleaning - Grounds Maintenance Workers - Occ Ed Class	6	High School Diploma or GED - Exception to GED if 480+ hours achieved	BOP Employee BOP Certificate Only Grounds Keeper/Landscaper	0 / 0
VT Google SketchUp Location: Main	Construction and Extraction - Construction and Building Inspectors - Occ Ed Class	3	High School Diploma or GED	BOP Employee BOP Certificate Only Construction Contractor	0 / 0
VT Google SketchUp Location: Camp	Construction and Extraction - Construction and Building Inspectors - Occ Ed Class	3	High School Diploma or GED	BOP Employee BOP Certificate Only Construction Contractor	0 / 0

Institution: SHERIDAN FCI　　　(Cont'd)

VT Microsoft Excel Location: Main	Office and Administrative Support - General Office Clerks - Occ Ed Class	4	High School Diploma or GED - Type 30 WPM	BOP Employee BOP Certificate Only Administrative Support	0 / 0
VT Microsoft Excel Location: Camp	Office and Administrative Support - General Office Clerks - Occ Ed Class	3	High School Diploma or GED - Type 30 WPM	BOP Employee BOP Certificate Only Administrative Support	0 / 0
VT Microsoft PowerPoint/Publisher Location: Camp	Office and Administrative Support - General Office Clerks - Occ Ed Class	3	High School Diploma or GED - Type 30 WPM	BOP Employee BOP Certificate Only Administrative Support	0 / 0
VT Microsoft Word Location: Main	Office and Administrative Support - General Office Clerks - Occ Ed Class	3	High School Diploma or GED - Typing 30 WPM	BOP Employee BOP Certificate Only Administrative Support	0 / 0
VT Microsoft Word Location: Camp	Office and Administrative Support - General Office Clerks - Occ Ed Class	4	High School Diploma or GED - Typing 30 WPM	BOP Employee BOP Certificate Only Administrative Support	0 / 0

Program / Location	Occupation		Requirements	Outcomes	
VT Personal Fitness Trainer Location: Main	Personal Care and Service - Fitness Trainers and Instructors - Occ Ed Class	6	High School Diploma or GED - Successful completion of Anatomy and Physiology course	BOP Employee BOP Certificate & Industry Recognized Certificate Personal Trainer	0 / 0
VT Personal Trainer Location: Camp	Personal Care and Service - Fitness Trainers and Instructors - Occ Ed Class	6	High School Diploma or GED - Successful completion of Anatomy and Physiology course	BOP Employee BOP Certificate & Industry Recognized Certificate Personal Trainer	0 / 0
VT Pesticide Applications Location: Camp	Building and Grounds Cleaning - Pest Control Workers - Occ Ed Class	6	High School Diploma or GED - Exception to GED if 480+ hours achieved	BOP Employee BOP Certificate Only Pesticide Control / Landscaping	0 / 0
VT PowerPoint/Publisher Location: Main	Office and Administrative Support - General Office Clerks - Occ Ed Class	3	High School Diploma or GED - Type 30 WPM	BOP Employee BOP Certificate Only Administrative Support	0 / 0
VT Quick Books Location: Main	Business and Financial - Accountants and Auditors - Occ Ed Class	3	High School Diploma or GED	BOP Employee BOP Certificate Only Bookkeeping/Accounting	0 / 0
VT Quick Books Location: Camp	Business and Financial - Accountants and Auditors - Occ Ed Class	3	High School Diploma or GED	BOP Employee BOP Certificate Only Book Keeping, accounting	0 / 0

Institution: SHERIDAN FCI   (Cont'd)

Wood Turning Lathe Operator	Production	20	High School Diploma or GED	BOP Employee	20 / 0
Location: Main	- Woodworkers			BOP Certificate & Department of Labor Certificate	
	- Apprenticeship			Lathe Operator/Wood Turner	

Institution: SOUTH CENTRAL REGIONAL OFFICE

POLLOCK USP	Food Preparation and Serving	12	High School Diploma or GED	BOP Employee	0 / 0
Location: Camp	- Food and Beverage Serving and Related Workers			BOP Certificate & Industry Recognized Certificate	
	- Occ Ed Class			Food Service Worker	
POLLOCK USP	Food Preparation and Serving	12	High School Diploma or GED	BOP Employee	0 / 0
Location: Camp	- Food and Beverage Serving and Related Workers			BOP Certificate & Industry Recognized Certificate	
	- Occ Ed Class			Food Service Worker	

Institution: SPRINGFIELD USMCFP

Advanced Small Engine Repair Location: Main	Installation, Maintenance, and Repair - Small Engine Mechanics - Occ Ed Class	9	High School Diploma or GED	BOP Employee BOP Certificate Only Small Engine Mechanic	0 / 0
Baker Location: Main	Food Preparation and Serving - Cooks - Apprenticeship	36	High School Diploma or GED	BOP Employee BOP Certificate & Department of Labor Certificate Baker	0 / 0
Barber Location: Main	Personal Care and Service - Barbers, Hairdressers, and Cosmetologists - Apprenticeship	12	High School Diploma or GED	BOP Employee BOP Certificate & Department of Labor Certificate Barber	0 / 0
Biomedical Equipment Technician Location: Main	Installation, Maintenance, and Repair - Medical Equipment Repairers - Apprenticeship	48	High School Diploma or GED	BOP Employee BOP Certificate & Department of Labor Certificate Biomedical Equipment Technician	0 / 0
Carpenter Location: Main	Construction and Extraction - Carpenters - Apprenticeship	48	High School Diploma or GED	BOP Employee BOP Certificate & Department of Labor Certificate Journeyman Carpenter	0 / 0

Institution: SPRINGFIELD USMCFP (Cont'd)

Dental Assistant	Community and Social Service	12	High School Diploma or GED	BOP Employee	0 / 0
Location: Main	- Health Educators			BOP Certificate & Department of Labor Certificate	
	- Apprenticeship			Dental Assistant	
Electrician	Construction and Extraction	48	High School Diploma or GED	BOP Employee	0 / 0
Location: Main	- Electricians			BOP Certificate & Department of Labor Certificate	
	- Apprenticeship			Maintenance Electrician	
Housekeeping	Building and Grounds Cleaning	12	High School Diploma or GED	BOP Employee	0 / 0
Location: Main	- Janitors and Building Cleaners			BOP Certificate & Department of Labor Certificate	
	- Apprenticeship			Housekeeper/Janitor	
HVAC	Installation, Maintenance, and Repair	36	High School Diploma or GED	BOP Employee	0 / 0
Location: Main	- Heating, Air Conditioning, and Refrigeration Mechanics and Installers			BOP Certificate & Department of Labor Certificate	
	- Apprenticeship			HVAC Technician	
Landscape Maintenance	Building and Grounds Cleaning	9	High School Diploma or GED	BOP Employee	0 / 0
Location: Main	- Grounds Maintenance Workers			BOP Certificate Only	
	- Occ Ed Class			Landscaper	

379

Institution: SPRINGFIELD USMCFP (Cont'd)

Machinist	Production	48	High School Diploma or GED	BOP Employee	0 / 0
Location: Main	- Machinists and Tool and Die Makers			BOP Certificate & Department of Labor Certificate	
	- Apprenticeship			Machinist	
Masonry	Construction and Extraction	36	High School Diploma or GED	BOP Employee	0 / 0
Location: Main	- Brickmasons, Blockmasons, and Stonemasons			BOP Certificate & Department of Labor Certificate	
	- Apprenticeship			Bricklayer	
Meat cutter	Food Preparation and Serving	36	High School Diploma or GED	BOP Employee	0 / 0
Location: Main	- Food Preparation Workers			BOP Certificate & Department of Labor Certificate	
	- Apprenticeship			Meat cutter	
Orthotics Technician	Production	12	High School Diploma or GED	BOP Employee	0 / 0
Location: Main	- Medical Appliance Technicians			BOP Certificate & Department of Labor Certificate	
	- Apprenticeship			Orthotics Technician	
Painter	Construction and Extraction	36	High School Diploma or GED	BOP Employee	0 / 0
Location: Main	- Painters, Construction and Maintenance			BOP Certificate & Department of Labor Certificate	
	- Apprenticeship			Painter	

Program	Detail	Months	Education	Certification	Enrolled/Completed
Plumber Location: Main	Construction and Extraction - Plumbers, Pipefitters, and Steamfitters - Apprenticeship	48	High School Diploma or GED	BOP Employee BOP Certificate & Department of Labor Certificate Plumber	0 / 0
Prosthetic Technician Location: Main	Production - Medical Appliance Technicians - Apprenticeship	12	High School Diploma or GED	BOP Employee BOP Certificate & Department of Labor Certificate Prosthetic Technician	0 / 0
Sheet Metal Location: Main	Construction and Extraction - Sheet Metal Workers - Apprenticeship	48	High School Diploma or GED	BOP Employee BOP Certificate & Department of Labor Certificate Sheet Metal Worker	0 / 0
Stationary Engineer Location: Main	Production - Stationary Engineers and Boiler Operators - Apprenticeship	48	High School Diploma or GED	BOP Employee BOP Certificate & Department of Labor Certificate Powerhouse Operator	0 / 0
Steamfitter Location: Main	Construction and Extraction - Plumbers, Pipefitters, and Steamfitters - Apprenticeship	48	High School Diploma or GED	BOP Employee BOP Certificate & Department of Labor Certificate Steamfitter	0 / 0

Institution: TALLADEGA FCI

Bakery	Food Preparation and Serving	36	High School Diploma or GED	BOP Employee	0 / 0
Location: Main	- Cooks		- Must Complete the ServSafe Class	Department of Labor Certificate	
	- Apprenticeship			Baker	
Barber	Personal Care and Service	12	Concurrent GED Enrollment	BOP Employee	0 / 0
Location: Main	- Barbers, Hairdressers, and Cosmetologists			Department of Labor Certificate	
	- Apprenticeship			Barber	
Camp ServSafe	Food Preparation and Serving	6	High School Diploma or GED	BOP Employee	0 / 0
Location: Camp	- Food Preparation Workers			Industry-Recognized Certificate	
	- Occ Ed Class			Restaurant Food Service Worker	
Carpentry	Construction and Extraction	48	Concurrent GED Enrollment	BOP Employee	0 / 0
Location: Main	- Carpenters			Department of Labor Certificate	
	- Apprenticeship			Carpenter	
Carpentry 1	Construction and Extraction	6	Concurrent GED Enrollment	BOP Employee	0 / 0
Location: Camp	- Carpenters			Industry-Recognized Certificate	
	- Occ Ed Class			Carpentry Helper	
Carpentry 2	Construction and Extraction	8	Concurrent GED Enrollment	BOP Employee	0 / 0
Location: Main	- Carpenters		- Completion of CORE Program	Industry-Recognized Certificate	
	- Occ Ed Class			Intermediate Carpenter	
Cook	Food Preparation and Serving	36	Concurrent GED Enrollment	BOP Employee	0 / 0
Location: Main	- Cooks			Department of Labor Certificate	
	- Apprenticeship			Cook	

Institution: TALLADEGA FCI (Cont'd)

Dental Assistant Location: Main	Production - Dental Laboratory Technicians - Apprenticeship	12	Concurrent GED Enrollment	BOP Employee Department of Labor Certificate Dental Assistant	0 / 0
Electrical 1 Location: Main	Construction and Extraction - Carpenters - Occ Ed Class	6	High School Diploma or GED - CORE NCCER	BOP Employee Industry-Recognized Certificate Electrical Helper	0 / 0
Electrical 2 Location: Main	Construction and Extraction - Electricians - Occ Ed Class	8	High School Diploma or GED - Completion of Elec 1 and CORE	BOP Employee Industry-Recognized Certificate Electrical Technician	0 / 0
Electrician Location: Main	Construction and Extraction - Electricians - Apprenticeship	48	Concurrent GED Enrollment	BOP Employee Department of Labor Certificate Electrician	0 / 0
Forklift Location: Main	Construction and Extraction - Construction Equipment Operators - Occ Ed Class	6	Concurrent GED Enrollment	BOP Employee BOP Certificate & Industry Recognized Certificate Powered Industrial Truck Operator	0 / 0
Forklift Location: Camp	Construction and Extraction - Construction Equipment Operators - Occ Ed Class	6	Concurrent GED Enrollment	BOP Employee Industry-Recognized Certificate Power Industrial Truck Operator	0 / 0

Institution: TALLADEGA FCI   **(Cont'd)**

Program / Location	Occupation		Prerequisites	Certifications	
HVAC 1 Location: Main	Installation, Maintenance, and Repair - Heating, Air Conditioning, and Refrigeration Mechanics and Installers - Occ Ed Class	6	High School Diploma or GED - Completion of CORE Class from NCCER	BOP Employee Industry-Recognized Certificate HVAC Helper	0 / 0
HVAC 2 Location: Main	Installation, Maintenance, and Repair - Heating, Air Conditioning, and Refrigeration Mechanics and Installers - Occ Ed Class	8	High School Diploma or GED - HVAC 1 and CORE Program for NCCER	BOP Employee Industry-Recognized Certificate HVAC Technician	0 / 0
Job Readiness Location: Main	Office and Administrative Support - Customer Service Representatives - Occ Ed Class	6	Concurrent GED Enrollment	BOP Employee BOP Certificate & Industry Recognized Certificate Customer Service	0 / 0
Landscape Technician Location: Main	Building and Grounds Cleaning - Grounds Maintenance Workers - Apprenticeship	24	Concurrent GED Enrollment	BOP Employee Department of Labor Certificate Landscaping Technician	0 / 0
Mason 1 Location: Main	Construction and Extraction - Brickmasons, Blockmasons, and Stonemasons - Occ Ed Class	6	Concurrent GED Enrollment - Completion of CORE Program	BOP Employee Industry-Recognized Certificate Masonry Helper	0 / 0

Institution: TALLADEGA FCI   **(Cont'd)**

Program / Location	Occupation		Prerequisites	Outcomes	
Mason 2 Location: Main	Construction and Extraction - Brickmasons, Blockmasons, and Stonemasons - Occ Ed Class	6	Concurrent GED Enrollment - Completion of CORE, Mason 1	BOP Employee Industry-Recognized Certificate Intermediate Mason	0 / 0
Masonry Location: Main	Construction and Extraction - Brickmasons, Blockmasons, and Stonemasons - Apprenticeship	48	Concurrent GED Enrollment	BOP Employee Department of Labor Certificate Mason	0 / 0
Masonry 3 Location: Main	Construction and Extraction - Brickmasons, Blockmasons, and Stonemasons - Occ Ed Class	6	Concurrent GED Enrollment - Completion of Mason 1 and 2 and CORE Programs	BOP Employee Industry-Recognized Certificate Intermediate Mason	0 / 0
NCCER CORE Location: Main	Construction and Extraction - Construction Laborers and Helpers - Occ Ed Class	6	Concurrent GED Enrollment	BOP Employee Industry-Recognized Certificate Construction Helper or Laborer	0 / 0
Office Technology Location: Main	Office and Administrative Support - Secretaries and Administrative Assistants - Occ Ed Class	6	High School Diploma or GED - Basic Computer Skills	BOP Employee Industry-Recognized Certificate Secretary or Administrative Assistant	0 / 0

385

Institution: TALLADEGA FCI (Cont'd)

Program / Location	Occupation Category		Prerequisite	Credential	
Painter Location: Main	Construction and Extraction - Painters, Construction and Maintenance - Apprenticeship	36	Concurrent GED Enrollment	BOP Employee Department of Labor Certificate Painter	0 / 0
Plumber Location: Main	Construction and Extraction - Plumbers, Pipefitters, and Steamfitters - Apprenticeship	48	Concurrent GED Enrollment	BOP Employee Department of Labor Certificate Plumber or Pipefitter	0 / 0
Quality Assurance Location: Main	Production - Quality Control Inspectors - Apprenticeship	24	Concurrent GED Enrollment	BOP Employee Department of Labor Certificate Quality Control Inspector	0 / 0
ServSafe Location: Main	Food Preparation and Serving - Food Preparation Workers - Occ Ed Class	6	High School Diploma or GED	BOP Employee Industry-Recognized Certificate Restaurant Food Service Worker	0 / 0
Sheet Metal Location: Main	Construction and Extraction - Sheet Metal Workers - Apprenticeship	48	Concurrent GED Enrollment	BOP Employee Department of Labor Certificate Sheet Metal Worker or Installer	0 / 0
Teacher's Aide Location: Main	Education, Training, and Library - Teacher Assistants - Apprenticeship	24	High School Diploma or GED	BOP Employee Department of Labor Certificate Teacher's Aide	0 / 0

Institution: TALLADEGA FCI (Cont'd)

Weld 1	Production	8	Concurrent GED Enrollment	BOP Employee
Location: Main	- Welders, Cutters, Solderers, and Brazers		- Completion of CORE Program	Industry-Recognized Certificate
	- Occ Ed Class			Welding Helper/Technician
				0 / 0
Welding	Production	48	Concurrent GED Enrollment	BOP Employee
Location: Main	- Welders, Cutters, Solderers, and Brazers			Department of Labor Certificate
	- Apprenticeship			Welder
				0 / 0
Welding	Production	48	Concurrent GED Enrollment	BOP Employee
Location: Main	- Welders, Cutters, Solderers, and Brazers			Department of Labor Certificate
	- Apprenticeship			Welder
				0 / 0

Institution: TALLAHASSEE FCI

Program / Location	Occupational Area		Prerequisite	Credential	
Business Education I Location: Main	Office and Administrative Support - Secretaries and Administrative Assistants - Occ Ed Class	6	High School Diploma or GED	BOP Employee Industry-Recognized Certificate Administrative Assistant	0 / 0
Business Education II Location: Main	Office and Administrative Support - General Office Clerks - Occ Ed Class	6	High School Diploma or GED	BOP Employee Industry-Recognized Certificate Office Clerk	0 / 0
Construction Craft Laborer Location: Main	Construction and Extraction - Construction Equipment Operators - Apprenticeship	24	High School Diploma or GED	BOP Employee Department of Labor Certificate Construction Operator	0 / 0
Cook Location: Main	Food Preparation and Serving - Cooks - Apprenticeship	24	High School Diploma or GED	BOP Employee Department of Labor Certificate Cook	0 / 0
Cosmetology Location: Main	Personal Care and Service - Barbers, Hairdressers, and Cosmetologists - Occ Ed Class	15	High School Diploma or GED	Independent Contractor State Certificate Cosmetologist	0 / 0
Electrician Apprenticeship Location: Main	Construction and Extraction - Electricians - Apprenticeship	48	High School Diploma or GED	BOP Employee Department of Labor Certificate Electrician	0 / 0

Institution: TALLAHASSEE FCI (Cont'd)

Horticulture Location: Main	Building and Grounds Cleaning - Grounds Maintenance Workers - Occ Ed Class	6	Concurrent GED Enrollment	BOP Employee Industry-Recognized Certificate Landscape/Grounds Maintenance Worker	0 / 0
Office Apprenticeship Location: Main	Office and Administrative Support - Secretaries and Administrative Assistants - Apprenticeship	24	High School Diploma or GED	BOP Employee Department of Labor Certificate Secretary	0 / 0
Plumber Apprenticeship Location: Main	Construction and Extraction - Plumbers, Pipefitters, and Steamfitters - Apprenticeship	48	High School Diploma or GED	BOP Employee Department of Labor Certificate Plumber	0 / 0
Refrigeration Apprenticeship Location: Main	Installation, Maintenance, and Repair - Heating, Air Conditioning, and Refrigeration Mechanics and Installers - Apprenticeship	36	High School Diploma or GED	BOP Employee Department of Labor Certificate HVAC Technician	0 / 0
VT Culinary Arts Location: Main	Food Preparation and Serving - Food Preparation Workers - Occ Ed Class	6	High School Diploma or GED	BOP Employee BOP Certificate & Industry Recognized Certificate Food Service Worker	0 / 0

Institution: TERMINAL ISLAND FCI

Program / Location	Occupational Area	Months	Requirements	Credentials	Enrollment
Apprenticeship Baker Location: Main	Food Preparation and Serving - Food Preparation Workers - Apprenticeship	36	Concurrent GED Enrollment - Job Supervisor Recommendation	BOP Employee BOP Certificate & Department of Labor Certificate Journeyman Baker	0 / 0
Apprenticeship Cook Location: Main	Food Preparation and Serving - Cooks - Apprenticeship	36	Concurrent GED Enrollment - Job Supervisor Recommendation	BOP Employee BOP Certificate & Department of Labor Certificate Journeyman Cook	0 / 0
AutoCAD Apprenticeship Location: Main	Construction and Extraction - Construction and Building Inspectors - Apprenticeship	48	High School Diploma or GED - Recommendation from Supervisor	BOP Employee BOP Certificate & Department of Labor Certificate Journeyman Drafter	0 / 0
Cabinet Maker Apprenticeship Location: Main	Construction and Extraction - Carpenters - Apprenticeship	48	Concurrent GED Enrollment - Job Supervisor Recommendation	BOP Employee BOP Certificate & Department of Labor Certificate Journeyman Cabinetmaker	0 / 0
Carpentry Location: Main	Construction and Extraction - Carpenters - Occ Ed Class	3	High School Diploma or GED -	BOP Employee BOP Certificate Only Construction Helper	0 / 0

Institution: TERMINAL ISLAND FCI (Cont'd)

CFC Certification	Installation, Maintenance, and Repair	2	High School Diploma or GED	BOP Employee	1 / 0
Location: Main	- Heating, Air Conditioning, and Refrigeration Mechanics and Installers			BOP Certificate & Industry Recognized Certificate	
	- Occ Ed Class			Refrigerant Material Handler	
Dental Assistant	Personal Care and Service	12	High School Diploma or GED	BOP Employee	0 / 0
Location: Main	- Skincare Specialists		- Interview by Dentist	BOP Certificate & Department of Labor Certificate	
	- Apprenticeship			Dental Assistant	
Electrical Apprenticeship	Construction and Extraction	48	High School Diploma or GED	BOP Employee	0 / 0
Location: Main	- Construction Laborers and Helpers		- Job Supervisor Recommendation	BOP Certificate & Department of Labor Certificate	
	- Apprenticeship			Journeyman Electrician	
Electrical Home Wiring	Construction and Extraction	3	High School Diploma or GED	BOP Employee	0 / 0
Location: Main	- Electricians			BOP Certificate Only	
	- Occ Ed Class			Electrician Helper	
Electrical Home Wiring	Construction and Extraction	3	High School Diploma or GED	BOP Employee	0 / 0
Location: Main	- Electricians			BOP Certificate Only	
	- Occ Ed Class			Electrician Helper	

Institution: TERMINAL ISLAND FCI   (Cont'd)

Program	Occupational Area		Requirements	Certificates	0 / 0
Electrostatic Powder Paint Machine Apprenticeship Location: Main	Production - Painting and Coating Workers - Apprenticeship	24	Concurrent GED Enrollment - Job Supervisor Recommendation	BOP Employee BOP Certificate & Department of Labor Certificate Journeyman Powder Paint Machine Operator	0 / 0
Electrostatic Powder Paint Technician Location: Main	Production - Assemblers and Fabricators - Apprenticeship	48	Concurrent GED Enrollment - Job Supervisor Recommendation	BOP Employee BOP Certificate & Department of Labor Certificate Journeyman Electrostatic Powder Paint Technician	0 / 0
Engraver Apprenticeship Location: Main	Production - Jewelers and Precious Stone and Metal Workers - Apprenticeship	24	High School Diploma or GED - Job Supervisor Recommendation	BOP Employee BOP Certificate & Department of Labor Certificate Engraver	0 / 0
Home Inspection Location: Main	Construction and Extraction - Construction and Building Inspectors - Occ Ed Class	3	High School Diploma or GED - Job Supervisor Recommendation	BOP Employee BOP Certificate & Department of Labor Certificate Home Inspector	0 / 0
HVAC Apprenticeship Location: Main	Construction and Extraction - Plumbers, Pipefitters, and Steamfitters - Apprenticeship	48	High School Diploma or GED - Job Supervisor Recommendation	BOP Employee BOP Certificate & Department of Labor Certificate Journeyman HVAC Technician	0 / 0

Institution: TERMINAL ISLAND FCI   (Cont'd)

Program	Occupation	Hours	Requirements	Certification	
Industrial Truck Mechanic Location: Main	Installation, Maintenance, and Repair - Automotive Service Technicians and Mechanics - Apprenticeship	48	Concurrent GED Enrollment - Job Supervisor Recommendation	BOP Employee BOP Certificate & Department of Labor Certificate Journeyman Forklift Mechanic	0 / 0
Machine Setter Apprenticeship Location: Main	Installation, Maintenance, and Repair - General Maintenance and Repair Workers - Apprenticeship	48	Concurrent GED Enrollment - Job Supervisor Recommendation	BOP Employee BOP Certificate & Department of Labor Certificate Journeyman Machine Setter	0 / 0
Maintenance Repairer Apprenticeship Location: Main	Installation, Maintenance, and Repair - General Maintenance and Repair Workers - Apprenticeship	48	Concurrent GED Enrollment - Job Supervisor Recommendation	BOP Employee BOP Certificate & Department of Labor Certificate Journeyman Maintenance Mechanic	0 / 0
Material Coordinator Apprenticeship Location: Main	Production - Quality Control Inspectors - Apprenticeship	24	Concurrent GED Enrollment - Job Supervisor Recommendation	BOP Employee BOP Certificate & Department of Labor Certificate Journeyman Material Coordinator	0 / 0
Pipefitter Apprenticeship Location: Main	Construction and Extraction - Plumbers, Pipefitters, and Steamfitters - Apprenticeship	48	Concurrent GED Enrollment - Powerhouse Operator Recommendation	BOP Employee BOP Certificate & Department of Labor Certificate Journeyman Pipefitter	0 / 0

Plumbing Location: Main	Construction and Extraction - Plumbers, Pipefitters, and Steamfitters - Occ Ed Class	3	High School Diploma or GED	BOP Employee BOP Certificate Only Plumber Helper	0 / 0
Plumbing Apprenticeship Location: Main	Construction and Extraction - Plumbers, Pipefitters, and Steamfitters - Apprenticeship	48	Concurrent GED Enrollment - Job Supervisor Recommendation	BOP Employee BOP Certificate & Department of Labor Certificate Journeyman Plumber	0 / 0
Production Planner-Shipping Clerk Location: Main	Production - Quality Control Inspectors - Apprenticeship	24	Concurrent GED Enrollment - Job Supervisor Recommendation	BOP Employee BOP Certificate & Department of Labor Certificate Journeyman Production Clerk	0 / 0
Quality Control Apprenticeship Location: Main	Production - Quality Control Inspectors - Apprenticeship	24	Concurrent GED Enrollment - Job Supervisor Recommendation	BOP Employee BOP Certificate & Department of Labor Certificate Journeyman Quality Control Manager	0 / 0
Stationary Engineer (Powerhouse) Apprenticeship Location: Main	Construction and Extraction - Boilermakers - Apprenticeship	48	Concurrent GED Enrollment - Powerhouse Operator Recommendation	BOP Employee BOP Certificate & Department of Labor Certificate Journeyman Powerhouse Operator	0 / 0

Institution: TERMINAL ISLAND FCI   (Cont'd)

Tool and Die (Machinist) Apprenticeship	Production	48	Concurrent GED Enrollment	BOP Employee	0 / 0
Location: Main	- Machinists and Tool and Die Makers		- Job Supervisor Recommendation	BOP Certificate & Department of Labor Certificate	
	- Apprenticeship			Journeyman Machinist	
Welding	Construction and Extraction	4	High School Diploma or GED	Accredited Post Secondary Institution	0 / 0
Location: Main	- Reinforcing Iron and Rebar Workers		- Release Date more than six months	Industry-Recognized Certificate	
	- Occ Ed Class			Welder	

Institution: TERRE HAUTE FCI

Program / Location	Occupation	Months	Education	Credentials	0/0
Baker Location: Main	Food Preparation and Serving - Cooks - Apprenticeship	36	High School Diploma or GED	BOP Employee BOP Certificate & Department of Labor Certificate Baker	0 / 0
Barbering Location: Main	Personal Care and Service - Barbers, Hairdressers, and Cosmetologists - Apprenticeship	12	High School Diploma or GED	BOP Employee BOP Certificate & Department of Labor Certificate Barber	0 / 0
Cook Location: Main	Food Preparation and Serving - Cooks - Apprenticeship	36	High School Diploma or GED	BOP Employee BOP Certificate & Department of Labor Certificate Cook	0 / 0
FISH HATCHERY WORKER Location: Camp	Farming, Fishing, and Forestry - Fishers and Related Fishing Workers - Apprenticeship	12	High School Diploma or GED	BOP Employee BOP Certificate & Department of Labor Certificate FISH HATCHERY WORKER	0 / 0
Housekeeping Location: Main	Building and Grounds Cleaning - Janitors and Building Cleaners - Apprenticeship	12	High School Diploma or GED	BOP Employee BOP Certificate & Department of Labor Certificate Janitor, Housekeeper	0 / 0

Institution: TERRE HAUTE FCI (Cont'd)

Program	Category		Education Requirement	Certifications / Outcomes	
Office Manager Location: Main	Office and Administrative Support	- General Office Clerks - Apprenticeship	24	High School Diploma or GED	BOP Employee BOP Certificate & Department of Labor Certificate Office Manager	0 / 0
Office Manager Location: Camp	Office and Administrative Support	- General Office Clerks - Apprenticeship	24	High School Diploma or GED	BOP Employee BOP Certificate & Department of Labor Certificate Office Manager	0 / 0
Tutor Location: Main	Education, Training, and Library	- Teacher Assistants - Apprenticeship	18	High School Diploma or GED	BOP Employee BOP Certificate & Department of Labor Certificate Tutor	0 / 0
Vocational Training Building Trades Location: Main	Construction and Extraction	- Construction Laborers and Helpers - Occ Ed Class	6	High School Diploma or GED	BOP Employee BOP Certificate Only Construction Laborer	0 / 0
Vocational Training Computers Location: Main	Office and Administrative Support	- General Office Clerks - Occ Ed Class	6	High School Diploma or GED	BOP Employee BOP Certificate Only Entry Level Administrative Assistant	0 / 0

Institution: TERRE HAUTE FCI   **(Cont'd)**

Vocational Training Diesel Mechanic	Installation, Maintenance, and Repair	6	High School Diploma or GED	Accredited Vocational/Technical School	0 / 0
Location: Camp	- Diesel Service Technicians and Mechanics			Post-Secondary (College) Certificate Only	
	- Apprenticeship			Diesel Mechanic	
VT COMPUTER APPLICATIONS	Office and Administrative Support	12	High School Diploma or GED	BOP Employee	0 / 0
Location: Camp	- Customer Service Representatives			BOP Certificate & Industry Recognized Certificate	
	- Occ Ed Class			N/A	

Institution: TERRE HAUTE USP

Baker	Food Preparation and Serving	36	High School Diploma or GED	BOP Employee	0 / 0
Location: Main	- Cooks			BOP Certificate & Department of Labor Certificate	
	- Apprenticeship			Baker	
Barbering	Personal Care and Service	12	High School Diploma or GED	BOP Employee	0 / 0
Location: Main	- Barbers, Hairdressers, and Cosmetologists			BOP Certificate & Department of Labor Certificate	
	- Apprenticeship			Barber	
Cook	Food Preparation and Serving	36	High School Diploma or GED	BOP Employee	0 / 0
Location: Main	- Cooks			BOP Certificate & Department of Labor Certificate	
	- Apprenticeship			Cook	
Housekeeping	Building and Grounds Cleaning	12	High School Diploma or GED	BOP Employee	0 / 0
Location: Main	- Janitors and Building Cleaners			BOP Certificate & Department of Labor Certificate	
	- Apprenticeship			Janitor, Housekeeper	
Office Manager	Office and Administrative Support	24	High School Diploma or GED	BOP Employee	0 / 0
Location: Main	- General Office Clerks			BOP Certificate & Department of Labor Certificate	
	- Apprenticeship			Office Manager	

Institution: TERRE HAUTE USP   **(Cont'd)**

Tutor	Education, Training, and Library	18	High School Diploma or GED	BOP Employee	0 / 0
Location: Main	- Teacher Assistants			BOP Certificate & Department of Labor Certificate	
	- Apprenticeship			Tutor	
VT COMPUTER APPLICATIONS	Office and Administrative Support	12	High School Diploma or GED	BOP Employee	0 / 0
Location: Main	- Customer Service Representatives			BOP Certificate & Industry Recognized Certificate	
	- Occ Ed Class			N/A	

Institution: TEXARKANA FCI

Automotive/Diesel Mechanics Location: Camp	Installation, Maintenance, and Repair - Automotive Service Technicians and Mechanics - Occ Ed Class	12	High School Diploma or GED	Accredited Post Secondary Institution Post-Secondary (College) Certificate Only Automotive/Diesel Repair	24 / 0
Building and Trades Location: Camp	Construction and Extraction - Construction Laborers and Helpers - Occ Ed Class	12	High School Diploma or GED	Accredited Post Secondary Institution Post-Secondary (College) Certificate Only Construction Laborer	24 / 0
Business Computer Applications Location: Camp	Office and Administrative Support - General Office Clerks - Occ Ed Class	12	High School Diploma or GED	Accredited Post Secondary Institution Post-Secondary (College) Certificate Only Office Clerk	24 / 0
Business Computer Applications Location: Main	Office and Administrative Support - General Office Clerks - Occ Ed Class	12	Concurrent GED Enrollment	Accredited Post Secondary Institution Post-Secondary (College) Certificate Only Office Clerk	24 / 0
Culinary Arts Location: Main	Food Preparation and Serving - Food Preparation Workers - Occ Ed Class	12	High School Diploma or GED	Accredited Post Secondary Institution Post-Secondary (College) Certificate Only Cook or Food Prep Worker	24 / 0

Institution: TEXARKANA FCI   (Cont'd)

Dental Assistant Location: Main	Production - Dental Laboratory Technicians - Apprenticeship	18	High School Diploma or GED	BOP Employee BOP Certificate & Department of Labor Certificate Dental Assistant	0 / 0
Dental Assistant Apprenticeship Location: Camp	Production - Dental Laboratory Technicians - Apprenticeship	18	High School Diploma or GED	BOP Employee BOP Certificate & Department of Labor Certificate Dental Assistant	0 / 0
Dental Technician Location: Main	Production - Dental Laboratory Technicians - Apprenticeship	24	High School Diploma or GED	BOP Employee BOP Certificate & Department of Labor Certificate Dental Technician	0 / 0
Dental Technician Apprenticeship Location: Camp	Production - Dental Laboratory Technicians - Apprenticeship	24	High School Diploma or GED	BOP Employee BOP Certificate & Department of Labor Certificate Dental Technician	0 / 0
Electrical Apprenticeship Location: Main	Installation, Maintenance, and Repair - Electrical and Electronics Installers and Repairers - Apprenticeship	60	High School Diploma or GED	BOP Employee BOP Certificate & Department of Labor Certificate Electrician	0 / 0

Institution: TEXARKANA FCI   (Cont'd)

Electrical Apprenticeship Location: Camp	Installation, Maintenance, and Repair - Electrical and Electronics Installers and Repairers - Apprenticeship	60	High School Diploma or GED	BOP Employee BOP Certificate & Department of Labor Certificate Electrician	0 / 0
Graphic Design Location: Main	Office and Administrative Support - Desktop Publishers - Occ Ed Class	12	High School Diploma or GED	Accredited Post Secondary Institution Post-Secondary (College) Certificate Only Graphic Designer	24 / 0
Heating and Air Conditioning Location: Main	Installation, Maintenance, and Repair - Heating, Air Conditioning, and Refrigeration Mechanics and Installers - Occ Ed Class	12	High School Diploma or GED	Accredited Post Secondary Institution Post-Secondary (College) Certificate Only HVAC Repairman	24 / 0
Heating and Air Conditioning Location: Camp	Installation, Maintenance, and Repair - Heating, Air Conditioning, and Refrigeration Mechanics and Installers - Occ Ed Class	12	High School Diploma or GED	Accredited Post Secondary Institution Post-Secondary (College) Certificate Only HVAC Repairman	24 / 0

Institution: TEXARKANA FCI   (Cont'd)

Program / Location		Requirement	Occupation	Credential	Count
Heating and Air Conditioning Location: Main	36	High School Diploma or GED	Installation, Maintenance, and Repair - Heating, Air Conditioning, and Refrigeration Mechanics and Installers - Apprenticeship	BOP Employee BOP Certificate & Department of Labor Certificate HVAC Repairman	0 / 0
Heating and Air Conditioning Apprenticeship Location: Camp	36	High School Diploma or GED	Installation, Maintenance, and Repair - Heating, Air Conditioning, and Refrigeration Mechanics and Installers - Apprenticeship	BOP Employee BOP Certificate & Department of Labor Certificate HVAC Repairman	0 / 0
Introduction to Culinary Arts Location: Main	3	High School Diploma or GED	Food Preparation and Serving - Food Preparation Workers - Occ Ed Class	Accredited Post Secondary Institution Industry-Recognized Certificate Food Preparation Worker	6 / 0
Introduction to Culinary Arts Location: Camp	3	High School Diploma or GED	Food Preparation and Serving - Food Preparation Workers - Occ Ed Class	Accredited Post Secondary Institution Industry-Recognized Certificate Food Preparation Worker	6 / 0
Upholstery Location: Main	9	High School Diploma or GED	Production - Upholsterers - Occ Ed Class	Accredited Post Secondary Institution Post-Secondary (College) Certificate Only Upholstery Worker	18 / 0

Institution: TEXARKANA FCI   (Cont'd)

Welding	Production	12	High School Diploma or GED	Accredited Post Secondary Institution	24 / 0
Location: Main	- Welders, Cutters, Solderers, and Brazers			Post-Secondary (College) Certificate Only	
	- Occ Ed Class			Welder	

Institution: THREE RIVERS FCI

Program	Occupation / Area		Pre-Requisites	Certifications	Enrolled/Completed
Building Trades Location: Main	Construction and Extraction - Carpenters - Occ Ed Class	12	No Pre-Requisites Required	Accredited Post Secondary Institution Post-Secondary (College) Certificate Only Framer/Carpenter Apprentice/Carpenter	0 / 0
Electrical Apprentice Location: Camp	Construction and Extraction - Electricians - Apprenticeship	60	High School Diploma or GED	BOP Employee Department of Labor Certificate Electrician	0 / 0
Electrical Apprentice program Location: Main	Installation, Maintenance, and Repair - Electrical and Electronics Installers and Repairers - Apprenticeship	60	High School Diploma or GED	BOP Employee Department of Labor Certificate Electrician	0 / 0
General Automotive Location: Camp	Installation, Maintenance, and Repair - Automotive Service Technicians and Mechanics - Occ Ed Class	12	No Pre-Requisites Required	Accredited Post Secondary Institution Post-Secondary (College) Certificate Only Automotive Technician	0 / 0
HVAC Location: Main	Installation, Maintenance, and Repair - Heating, Air Conditioning, and Refrigeration Mechanics and Installers - Occ Ed Class	12	No Pre-Requisites Required	Accredited Post Secondary Institution Post-Secondary (College) Certificate Only A/C technician	0 / 0

Institution: THREE RIVERS FCI   (Cont'd)

HVAC Apprentice Location: Camp	Installation, Maintenance, and Repair - Heating, Air Conditioning, and Refrigeration Mechanics and Installers - Apprenticeship	60	High School Diploma or GED	BOP Employee Department of Labor Certificate HVAC Technician	0 / 0
HVAC Apprentice Location: Main	Installation, Maintenance, and Repair - Heating, Air Conditioning, and Refrigeration Mechanics and Installers - Apprenticeship	60	High School Diploma or GED	BOP Employee Department of Labor Certificate HVAC Technician	0 / 0
Plumbing Apprentice Location: Main	Construction and Extraction - Plumbers, Pipefitters, and Steamfitters - Apprenticeship	60	High School Diploma or GED	BOP Employee Department of Labor Certificate Plumber	0 / 0
Plumbing Apprentice Location: Camp	Construction and Extraction - Plumbers, Pipefitters, and Steamfitters - Apprenticeship	60	High School Diploma or GED	BOP Employee Department of Labor Certificate Plumber	0 / 0
Welding Location: Main	Construction and Extraction - Structural Iron and Steel Workers - Occ Ed Class	8	No Pre-Requisites Required	Accredited Post Secondary Institution Post-Secondary (College) Certificate Only Welder	0 / 0

Institution: TUCSON FCI

Program / Location		Requirements	Certifications	

Advanced Baking
Location: Main
  - Bakers
  - Occ Ed Class
	Production
	4
		High School Diploma or GED
		- Cleared to work in Food Service, 2 years remaining on sentence, 1 year clear conduct, complete the Basic Baking course
			BOP Employee
			Industry-Recognized Certificate
			ACF Certified Advanced Baker
				2 / 0

Basic Baking
Location: Main
  - Bakers
  - Occ Ed Class
	Production
	4
		High School Diploma or GED
		- Cleared to work in Food Service, 2 years remaining on sentence, 1 year clear conduct
			BOP Employee
			Industry-Recognized Certificate
			ACF Certified Basic Baker
				2 / 0

Cook Apprenticeship
Location: Main
  - Cooks
  - Apprenticeship
	Food Preparation and Serving
	36
		High School Diploma or GED
		- Cleared to work in Food Service, working in Food Service for at least 6 months, 4 years remaining on sentence, 1 year clear conduct
			BOP Employee
			Department of Labor Certificate
			Journeyman Cook
				0 / 0

Custodial Maintenance
Location: Main
  - Janitors and Building Cleaners
  - Occ Ed Class
	Building and Grounds Cleaning
	6
		High School Diploma or GED
		- - Have a minimum 1 year left on sentence, 1 year clear conduct
			BOP Employee
			Industry-Recognized Certificate
			TPC Certified Custodian
				0 / 0

Institution: TUCSON FCI   **(Cont'd)**

Electrician Apprenticeship Location: Main	Construction and Extraction - Electricians - Apprenticeship	48	High School Diploma or GED - Must work in assigned occupation within institution, have minimum 5 years left on sentence, and medically cleared	BOP Employee Department of Labor Certificate Journeyman Electrician	0 / 0
HVAC Apprenticeship Location: Main	Installation, Maintenance, and Repair - Heating, Air Conditioning, and Refrigeration Mechanics and Installers - Apprenticeship	48	High School Diploma or GED - Must work in assigned occupation within institution, have minimum 5 years left on sentence, and medically cleared	BOP Employee Department of Labor Certificate Journeyman HVAC Technician	0 / 0
Management Business Basics Location: Main	Office and Administrative Support - Customer Service Representatives - Occ Ed Class	12	High School Diploma or GED - - Have a minimum 2 years left on sentence, 1 year clear conduct, completion of Basic Business I certificate	Accredited Post Secondary Institution Post-Secondary (College) Certificate & Industry Recognized Certificate Management Business Certificate	0 / 12
Pastry Cook Apprenticeship Location: Main	Food Preparation and Serving - Food Preparation Workers - Apprenticeship	36	High School Diploma or GED - Must be cleared to work Food Service, work in assigned occupation within institution for at least 6 months, and have minimum 4 years left on sentence	BOP Employee Department of Labor Certificate Journeyman Pastry Cook	0 / 0

Institution: TUCSON FCI   **(Cont'd)**

Plumber Apprenticeship Location: Main	Construction and Extraction - Plumbers, Pipefitters, and Steamfitters - Apprenticeship	48	High School Diploma or GED - Must work in assigned occupation within institution, have minimum 5 years left on sentence, and be medically cleared	BOP Employee Department of Labor Certificate Journeyman Plumber	0 / 0
ServSafe Location: Main	Food Preparation and Serving - Food Preparation Workers - Occ Ed Class	4	High School Diploma or GED - Cleared to work in Food Service, 2 years remaining on sentence, 1 year clear conduct	BOP Employee Industry-Recognized Certificate ServSafe Certified Food Handler	2 / 0

Institution: TUCSON USP

Advanced Baking Location: Camp	Production - Bakers - Occ Ed Class	2	High School Diploma or GED - Cleared to work in Food Service, 2 years remaining on sentence, 1 year clear conduct, complete the basic Baking Course	BOP Employee Industry-Recognized Certificate ACF Certified Advanced Baker	2 / 0
Advanced Baking Location: Main	Production - Bakers - Occ Ed Class	4	High School Diploma or GED - Cleared to work in Food Service, 2 years remaining on sentence, 1 year clear conduct, complete the Basic Baking course	BOP Employee Industry-Recognized Certificate ACF Certified Advanced Baker	2 / 0
Basic Baking Location: Camp	Production - Bakers - Occ Ed Class	4	High School Diploma or GED - Cleared to work in food service, 2 years remaining on sentence, 1 year clear conduct	BOP Employee Industry-Recognized Certificate ACF Certified Basic Baker	2 / 0
Basic Baking Location: Main	Production - Bakers - Occ Ed Class	4	High School Diploma or GED - Cleared to work in Food Service, 2 years remaining on sentence, 1 year clear conduct	BOP Employee Industry-Recognized Certificate ACF Certified Basic Baker	2 / 0

411

Institution: TUCSON USP   (Cont'd)

Program	Hours	Requirements	Certification	
Cook Apprenticeship Location: Main Food Preparation and Serving - Cooks - Apprenticeship	36	High School Diploma or GED - Cleared to work in Food Service and working in Food Service for at least 6 months, 4 years remaining on sentence, 1 year clear conduct	BOP Employee Department of Labor Certificate Journeyman Cook	0 / 0
Custodial Maintenance Location: Main Building and Grounds Cleaning - Janitors and Building Cleaners - Occ Ed Class	6	High School Diploma or GED - 1 year left on sentence, 1 year clear conduct	BOP Employee Industry-Recognized Certificate TPC Certified Custodian	0 / 0
Electrician Apprenticeship Location: Main Construction and Extraction - Electricians - Apprenticeship	48	High School Diploma or GED - Must work in assigned occupation within institution, have minimum 5 years left on sentence, and medically cleared	BOP Employee Department of Labor Certificate Journeyman Electrician	0 / 0
Electrician Apprenticeship Location: Camp Construction and Extraction - Electricians - Apprenticeship	48	High School Diploma or GED - Must work in assigned occupation within institution, have minimum of five years left on sentence and medically cleared	BOP Employee Department of Labor Certificate Journeyman Electrician	0 / 0

412

Institution: TUCSON USP　　(Cont'd)

HVAC Apprenticeship Location: Main	Installation, Maintenance, and Repair - Heating, Air Conditioning, and Refrigeration Mechanics and Installers - Apprenticeship	48	High School Diploma or GED - Must work in assigned occupation within institution, have minimum 5 years left on sentence, and be medically cleared	BOP Employee Department of Labor Certificate Journeyman HVAC Technician	0 / 0
Management Business Basics Location: Camp	Office and Administrative Support - Customer Service Representatives - Occ Ed Class	12	High School Diploma or GED - - Have a minimum 2 years left on sentence, 1 year clear conduct, completion of Basic Business I certificate	Accredited Post Secondary Institution Post-Secondary (College) Certificate Only Management Business Certificate	0 / 12
Management Business Basics Location: Main	Office and Administrative Support - Customer Service Representatives - Occ Ed Class	12	High School Diploma or GED - - Have a minimum 2 years left on sentence, 1 year clear conduct, completion of Basic Business I certificate	Accredited Post Secondary Institution Post-Secondary (College) Certificate Only Management Business Certificate	0 / 12
Pastry Cook Apprenticeship Location: Main	Food Preparation and Serving - Food Preparation Workers - Apprenticeship	36	High School Diploma or GED - Must be cleared to work Food Service, work in assigned occupation within institution for at least 6 months, and have minimum 4 years left on sentence	BOP Employee Department of Labor Certificate Journeyman Pastry Cook	0 / 0

Institution: TUCSON USP (Cont'd)

Program / Location	Occupation		Requirements	Certifications	
Plumbing Apprenticeship Location: Main	Construction and Extraction - Plumbers, Pipefitters, and Steamfitters - Apprenticeship	48	High School Diploma or GED - Must work in assigned occupation within institution, have minimum 5 years left on sentence, and medically cleared	BOP Employee Department of Labor Certificate Journeyman Plumber	0 / 0
ServSafe Location: Main	Food Preparation and Serving - Food Preparation Workers - Occ Ed Class	4	High School Diploma or GED - Cleared to work in Food Service, 2 years remaining on sentence, and 1 year clear conduct	BOP Employee Industry-Recognized Certificate ServSafe Certified Food Handler	2 / 0
ServSafe Location: Camp	Food Preparation and Serving - Food Preparation Workers - Occ Ed Class	4	High School Diploma or GED - Cleared to work in Food Service, 2 years remaining on sentence, and 1 year clear conduct	BOP Employee Industry-Recognized Certificate Servsafe Certified Food Handler	2 / 0

Institution: VICTORVILLE MED I FCI

Program / Location	Occupation		Prerequisite	Outcome	
Automotive Service Excellence Location: Main	Education, Training, and Library - Career and Technical Education Teachers - Occ Ed Class	27	High School Diploma or GED	Accredited Vocational/Technical School Post-Secondary (College) Certificate & Industry Recognized Certificate Automotive Maintenance Repairman	0 / 9
Construction & Building Trades Location: Main	Construction and Extraction - Construction Laborers and Helpers - Occ Ed Class	6	Concurrent GED Enrollment	BOP Employee BOP Certificate Only Construction Worker	0 / 0
Culinary Arts Location: Main	Food Preparation and Serving - Chefs and Head Cooks - Occ Ed Class	12	High School Diploma or GED - Concurrent Enrollment in ServSafe	BOP Employee BOP Certificate & Industry Recognized Certificate Cook; Server; Chef	0 / 0
Dental Assistant Location: Main	Production - Dental Laboratory Technicians - Apprenticeship	24	High School Diploma or GED -	BOP Employee Department of Labor Certificate Dental Assistant	0 / 0
HVAC Mechanic/Installer Location: Main	Installation, Maintenance, and Repair - Heating, Air Conditioning, and Refrigeration Mechanics and Installers - Apprenticeship	24	High School Diploma or GED -	BOP Employee Department of Labor Certificate HVAC Mechanic/Installer	0 / 0

415

Institution: VICTORVILLE MED I FCI (Cont'd)

Manage First	Food Preparation and Serving	12	High School Diploma or GED	BOP Employee	0 / 0
Location: Main	- Food and Beverage Serving and Related Workers			BOP Certificate & Industry Recognized Certificate	
	- Occ Ed Class			Restaurant Management	
Microsoft Office 2010	Office and Administrative Support	6	Concurrent GED Enrollment	BOP Employee	0 / 0
Location: Main	- General Office Clerks			BOP Certificate Only	
	- Occ Ed Class			General Office Clerk	
Plumber	Construction and Extraction	24	High School Diploma or GED	BOP Employee	0 / 0
Location: Main	- Plumbers, Pipefitters, and Steamfitters		-	Department of Labor Certificate	
	- Apprenticeship			Plumber	
Recycling/Solid Waste Management	Construction and Extraction	3	High School Diploma or GED	Accredited Vocational/Technical School	0 / 0
Location: Main	- Hazardous Materials Removal Workers			Vocational/Technical School Certificate Only	
	- Occ Ed Class			Recycling Worker	
ServSafe	Food Preparation and Serving	3	Concurrent GED Enrollment	BOP Employee	0 / 0
Location: Main	- Food Preparation Workers			Industry-Recognized Certificate	
	- Occ Ed Class			Food Preparation Worker	

Institution: VICTORVILLE MED I FCI   (Cont'd)

Solar Panel Installation Location: Main	Installation, Maintenance, and Repair - Heating, Air Conditioning, and Refrigeration Mechanics and Installers - Occ Ed Class	3	High School Diploma or GED	Accredited Vocational/Technical School Post-Secondary (College) Certificate & Industry Recognized Certificate Solar Panel Installer	0 / 1

Institution: VICTORVILLE MED II FCI

Automotive Service Excellence Location: Main	Installation, Maintenance, and Repair - Automotive Service Technicians and Mechanics - Occ Ed Class	27	High School Diploma or GED	Accredited Vocational/Technical School Vocational/Technical School Certificate Only Automotive Service Technician	0 / 9
Automotive Service Excellence Location: Camp	Installation, Maintenance, and Repair - Automotive Service Technicians and Mechanics - Occ Ed Class	27	High School Diploma or GED	Accredited Vocational/Technical School Vocational/Technical School Certificate Only Automotive Service Technician	0 / 9
Culinary Arts Location: Main	Food Preparation and Serving - Chefs and Head Cooks - Occ Ed Class	12	High School Diploma or GED	BOP Employee BOP Certificate Only Cook; Chef; Server	0 / 0
Culinary Arts Location: Camp	Food Preparation and Serving - Chefs and Head Cooks - Occ Ed Class	12	High School Diploma or GED	BOP Employee BOP Certificate Only Cook; Chef; Server	0 / 0
Dental Assistant Location: Camp	Production - Dental Laboratory Technicians - Apprenticeship	24	High School Diploma or GED	BOP Employee Department of Labor Certificate Dental Assistant	0 / 0
Horticulture Location: Camp	Farming, Fishing, and Forestry - Forest and Conservation Workers - Occ Ed Class	3	Concurrent GED Enrollment	BOP Employee BOP Certificate Only Horticultural Worker	0 / 0

Institution: VICTORVILLE MED II FCI   (Cont'd)

Program / Location	Occupation	Count	Prerequisite	Outcome	
Horticulture Location: Main	Farming, Fishing, and Forestry - Forest and Conservation Workers - Occ Ed Class	3	Concurrent GED Enrollment	BOP Employee BOP Certificate Only Horticultural Worker	0 / 0
HVAC Location: Main	Installation, Maintenance, and Repair - Heating, Air Conditioning, and Refrigeration Mechanics and Installers - Apprenticeship	24	High School Diploma or GED -	BOP Employee Department of Labor Certificate HVAC Mechanic & Installer	0 / 0
Manage First Location: Camp	Food Preparation and Serving - Food and Beverage Serving and Related Workers - Occ Ed Class	12	High School Diploma or GED	BOP Employee BOP Certificate & Industry Recognized Certificate Restaurant Management	0 / 0
Manage First Location: Main	Food Preparation and Serving - Food and Beverage Serving and Related Workers - Occ Ed Class	12	High School Diploma or GED	BOP Employee BOP Certificate & Industry Recognized Certificate Restaurant Management	0 / 0
Microsoft Office 2010 Location: Camp	Office and Administrative Support - General Office Clerks - Occ Ed Class	6	Concurrent GED Enrollment	BOP Employee BOP Certificate Only General Office Clerk	0 / 0

Institution: VICTORVILLE MED II FCI (Cont'd)

Program / Location	Count	Requirement	Occupation	Credential	
Microsoft Office 2010 Location: Main	6	Concurrent GED Enrollment	Office and Administrative Support - General Office Clerks - Occ Ed Class	BOP Employee BOP Certificate Only General Office Clerk	0 / 0
Plumber Location: Main	24	High School Diploma or GED -	Construction and Extraction - Plumbers, Pipefitters, and Steamfitters - Apprenticeship	BOP Employee Department of Labor Certificate Plumber	0 / 0
Recycling/Solid Waste Management Location: Main	3	High School Diploma or GED	Construction and Extraction - Hazardous Materials Removal Workers - Occ Ed Class	Accredited Vocational/Technical School Vocational/Technical School Certificate Only Recycling Worker	0 / 0
Recycling/Solid Waste Management Location: Camp	3	High School Diploma or GED	Construction and Extraction - Hazardous Materials Removal Workers - Occ Ed Class	Accredited Vocational/Technical School Vocational/Technical School Certificate Only Recycling Worker	0 / 0
ServSafe Location: Camp	3	Concurrent GED Enrollment	Food Preparation and Serving - Food Preparation Workers - Occ Ed Class	BOP Employee Industry-Recognized Certificate Food Preparation Worker	0 / 0

Institution: VICTORVILLE MED II FCI   (Cont'd)

ServSafe	Food Preparation and Serving	3	Concurrent GED Enrollment	BOP Employee	0 / 0
Location: Main	- Food Preparation Workers			Industry-Recognized Certificate
	- Occ Ed Class			Food Preparation Worker
Solar Panel Installation	Installation, Maintenance, and Repair	3	High School Diploma or GED	Accredited Vocational/Technical School	0 / 1
Location: Main	- Heating, Air Conditioning, and Refrigeration Mechanics and Installers			Both Vo-Tech School and Industry-Recognized Certificates
	- Occ Ed Class			Solar Panel Installer
Wheelchair Repair	Installation, Maintenance, and Repair	3	Concurrent GED Enrollment	BOP Employee	0 / 0
Location: Main	- General Maintenance and Repair Workers			BOP Certificate Only
	- Occ Ed Class			Wheelchair Repairman

Institution: VICTORVILLE USP

Program / Location	Occupation	#	Education Requirement	Certification	Ratio
Automotive Service Excellence Location: Main	Installation, Maintenance, and Repair - Automotive Service Technicians and Mechanics - Occ Ed Class	27	High School Diploma or GED	Accredited Vocational/Technical School Vocational/Technical School Certificate Only Automotive Service Technician	0 / 9
Culinary Arts Location: Main	Food Preparation and Serving - Food Preparation Workers - Occ Ed Class	12	High School Diploma or GED	BOP Employee BOP Certificate & Industry Recognized Certificate Cook; Chef; Food Preparer	0 / 0
HVAC Location: Main	Installation, Maintenance, and Repair - Heating, Air Conditioning, and Refrigeration Mechanics and Installers - Apprenticeship	24	High School Diploma or GED -	BOP Employee Department of Labor Certificate HVAC Mechanic/Installer	0 / 0
Manage First Location: Main	Food Preparation and Serving - Food and Beverage Serving and Related Workers - Occ Ed Class	12	High School Diploma or GED	BOP Employee BOP Certificate & Industry Recognized Certificate Restaurant Management	0 / 0
Microsoft Office 2010 Location: Main	Office and Administrative Support - General Office Clerks - Occ Ed Class	6	Concurrent GED Enrollment	BOP Employee BOP Certificate Only General Office Clerk	0 / 0

Institution: VICTORVILLE USP   (Cont'd)

Plumber		High School Diploma or GED	BOP Employee	0 / 0
Location: Main	Construction and Extraction	24	Department of Labor Certificate	
	- Plumbers, Pipefitters, and Steamfitters	-	Plumber	
	- Apprenticeship			
Recycling/Solid Waste Management	Construction and Extraction	3	High School Diploma or GED	Accredited Vocational/Technical School	0 / 0
Location: Main	- Hazardous Materials Removal Workers			Vocational/Technical School Certificate Only	
	- Occ Ed Class			Recycling Worker	
ServSafe	Food Preparation and Serving	3	Concurrent GED Enrollment	BOP Employee	0 / 0
Location: Main	- Food Preparation Workers			Industry-Recognized Certificate	
	- Occ Ed Class			Food Preparation Worker	

Institution: WASECA FCI

Program / Location	Occupation Area	Months	Prerequisites	Credential	
Animal Trainer Location: Main	Personal Care and Service - Animal Care and Service Workers - Apprenticeship	24	High School Diploma or GED	BOP Employee BOP Certificate & Department of Labor Certificate Service Dog Trainer	0 / 0
Business Office Specialist Location: Main	Office and Administrative Support - General Office Clerks - Occ Ed Class	36	High School Diploma or GED	Accredited Post Secondary Institution Post-Secondary (College) Certificate Only Office Assistant	0 / 28
Cosmetology Program Location: Main	Personal Care and Service - Barbers, Hairdressers, and Cosmetologists - Occ Ed Class	12	High School Diploma or GED - 12 Months Clear Conduct	Accredited Post Secondary Institution Post-Secondary (College) Certificate & Industry Recognized Certificate Cosmetologist	0 / 60
Electrician, Maintenance Location: Main	Construction and Extraction - Electricians - Apprenticeship	48	High School Diploma or GED	BOP Employee BOP Certificate & Department of Labor Certificate Electrician	0 / 0
Housekeeper, Commercial, Residential, or Industrial Location: Main	Building and Grounds Cleaning - Janitors and Building Cleaners - Apprenticeship	12	High School Diploma or GED	BOP Employee BOP Certificate & Department of Labor Certificate Housekeeper	0 / 0

424

Institution: WASECA FCI (Cont'd)

Landscape Management Technician Location: Main Building and Grounds Cleaning - Grounds Maintenance Workers - Apprenticeship	12	High School Diploma or GED	BOP Employee BOP Certificate & Department of Labor Certificate Landscaper	0 / 0
Landscape Technician Location: Main Farming, Fishing, and Forestry - Agricultural Workers - Apprenticeship	24	High School Diploma or GED	BOP Employee BOP Certificate & Department of Labor Certificate Landscape Technician	0 / 0
Patternmaker (textiles) Location: Main Production - Sewers and Tailors - Apprenticeship	36	High School Diploma or GED	BOP Employee Department of Labor Certificate Textile cutting machine setter, operator, and tender	0 / 0
Pipefitter Location: Main Construction and Extraction - Plumbers, Pipefitters, and Steamfitters - Apprenticeship	48	High School Diploma or GED	BOP Employee Department of Labor Certificate Pipefitter	0 / 0
Quality Control Inspector Location: Main Production - Quality Control Inspectors - Apprenticeship	24	High School Diploma or GED	BOP Employee Department of Labor Certificate QA Inspector	0 / 0
Sewing Machine Operator Location: Main Production - Sewers and Tailors - Apprenticeship	12	High School Diploma or GED	BOP Employee Department of Labor Certificate Sewing Machine Operator	0 / 0

Institution: WASECA FCI   (Cont'd)

Sewing Machine Repairer	Production	36	High School Diploma or GED	BOP Employee
Location: Main	- Sewers and Tailors			Department of Labor Certificate
	- Apprenticeship			Sewing Machine Repairer
Stationary Engineer	Production	36	High School Diploma or GED	BOP Employee
Location: Main	- Stationary Engineers and Boiler Operators			Department of Labor Certificate
	- Apprenticeship			Stationary Engineer
VT Horticulture	Farming, Fishing, and Forestry	12	High School Diploma or GED	BOP Employee
Location: Main	- Agricultural Workers			Post-Secondary (College) Certificate Only
	- Occ Ed Class			Grounds and Turf Management Specialist
VT P.A.W.S. (Prisoners Assisting With Service Dogs) Program	Personal Care and Service	12	High School Diploma or GED	Independent Contractor
Location: Main	- Animal Care and Service Workers			Post-Secondary (College) Certificate Only
	- Occ Ed Class			Dog Trainer Specialist
VT Woodworking	Construction and Extraction	12	High School Diploma or GED	BOP Employee
Location: Main	- Construction Laborers and Helpers			Post-Secondary (College) Certificate Only
	- Occ Ed Class			Cabinet Maker/Framer

Column (enrollment): 0 / 0, 0 / 0, 60 / 0, 60 / 0, 60 / 0

Institution: WILLIAMSBURG FCI

Program	Area	Count	Requirement	Credentials	
Culinary Arts Location: Main	Food Preparation and Serving - Chefs and Head Cooks - Occ Ed Class	6	High School Diploma or GED	BOP Employee Both Vo-Tech School and Industry-Recognized Certificates Chef	0 / 0
Custodial Maintenance Apprenticeship Location: Main	Building and Grounds Cleaning - Janitors and Building Cleaners - Apprenticeship	24	High School Diploma or GED	BOP Employee Department of Labor Certificate Custodian	0 / 0
Electrician Apprenticeship Location: Main	Construction and Extraction - Electricians - Apprenticeship	48	High School Diploma or GED	BOP Employee Department of Labor Certificate Electrician	0 / 0
HVAC Apprenticeship Location: Main	Installation, Maintenance, and Repair - Heating, Air Conditioning, and Refrigeration Mechanics and Installers - Apprenticeship	36	High School Diploma or GED	BOP Employee Department of Labor Certificate Heating, Ventilation & Air Condition Installer	0 / 0
NCCER Core Location: Main	Construction and Extraction - Construction and Building Inspectors - Occ Ed Class	3	High School Diploma or GED	BOP Employee Industry-Recognized Certificate Safety Technician	0 / 0

Institution: WILLIAMSBURG FCI   **(Cont'd)**

Plumbing Apprenticeship Location: Main	Construction and Extraction - Plumbers, Pipefitters, and Steamfitters - Apprenticeship	48	High School Diploma or GED	BOP Employee Department of Labor Certificate Plumber	0 / 0
Residential Carpentry Location: Main	Construction and Extraction - Carpenters - Occ Ed Class	6	High School Diploma or GED	BOP Employee Industry-Recognized Certificate Carpenter	0 / 0
Serve Safe Location: Main	Food Preparation and Serving - Food Preparation Workers - Occ Ed Class	3	High School Diploma or GED	BOP Employee Both Vo-Tech School and Industry-Recognized Certificates Cook	0 / 0

Institution: YANKTON FPC

Program	Duration	Requirement	Outcome	Occupation	Ratio
Associate of Arts - Accounting Location: Camp Business and Financial - Accountants and Auditors - Occ Ed Class	36	High School Diploma or GED	Accredited Post Secondary Institution A.A, A.S., or A.A.S. Diploma Accounting Technician		0 / 64
Associate of Arts - Business Administration Location: Camp Business and Financial - Management Analysts - Occ Ed Class	36	High School Diploma or GED	Accredited Post Secondary Institution A.A, A.S., or A.A.S. Diploma Office Manager		0 / 64
Associate of Science - Horticulture Location: Camp Building and Grounds Cleaning - Grounds Maintenance Workers - Occ Ed Class	36	High School Diploma or GED	Accredited Post Secondary Institution A.A, A.S., or A.A.S. Diploma Grounds Keeper		0 / 65
AWS Certified Welding Course Location: Camp Production - Welders, Cutters, Solderers, and Brazers - Occ Ed Class	4	High School Diploma or GED	Independent Contractor Industry-Recognized Certificate Welder		0 / 0
Baker Apprenticeship Location: Camp Production - Bakers - Apprenticeship	36	Concurrent GED Enrollment	BOP Employee Department of Labor Certificate Baker		0 / 0

Institution: YANKTON FPC (Cont'd)

Program	Occupation	Months	Prerequisite	Credential	Enrollment
Boiler Operator/Mechanic Apprenticeship Location: Camp	Installation, Maintenance, and Repair - Heating, Air Conditioning, and Refrigeration Mechanics and Installers - Apprenticeship	48	Concurrent GED Enrollment	BOP Employee Department of Labor Certificate Boiler Operator	0 / 0
Building Maintenance Apprenticeship Location: Camp	Installation, Maintenance, and Repair - General Maintenance and Repair Workers - Apprenticeship	36	Concurrent GED Enrollment	BOP Employee Department of Labor Certificate General Maintenance Foreman	0 / 0
Carpentry Apprenticeship Location: Camp	Construction and Extraction - Carpenters - Apprenticeship	48	Concurrent GED Enrollment	BOP Employee Department of Labor Certificate Carpenter	0 / 0
CNC Machine Operator Location: Camp	Production - Machinists and Tool and Die Makers - Occ Ed Class	4	High School Diploma or GED	Independent Contractor Industry-Recognized Certificate CNC Machine Operator	0 / 0
Cook Apprenticeship Location: Camp	Food Preparation and Serving - Cooks - Apprenticeship	24	Concurrent GED Enrollment	BOP Employee Department of Labor Certificate Cook	0 / 0

Institution: YANKTON FPC   (Cont'd)

Program	Occupation	Months		Credential	0 / 0
Dental Assistant Apprenticeship Location: Camp	Personal Care and Service - Animal Care and Service Workers - Apprenticeship	12	Concurrent GED Enrollment	Independent Contractor Department of Labor Certificate Dental Assistant	0 / 0
Electrician Maintenance Apprenticeship Location: Camp	Construction and Extraction - Electricians - Apprenticeship	48	Concurrent GED Enrollment	BOP Employee Department of Labor Certificate Electrician	0 / 0
Human Services Direct Support Professional Apprenticeship Location: Camp	Education, Training, and Library - Instructional Coordinators - Apprenticeship	36	Concurrent GED Enrollment	BOP Employee Department of Labor Certificate Human Services Specialist	0 / 0
HVAC Apprenticeship Location: Camp	Installation, Maintenance, and Repair - Heating, Air Conditioning, and Refrigeration Mechanics and Installers - Apprenticeship	36	Concurrent GED Enrollment	BOP Employee Department of Labor Certificate HVAC Maintenance Worker	0 / 0
Industrial Housekeeper Location: Camp	Building and Grounds Cleaning - Janitors and Building Cleaners - Apprenticeship	12	Concurrent GED Enrollment	BOP Employee Department of Labor Certificate Janitor	0 / 0
Landscape Management Technician Apprenticeship Location: Camp	Building and Grounds Cleaning - Grounds Maintenance Workers - Apprenticeship	12	Concurrent GED Enrollment	BOP Employee Department of Labor Certificate Grounds Keeper	0 / 0

431

Landscape Technician Apprenticeship Location: Camp	Building and Grounds Cleaning - Grounds Maintenance Workers - Apprenticeship	24	Concurrent GED Enrollment	BOP Employee Department of Labor Certificate Grounds Keeper	0 / 0
Painting Apprenticeship Location: Camp	Construction and Extraction - Painters, Construction and Maintenance - Apprenticeship	36	Concurrent GED Enrollment	BOP Employee Department of Labor Certificate Painter	0 / 0
Plumbing Apprenticeship Location: Camp	Construction and Extraction - Plumbers, Pipefitters, and Steamfitters - Apprenticeship	48	Concurrent GED Enrollment	BOP Employee Department of Labor Certificate Plumber	0 / 0
Refrigeration Mechanic Apprenticeship Location: Camp	Installation, Maintenance, and Repair - Heating, Air Conditioning, and Refrigeration Mechanics and Installers - Apprenticeship	36	Concurrent GED Enrollment	BOP Employee Department of Labor Certificate Refrigeration Mechanic	0 / 0
Tape Recorder Repairer Apprenticeship Location: Camp	Production - Assemblers and Fabricators - Apprenticeship	48	Concurrent GED Enrollment	BOP Employee Department of Labor Certificate Electronics Technician	0 / 0

Institution: YANKTON FPC (Cont'd)

Undergraduate Certificate - Business Management	12	High School Diploma or GED	Accredited Post Secondary Institution	0 / 18
Location: Camp			Post-Secondary (College) Certificate & Industry Recognized Certificate
Office and Administrative Support			Office Manager
- General Office Clerks			
- Occ Ed Class			
Undergraduate Certificate - Fundamental Horticulture	12	High School Diploma or GED	Accredited Post Secondary Institution	0 / 17
Location: Camp			Post-Secondary (College) Certificate & Industry Recognized Certificate
Building and Grounds Cleaning			Landscape Maintenance Technician
- Grounds Maintenance Workers			
- Occ Ed Class			

Institution: YAZOO CITY FCI

Cabinet Maker	Construction and Extraction	48	High School Diploma or GED	BOP Employee	0 / 0
Location: Main	- Carpenters		- Must work in Vocational Training	Department of Labor Certificate	
	- Apprenticeship			Cabinetry Maker	
Custodial Maintenance	Building and Grounds Cleaning	12	High School Diploma or GED	BOP Employee	20 / 0
Location: Main	- Grounds Maintenance Workers		- Must have worked as an orderly	Department of Labor Certificate	
	- Apprenticeship			Custodian	
Custodial Maintenance	Building and Grounds Cleaning	12	High School Diploma or GED	BOP Employee	20 / 0
Location: Main	- Grounds Maintenance Workers		- Must have worked as an orderly	Department of Labor Certificate	
	- Apprenticeship			Custodian	
HVAC	Installation, Maintenance, and Repair	36	High School Diploma or GED	BOP Employee	0 / 0
Location: Main	- Heating, Air Conditioning, and Refrigeration Mechanics and Installers		- Must work in Facilities with HVAC foreman	Department of Labor Certificate	
	- Apprenticeship			HVAC	
Teacher's Assistant	Education, Training, and Library	24	High School Diploma or GED	BOP Employee	40 / 0
Location: Main	- Teacher Assistants		- Must work as a tutor	Department of Labor Certificate	
	- Apprenticeship			Teacher's Aide	

Institution: YAZOO CITY MED FCI

Program	Occupational Area	Months	Requirements	Certifications	Slots
Custodial Maintenance Location: Main	Building and Grounds Cleaning - Grounds Maintenance Workers - Apprenticeship	6	High School Diploma or GED - Must have worked as an orderly or in UNICOR	BOP Employee BOP Certificate & Department of Labor Certificate Custodian	20 / 0
Custodial Maintenance Location: Main	Building and Grounds Cleaning - Grounds Maintenance Workers - Apprenticeship	6	High School Diploma or GED - Must work or have worked as an orderly or in UNICOR	BOP Employee BOP Certificate & Department of Labor Certificate Custodian	20 / 0
Teacher Aide I Location: Main	Education, Training, and Library - Teacher Assistants - Apprenticeship	12	High School Diploma or GED - Must work as a tutor or teaching assistant	BOP Employee BOP Certificate & Department of Labor Certificate Teacher's Aide	40 / 0
Teacher's Assistant Location: Main	Education, Training, and Library - Teacher Assistants - Apprenticeship	12	High School Diploma or GED - Must work as an education tutor or assistant	BOP Employee BOP Certificate & Department of Labor Certificate Teacher's Aide	40 / 0
Welding Apprenticeship Location: Main	Installation, Maintenance, and Repair - Industrial Machinery Mechanics and Maintenance Workers - Apprenticeship	6	High School Diploma or GED	Accredited Vocational/Technical School Department of Labor Certificate Welder	20 / 0